DESIGNING UNDERGRADUATE EDUCATION

A Systematic Guide

PUBLISHED IN COOPERATION WITH
THE COUNCIL OF INDEPENDENT COLLEGES

William H. Bergquist

Ronald A. Gould

Elinor Miller Greenberg

DESIGNING
UNDERGRADUATE
EDUCATION

Jossey-Bass Publishers

San Francisco • Washington • London • 1981

DESIGNING UNDERGRADUATE EDUCATION
A Systematic Guide
        by William H. Bergquist, Ronald A. Gould, and
        Elinor Miller Greenberg

Copyright © 1981 by: Council of Independent Colleges
                      One Dupont Circle
                      Washington, D.C. 20036

                      Jossey-Bass Inc., Publishers
                      433 California Street
                      San Francisco, California 94104

                      Jossey-Bass Limited
                      28 Banner Street
                      London EC1Y 8QE

Library of Congress Cataloging in Publication Data

Bergquist, William H.
        Designing undergraduate education.

        Bibliography: p. 303
        Includes index.
        1. Universities and colleges—United States—
Curricula. 2. Curriculum planning—United States.
I. Gould, Ronald, Sir, 1904-   . II. Greenberg,
Elinor. III. Title.
LB2361.5.B47   378′.199′0973   81-47768
ISBN 0-87589-508-5   AACR2

Manufactured in the United States of America

JACKET DESIGN BY WILLI BAUM

FIRST EDITION

Code 8122

The Jossey-Bass
Series in Higher Education

FOREWORD

The Council of Independent Colleges (CIC)* is pleased to join
with Jossey-Bass in publishing *Designing Undergraduate Education* by William H. Bergquist, Ronald A. Gould, and Elinor Miller
Greenberg. This important new book offers a timely and comprehensive treatment of a subject that is central to the continued vitality of American higher education. It is timely because
it directs our attention to the fact that the future depends more
on the relentless search for high quality undergraduate education than on the resolution of economic and enrollment problems dominating the current period. It is comprehensive in that
it offers the most exhaustive description of contemporary collegiate curricular design and practice to date, with examples from

*Formerly the Council for the Advancement of Small Colleges
(CASC).

hundreds of colleges and universities, large and small, public and private.

Although many other books have recently been written about undergraduate education, this volume offers faculty members and administrators two distinct advantages. First, it is practical. Readers are given detailed descriptions from college and university catalogues, reports of noteworthy as well as representative curricular designs, and names of other institutions offering particular kinds of curriculums. Second, this volume provides the first systematic review and guide to the planning of all important aspects of the contemporary college curriculum: time, space, resources, organization, procedures, and outcomes. By using a systematic approach to curriculum description and analysis, the authors encourage a new perspective. When planning a new or revised curriculum, readers will no longer be content to look only at the content of an individual course or the sequencing of courses but will also want to consider the way time and space are used, resources allocated, curricular units organized, procedures employed, and outcomes defined to produce a successful undergraduate education.

Bergquist, Gould, and Greenberg are eminently qualified to make this new contribution to the literature of American higher education. They bring to the book years of consulting with hundreds of colleges, universities, associations, and agencies, as well as practical experience as teachers, trainers, and researchers. In addition to their other publications, Bergquist and Greenberg collaborated in coediting *New Directions for Higher Education: Educating Learners of All Ages* (with Kathleen O'Connell, Jossey-Bass, 1980). Bergquist and Greenberg are also consultants to CIC's Project on Quality Undergraduate Education (QUE), which incorporates all that has been learned about campus change over the past seven years from a dozen major CIC projects on faculty and administrator development, curricular reform, and institutional planning. A four-year project funded by the W. K. Kellogg Foundation to advance high quality education in liberal arts colleges, QUE inspired much of the content of *Designing Undergraduate Education*.

Students of higher education and campus practitioners

alike will find this work a valuable practical guide to improving existing undergraduate programs, or creating new ones, while maintaining institutional purpose and integrity. The book will be an especially important resource for both campus and national leaders who are committed to seeing America's colleges and universities become rededicated to the growth and learning of students of all ages and backgrounds.

September 1981   Gary H. Quehl, President
                               Council of Independent Colleges
                               Washington, D.C.

PREFACE

The pendulum swing has remained one predictable feature in the change and development of the collegiate curriculum in American higher education. In the late 1960s and early 1970s, many college and university curriculums became increasingly individualized and open to innovation and experiment. Particularly in response to the increased heterogeneity of student populations and the increased complexity of social and technological problems facing this country, colleges and universities were encouraged to move in distinctive directions that were tailored to meet the needs of particular student populations and/or solve social problems. In 1971, the Newman Commission (Newman and others, 1971) spoke of the need for increased diversification of institutions and curriculums. At about the same time, Hefferlin (1971), in his seminal piece on academic reform, argued for increased variety in curricular offerings. As late as 1976, David Mathews, Secretary of Health, Education, and Welfare, reiterated the need for colleges and universities to resist movement toward uniformity.

In the late 1970s, the pendulum swung back toward uniformity and a search for consensus in the collegiate curriculum. Ernest L. Boyer (past U.S. Commissioner of Education) and Martin Kaplan (his executive assistant) pointed to the need for a new core curriculum (Boyer and Kaplan, 1977, pp. 22-23): "While diversity necessarily and correctly affirms the individual, education for interdependence is just as vital. Only a common core of study confronts the fact that isolation and integration are both essential, that social connection points are crucial for greater understanding and survival."

Warren Bryan Martin, then vice-president of the Danforth Foundation, similarly spoke of the need to define the "limits to diversity": "Diversity has proven addictive. No matter how diverse colleges become, further diversity is called for; no matter how flexible and adaptive the system becomes, greater responsiveness is demanded. While a lot of people have been busy extending the definition of pluralism, too few have been defining its limits. Consequently, a new effort is now being made to reorder priorities, to sort things out. The limits of our tolerance for diversity, at least among many parents and students, faculty and governing bodies, have been reached" (1978, p. 48).

The concerns of Boyer and Kaplan (1977) and those of Martin (1978) speak not to a return to former times and to outmoded and irrelevant course distribution requirements and "History of Western Civilization" sequences, but to a new corecurriculum idea, based on the need for common skills, a body of common knowledge—competencies, if you will—that will enable our students not only to survive but actually to thrive as we face future challenges and problems. For many practitioners and theorists, this "movement back" toward a core curriculum and toward uniformity has not come easily, for it has often been led by those very faculty members and administrators who were advocates for individualization and diversity in the late 1960s and early 1970s. Ironically, many of those who believe that students should have maximum choice in the direction of their educational program also believe that each student should be exposed to certain central concepts, basic values, or trans-forming experiences that our times, problems, and potentials demand of each of us.

Every college and university must now face this central issue of *closing in* or *moving out* when considering revisions in its undergraduate curriculum. In closing in, a college or univer-sity has the opportunity to identify and clarify its current mis-sion and can plot more fully the implications of this mission for the curriculum of the college. In making the choice to *close in,* a college or university is faced with the challenge posed by Boyer and Kaplan (1977) and Martin (1978) of making this re-affirmation of the traditional a creative and renewing process. One cannot just return to the old. A changing student popula-tion and a changing world will not permit this.

Martin (1978) points out that there are now two tracks in our educational system: one track embraces institutions that are "narrowly academic" and committed to the traditional, whereas the second track embraces institutions that are "broadly educa-tional" and nontraditional. This second track, Martin persua-sively argues, is becoming increasingly important: "The number of people served, the money spent, and the political commit-ment today is toward nontraditional education and away from narrowly academic colleges and universities and toward broadly educational institutions" (p. 42). The college or university choosing to close in on an existing program should keep this trend toward the nontraditional in mind. A commitment to "the old" may jeopardize the institution's existence in the fu-ture.

A college or university may choose, alternatively, to move out into new undergraduate curricular areas and, in doing so, needs to keep in mind the problems associated with innova-tion and experimentation that Martin identifies: "The cost of a continuous expansion in educational offerings, as required to satisfy our insatiable appetite for variety, has become prohibi-tive. And so many kinds of people have been gathering together under one roof that the house of intellect seems to have become a circus tent. The types of programs instituted, and the range of people enrolled in them; the variety of colleges and universities developed, and the extensive claims they have made for these services; these and other developments have been carried to such extremes that an interest in differentiation has given way to a tolerance of contradiction" (p. 44). Martin seems to be cautioning the innovator and experimenter against indiscriminate use of new program ideas without systematic reflection on the implications and probable outcomes of program changes. The lack of this kind of thoughtfulness in many innovative and experimental programs has undermined intellectual credibility. Martin also identifies the problem of oversell that has accompanied many of these new program initiatives.

In this book we have provided ideas and resources that will enable a college or university to close in on and improve an existing undergraduate program or to move out into a new program area without sacrificing clarity of purpose or credibility. The six primary dimensions of all undergraduate curriculums are identified: time, space, resources, organization, procedures, and outcomes. Alternative ways in which colleges and universities have designed undergraduate curriculums with reference to each of these dimensions are described and discussed. Readers can review each of these dimensions and alternative program designs in a systematic manner. They can then apply these six dimensions and alternative program designs to undergraduate curricular purposes and the needs of their own institution, to its current or potential student clientele, and to the community that the institution is intended to serve.

The basic curricular taxonomy proposed in this book was first developed by Elinor Greenberg and William Bergquist as part of the Project on Quality Undergraduate Education (Project QUE) being conducted by the Council of Independent Colleges (CIC), formerly the Council for the Advancement of Small Colleges (CASC), under a generous grant from the W. K. Kellogg Foundation. Materials prepared for the Project QUE Work Manual by William Bergquist and Ronald Gould have been updated and expanded by Bergquist, Gould, and Greenberg for the more general audience that is likely to read this book. Some of the content in Chapter Five has been derived from a discussion about teaching methods in the third volume of *A Handbook for*

Faculty Development (Bergquist and Phillips, 1981), published by CIC. This material has been expanded and updated for use in the present volume.

We wish to thank the CIC staff for assistance in preparing this book. Our appreciation is extended in particular to Jack Armstrong, the director of Project QUE, Lucy Race and Nancy Mosier of the Project QUE staff, Jean Bernard, the editor at CIC, and Gary Quehl, president of CIC, who originally conceived of Project QUE and steadily encouraged the efforts leading to the publication of this book. We also wish to express our gratitude to Wilma Jean Connell for her highly professional services in preparing this manuscript and to acknowledge the invaluable contributions made by the colleagues at colleges and universities with whom we have worked. Faculty members and academic administrators at many collegiate institutions have graciously provided us with descriptions and analyses of their own undergraduate programs, linkages to other programs, and ideas about what undergraduate education can and should be.

September 1981   William H. Bergquist
                                                      Walnut Creek, California

                                                          Ronald A. Gould
                                                      Berkeley, California

                                                      Elinor Miller Greenberg
                                                      Littleton, Colorado

CONTENTS

THE AUTHORS

William H. Bergquist is faculty member and head of the Center for Organizational Studies at the Wright Institute, Berkeley, and an independent consultant for colleges and universities throughout the United States and Canada. He was awarded the B.A. degree in psychology from Occidental College (1962) and the M.A. and Ph.D. degrees in psychology from the University of Oregon (1967 and 1970, respectively). He has served on the faculty at the University of Oregon and the University of Idaho, as director of Special Higher Education (WICHE), and currently as chief consultant to the Council for Independent Colleges (CIC). He has written numerous articles and books, including such CIC publications as *A Handbook for Faculty Development* (3 vols.: 1975, 1977, 1981), *Developing the College Curriculum: A Handbook for Faculty and Administrators* (1977), *Handbook for College Administration* (1978), and *The College I Experience: Integrating Work, Leisure, and Service* (1980); among his other publications are *New Directions for Higher Education: A Comprehensive Approach to Institutional Development* (coeditor with William Shoemaker, 1976) and *Designing Teaching Improvement Programs* (1978).

Ronald A. Gould has been a higher education researcher during the past four years, first with the Educational Testing Service and most recently with Project QUE. Currently completing his doctorate in social action research at the Wright Institute, he was awarded the B.A. degree in psychology and philosophy from Ottawa University in Kansas (1976) and the M.A. degree in psychology from the University of Chicago (1978). He is specifically interested in the philosophy of time and how it relates to one's becoming an effective change agent; his primary areas of consultation work have been organizational and program evaluation.

Elinor Miller Greenberg is Mountains and Plains Regional Manager of the Council for the Advancement of Experiential Learning (CAEL) and senior consultant to CIC. She was awarded the B.A. degree in speech and psychology from Mount Holyoke College (1953), the M.A. degree in speech pathology from the University of Wisconsin (1954), and the Ed.D. degree in lifelong education from the University of Northern Colorado (1981). She has served on the faculty at Loretto Heights College and the University of Colorado at Denver, was founding director of the University Without Walls program at Loretto Heights, and has just been appointed by the governor to the Colorado State Board for Community Colleges and Occupational Education. Greenberg is also project director of Advancing Quality Education for Adult Learners, cosponsored by CAEL and CIC, and principal consultant to the Fund for the Improvement of Postsecondary Education's program on Better Strategies for Educating Adults. She has published numerous articles in a variety of publications, including the *Journal of Experiential Education* and the *Association of Governing Boards (AGB) Reports.*

DESIGNING UNDERGRADUATE EDUCATION

A Systematic Guide

PUBLISHED IN COOPERATION WITH
THE COUNCIL OF INDEPENDENT COLLEGES

INTRODUCTION

Describing the
Undergraduate Curriculum

During the past decade, several attempts have been made to categorize and systematically describe the variety of undergraduate curricular offerings found in American colleges and universities. In the early 1970s, the Carnegie Commission on Higher Education produced *An Inventory of Academic Innovation and Reform*. Prepared and written by Dr. Ann Heiss, this technical report identified and described new innovative institutions, new institutions within institutions, innovative changes by academic subunits within conventional colleges and universities, procedural innovations, and institutional self-studies. Under the procedures category, Heiss examined changes in the academic calendar, time blocks, admissions, counseling, general education, structural changes in the alignment of disciplines, and new degrees. In this last category, Heiss also examined changes in course or degree requirements, new fields of study, changes in modes of teaching and learning, changes in grading, course-

1

credit policies, testing and examinations, evaluation of teaching techniques, and changes in tenure policies. Heiss' inventory is of considerable value in the identification of innovative programs and institutions. However, one cannot help being impressed that by 1979, a considerable number of the innovative programs and institutions that Heiss had identified no longer existed. Many of these initiatives led short—though often productive—lives.

The value of Heiss' inventory seems to reside more in its comprehensive nature than in its organization. Heiss did not develop a systematic taxonomy or set of categories in which to place the programs and institutions she described.

Of an even less systematic nature is the *Yellow Pages of Undergraduate Innovations,* produced in 1974 by the Center for Improvement of Undergraduate Education at Cornell University. This directory provides brief descriptions of a variety of programs that were self-defined as being innovative by those administering them. No attempt was made to screen out those programs that were not truly innovative or were unsuccessful. This document is already out of date (more so than the Heiss report) though of some historical interest.

A more recent resource document, *Handbook on Undergraduate Curriculum,* has been prepared under the auspices of the Carnegie Foundation (the Carnegie Council for Policy Studies in Higher Education). Written by Arthur Levine, this substantial book is divided into nine sections: general education, majors or concentrations, basic and advanced skills and knowledge, tests and grades, education and work, advising, credits and degrees, methods of instruction, and structure of academic time. Like Heiss' report, Levine's handbook provides a comprehensive (and contemporary) inventory, yet does not offer a means for systematically analyzing or creating a collegiate curriculum.

A somewhat more systematic (though less comprehensive) attempt to describe the undergraduate curriculum has been made by William Bergquist (1977), who builds on the previous categorizations of Paul Dressel (1971) and Lewis Mayhew and Patrick Ford (1971). Bergquist identifies eight curricular models that he believes encompass most of the curricular offerings now found in American higher education:

1. *Heritage-Based:* The curriculum is primarily designed to provide students with a clear and meaningful sense of their own cultural and historical background(s), thereby providing them with the knowledge and skills to deal with current and future problems associated with this heritage.
2. *Thematic Based:* A specific, pressing problem or issue of our contemporary society is identified that encompasses a wide variety of academic disciplines; an educational program that will provide students with the resources needed to solve and/or cope with this problem or issue is then designed.
3. *Competency-Based:* A set of specific competencies which a student is to acquire and/or demonstrate prior to graduation is identified; educational resources (including course work) are developed, assembled, or identified in order for the student to diagnose current levels and achieve desired levels of competence.
4. *Career-Based:* Programs are specifically designed to prepare students for a certain vocation, admission to a professional training program, or a vocational decision-making process.
5. *Experience-Based:* On- and off-campus experiences that are in some sense educational are created or provided; the college takes some responsibility for controlling the quality of the experiences, sequencing the experiences, and relating the learnings from these experiences to principles that have been conveyed through more traditional modes (lecture, discussions, seminars).
6. *Student-Based:* Students are allowed a significant role in determining: (a) the nature of the formal educational experiences they are to receive, (b) the ways in which these experiences are to be interpreted, and (c) the criteria and means by which they are to be evaluated. Typically, some form of learning contract is developed between a student and mentor (teacher, adviser) or between several students (student-initiated and/or student-conducted courses).
7. *Values-Based:* Students are provided with the educational resources and experiences to clarify or expand on their current values or to acquire new values; these values are related to current social, political, or religious issues or to the students' life and career plans.
8. *Future-Based:* Conditions are created for students to acquire knowledge, skills, and attitudes that are appropriate to the creation of a desirable future or that are adaptive to a predictable future society [Bergquist, 1977, p. 83].

Bergquist (1977, pp. 83-84) further states that these eight models "tend to interrelate with one another with reference to two pervasive curricular questions . . . : (1) how general or specific should the curriculum be that is offered by this college? and (2) to what extent should the curriculum be prescriptive or elective with reference to the role played by students?"

Making use of these two curricular questions, Bergquist (1977) proposes a circular figure, Figure 1, that graphically portrays the interrelations among the eight curricular models with reference to their responses to these two questions.

Figure 1. The Curricular Wheel, Showing Relations Among Eight Curricular Models with Respect to the General/Specific and Prescriptive/Elective Dimensions.

Source: Bergquist, 1977, p. 84.

Bergquist's "curricular wheel" has proved to be of value to many colleges in curricular planning. It also served as a basis for Jerry Chance's description of alternative curricular approaches to general education, which appears in a resource guide prepared by Jerry Gaff (1980) for the Project on General Education Models (GEM). Bergquist's eight models (and Chance's adaptation of them) systematically categorize existing curricular offerings and can be useful to college curricular planning groups in selecting a program for quality development. These curricular categorizations, however, mix several dimensions of the curriculum together; hence, they often compare apples with oranges. Several categories, for instance, focus primarily on content (for example, "heritage" and "future-based" curriculums), whereas other categories focus on process or method (for example, "student-based" and "experience-based" curriculums). Perhaps even more important, Bergquist's categorization (and those of Heiss and Levine) does an excellent job of describing *current* offerings but does not describe all the *possible* curricular offerings (given the current state of the art). A curricular categorization system is needed that is generative as well as descriptive—that is, one that can be used to create entirely new curricular offerings.

In this book, we propose a generative system for the categorization of collegiate curriculums. This system more clearly identifies and isolates six generic dimensions of all curriculums. We have also described various alternative program designs to illustrate how colleges have actually used these six dimensions to develop creative and coherent curriculum patterns. By rearranging these six curricular dimensions, or variables, it is possible to free up the curriculum design process and to be both more creative and more explicit in curriculum development.

A Curricular Taxonomy

The structure of academic programs can be described in terms of six curricular dimensions:

1. *Time:* Duration and schedule of instructional units.
2. *Space:* Use of instructional and noninstructional areas both on and off the college campus.
3. *Resources:* Instructional use of people, situations, and materials, both on and off campus, from instructional and noninstructional areas.
4. *Organization:* Arrangement and sequencing of instructional units and arrangement of academic administrative units.
5. *Procedures:* Planning, implementing, evaluating, and crediting instructional units.
6. *Outcomes:* Defining the intended desired results of a particular instructional unit or academic program.

In most instances, a college curriculum can be described in terms of a series of decisions that the college has made with reference to each of these six dimensions. Furthermore, there is a hierarchy of the six dimensions with reference to the profundity of change required when a decision is made to alter existing curricular structures within one or another dimension. For example, changes in curricular time and space are less profound than changes in resources or organization, these latter changes being, in turn, less profound than changes in either procedures or outcomes. Whereas changes in time and space primarily require only structural change, changes in procedures and outcomes tend to require changes in processes and attitudes as well as structure (Watson and Johnson, 1972). Furthermore, changes in the procedural or outcome dimension almost inevitably will require changes in each of the other dimensions as well. Curricular changes, therefore, will be easiest to bring about, as a rule, if they involve lower-order (time, space) rather than higher-order (procedures, outcomes) dimensions.

Figure 2. Hierarchy of the Six Curricular Dimensions.

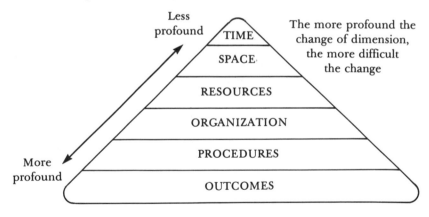

The following six chapters describe the six curricular dimensions and show how alternative program designs are responsive to each. In general, the first alternatives described under each dimension are most frequently found in the contemporary undergraduate college curriculum and are most compatible with prevalent norms, practices, and goals of contemporary collegiate institutions. The last alternatives described in each dimension generally represent significant departures from current practices for most contemporary colleges and universities. For most of the alternative program designs, one or more colleges or universities that are currently using or have recently used the design have been identified. We have not tried to identify all programs using any one design, nor do we imply that each design is necessarily being used successfully at the collegiate institutions we do identify. We also have not tried to differentiate between extant programs and those that no longer exist, for such an exercise is soon outdated; furthermore, even if a program no longer exists in an institution, those persons who designed or implemented the program may still be present and can provide valuable guidance to others who wish to initiate or adapt a similar program. We have identified the state (in parentheses) in which each institution is located. The reader who is interested in obtaining more information about a particular program is encouraged to contact the dean or academic vice-president of the appropriate college or university.

— I —

TIME

Scheduling Instructional Units

Many of the publicized changes in the curriculums of American colleges and universities over the past decade have involved the calendar or the clock. Collegiate institutions are no longer tied to the 8 A.M.-5 P.M. instructional day nor to the standard and often static semester or quarter system in which each student simultaneously takes three to five courses per term. Faculty members and administrators recognize that some students are best served by (and attracted to) a collegiate institution that offers a flexible schedule of courses given at nontraditional times of day and on nontraditional days of the week. They also have come to recognize that some course material is best presented and learned over a short, intensive period without the distraction of other subject matter, whereas other material is best presented and learned over a lengthy period, interspersed with material from other courses. In recent years, the curricular calen-

8

dar has also been altered for noneducational reasons, especially to save energy and to combat soaring heating costs. Following are descriptions of several approaches that have been taken to designing the curricular calendar and clock.

Curricular Calendar

Multiple Instructional Units of Constant Length. As Boyer (1975, p. 15) has noted, the precedence of the two-semester academic year is very strong, as is that of the four-year baccalaureate degree program. The two-semester (September to June) system is a compromise between the year-round, three-term system of Cambridge University (a highly influential model for early American universities) and the agricultural demand for low-cost youth labor during summer.

The "traditional" semester calendar, according to the American Association of Collegiate Registrars and Admissions Officers (AACRAO), "begins in approximately mid-September and has one semester running until late January and another from late January or early February through early June" (Eddy, 1979, p. 7). AACRAO also identifies an "early" semester variation that many colleges have adopted to avoid the "lame duck" period between Christmas vacation and final exams: "The first or fall semester runs from late August through mid to late December, and the second semester (called either winter or spring) continues from mid January through mid to late May" (p. 7).

Though still widely used, the semester calendar is declining in popularity. The traditional semester was found in only 6 percent of collegiate institutions in the United States during the 1978-79 academic year, whereas it was used by over one third of these institutions a decade ago. Two thirds of the colleges and universities that still use the traditional semester calendar are to be found in two states, New York and California, with large and often slow-changing postsecondary systems. Some collegiate institutions, however, have returned to the traditional semester system after finding that many students (especially recent high school graduates, reentering women, and students requiring summer jobs) cannot begin in August.

Levine (1978, p. 236) has identified several advantages and disadvantages of the traditional semester:

Advantages

1. It provides the most classroom hours per term.
2. It makes possible a review week at the end of each term.
3. It permits a lengthy, more thorough study of subjects.
4. It encourages a stable college community owing to common vacation and attendance patterns.
5. It enables students to find summer employment at the time when jobs are most available owing to worker vacations and good weather.
6. It minimizes the number of courses for which faculty must prepare, the number of times students must register for courses, and the number of examination periods for which grades must be recorded.

Disadvantages

1. It allows little flexibility regarding student attendance patterns and faculty teaching schedules.
2. It forces courses into a term or year length regardless of content or purpose.
3. It requires full-time students to study four or five different subjects at a time.
4. It limits students in the number of courses they can take in four years more severely than any other calendar system.
5. It may unnecessarily stretch subjects that could be covered more quickly in shorter terms.
6. Its three-month summer vacation period is not necessary for all students and faculty.

The early semester was used by one quarter of American colleges and universities in 1970-71, but by over half of these institutions in 1978-79. Several reasons have been given for the popularity of the early semester calendar: (1) ending the semester before Christmas, (2) freeing up student time over Christmas, (3) de-emphasizing final examinations and encouraging semester-long evaluation, (4) more efficient use of campus facilities because of decreased periods of low use, (5) greater flexibility in summer scheduling, (6) earlier end to the spring semester, enabling students to have a competitive edge in the summer job market, and (7) a more likely candidate than the traditional semester for a common systemwide calendar, given its current popularity.

A variant on the semester calendar, the trimester, is much less common. It has been used by 3 to 4 percent of collegiate institutions in the United States in recent years (Eddy, 1979). The trimester usually consists of three fifteen-week terms: "Full-time students attend ... two terms per year and take four courses per term or attend three terms per year and take three courses per term. The latter arrangement is called the 3-3 calendar. It was introduced at Goucher College in the early 1950s, but Dartmouth is generally credited with devising the calendar and [the University of] Pittsburgh with increasing its notoriety" (Levine, 1978, p. 236).

The University of Michigan, Harper College (Ill.), and the Florida State System of Higher Education, among others, moved to the trimester by the early 1970s (Heiss, 1973). Levine (1978, pp. 236-237) identifies the following advantages and disadvantages in the use of this calendar option:

Advantages

1. It is efficient in using time and facilities because the campus is in full operation all year long and there is no summer hiatus.
2. It allows for acceleration in that students can take nine or more courses per year versus eight in the semester curriculum.
3. It allows flexibility in student attendance patterns because students can take any of the three terms off.
4. It eliminates the January "lame duck" session.
5. It can be easily adapted from the semester calendar.
6. It provides a longer summer term, beginning in April and ending in August, for students who want or need the time for work.

7. It enables faculty to earn additional money by teaching during the summer.

Disadvantages

1. It makes transfer from a college on the semester system difficult during the spring, as the trimester term begins earlier than the spring semester.
2. It makes faculty exchange during the spring term difficult for the same reasons.
3. It offers in its 3-3 form less vacation time than many other calendars.
4. It leaves less time for faculty research and course preparation than many other calendars.
5. It entails more registration, bookkeeping, advising, and examination periods than two-term calendars.
6. It is incompatible with several financial aid programs that are based on semester or quarter calendars.
7. It requires a fairly constant year-round enrollment to be economical.
8. It is fatiguing to faculty and students.

One of the major curricular innovations early in the twentieth century was a change from the semester calendar to a four-term ("quarter") calendar. The quarter calendar is used currently by 18 percent of four-year arts and sciences colleges (Levine, 1978) and, together with the semester and trimester calendars, dominates American higher education (Levine, 1978, p. 235). Several other "constant length" calendars are used more sparingly. The College of Racine (Wisc.) employs a 7-7-7-7-7-7 calendar, while the "block" system of Colorado College (described in more detail below) offers nine instructional units ("modules") of constant length each year. Some of the advantages and disadvantages of this type of calendar, as identified by Levine (1978, pp. 238-239), are these:

Advantages

1. It permits students to take a greater number and variety of courses than is possible with two-term calendars.

2. It enables students to concentrate on a small number of courses per term.

3. It offers students the possibility of acceleration by attending additional terms or by taking four courses.

4. It provides students and faculty flexibility in choosing attendance or vacation patterns.

5. It offers more frequent breaks than the semester system.

6. It allows for courses of three lengths (one quarter, two quarters, three quarters), while the semester system allows for only two.

7. It is better adjusted to national holidays and traditional work-year breaks, as quarters fit into the spaces between Labor Day, Christmas, and Easter vacation.

Disadvantages

1. It makes inefficient use of time as contrasted with the trimester system (forty weeks of instruction versus forty-five weeks of instruction per year).

2. It involves twice as much registration and bookkeeping as the semester calendar.

3. It requires more preparation, tests, and grading by faculty.

4. It occasionally results in superficial courses because terms are only ten weeks long.

5. It keeps students on an academic treadmill owing to need to choose and complete new courses every ten weeks.

6. It makes faculty teaching at the summer session of other colleges difficult.

7. It makes unavoidable absences from class (by either faculty or students) more serious.

Given the large number of colleges and universities using one of these three calendars, there is no need to provide further references or descriptions. Several institutions, however, offer variations on these calendars that are worth noting.

Governors State University (Ill.) offers a trimester calendar in which each of the three fifteen-week terms is further divided into two seven-to-eight-week units: "Courses may be scheduled to meet for the entire fifteen weeks (designated as

Block 1), for the first seven to eight weeks (Block 2), or for the last seven to eight weeks (Block 3) of the trimester" (Governors State University, 1978, p. 19).

Stephens College (Mo.) offers a similar modified semester system: "The college's calendar consists of two fourteen-week terms of four sessions. Courses vary in length from three-and-a-half to seven to fourteen weeks. Credits earned are counted in course units rather than credit hours; one course is the equivalent of three semester hours. The advantage of the system is flexibility. Each instructor is encouraged to look critically at the content of each course and decide whether it is best suited to a three-and-a-half, seven, or fourteen-week format. Students can explore courses for a short period of time or delve into their areas of interest for a longer time" (Schmidtlein, 1980).

Several institutions have modified the traditional semester system by adding a "rump" term of seven to eight weeks that "allows students the option of enriching their programs, to graduate with a double major, or to complete the requirements in three years" (Heiss, 1973, p. 49). The University of Denver (Colo.) has made a similar modification in its quarter calendar, introducing a three-week period in December as an intersession. These variations on the standard calendar closely resemble a significant calendar change adopted by many colleges in the 1960s and 1970s: the 4-1-4 calendar. We turn now to this alternative.

Multiple Instructional Units of Variable Length. As Heiss (1973) has noted in her Carnegie-commissioned *Inventory of Academic Innovation and Reform,* "Changes in the structure of knowledge, in teaching methods, in career aspirations, and in academic life-styles prompted some institutions to experiment with new time frames around which new educational efficiencies might result" (p. 47). The most widespread of these recent innovations has been the movement to variable-length terms and, more specifically, to the introduction of short-length terms (two to four weeks) during January: "Introduced by Florida Presbyterian College [now Eckerd College] in the early 1960s, over 500 colleges and universities now [1973] have some counterpart of the January intersession which eliminates the "lame duck" period after the Christmas holiday. This innovation arranges the calendar so that the fall semester ends before the Christmas break. After Christmas vacation, there is a one-month term followed by another full semester. During this intermediate term, the student can devote his time to a single intensive experience: doing independent study, giving community service, engaging in a special seminar, traveling, doing research under supervision, or taking courses at some distant and/or appropriate setting" (Heiss, 1973, pp. 47-48).

The extent to which the 4-1-4 calendar has dominated innovations in the area of academic calendars is witnessed by a listing of calendars in the January 21, 1972, issue of the *Chronicle of Higher Education*. This list of 149 innovative calendars includes only a handful that are not 4-1-4. As of 1978, 21 percent of all four-year arts and sciences colleges had adopted 4-1-4 (Levine, 1978). The success of this calendar innovation was witnessed further by the establishment and growth of the 4-1-4 Conference, involving representatives from collegiate institutions that have adopted 4-1-4 calendars, and the subsequent growth of this conference into an organization with an expanded focus, the Association for Innovation in Higher Education. Levine (1978, pp. 237-238) identifies eight advantages and three disadvantages in using the 4-1-4 calendar:

Advantages

1. It provides a change of pace between semesters.
2. It accommodates an innovative enclave or laboratory for pedagogical experimentation.
3. It breaks down academic compartmentalization through mini-term interdisciplinary teaching and curriculum experimentation.
4. It enables students to accelerate their studies.
5. It allows for new courses without course proliferation.
6. It provides an opportunity for faculty not teaching during the mini-term to pursue research, study, or writing.
7. It eliminates the "lame duck" session.
8. It increases flexibility for students in undergraduate programs with few electives.

Disadvantages

1. The mini-term may be little more than a frill.
2. The mini-term costs faculty and students vacation time and results in extra work.
3. The mini-term adds financial and administrative costs to the regular semester systems.

The second and third advantages identified by Levine (pedagogical experimentation and interdisciplinarity) have been particularly important for many colleges, as noted by Halliburton (1977, p. 69): "The 4-1-4 calendar has provided . . . an area in which to develop innovative curricular approaches—approaches which are more difficult to experiment with during a conventional semester or quarter." Although colleges and universities have not always taken advantage of these faculty and curriculum development opportunities, they remain available to the 4-1-4 institution.

During the 1970s, several variations on 4-1-4 were tried. Probably the most common is the 4-4-1 calendar, in which the mini-term is placed at the end of the spring semester. Clark College (Ga.) and Elmira College (N.Y.) are among the institutions that have tried this calendar. Writing about the use of 4-4-1 at Wesleyan College (N.C.), Stewart (1976, p. 188) notes that "the first semester ends shortly before Christmas; the second semester ends late in April; and the final month of the academic year, called the May term or mini-mester, is devoted to concentrated study of a single subject, either on or off campus. The May term allows the student to pursue exciting independent or group study in the area of his or her special interests."

The mini-term at Hartwick College (N.Y.) has also been moved out of January. This short term has been placed in December, the college adopting a 10-3-10 calendar. Another variation on the 4-1-4 calendar is an expansion in the size (duration/credit hours) of the January intersession. Furman University (S.C.) provides a 3-2-3 program, and the College of Idaho has adopted a 12-6-12 calendar. Both these latter modifications on 4-1-4 blend many of the advantages (and disadvantages) of the trimester and 4-1-4 systems.

Most of the other modifications of 4-1-4 are more complex. Western Maryland College offers a four-month/one-month/five-month calendar; Seattle Pacific University (Wash.) provides four seven-week terms and two three-week terms; and the University of Wisconsin at Oshkosh has chosen two traditional semesters of seventeen weeks, each of which is broken into two seven-week sessions and a three-week session, as well as an eight-week summer session, which is broken into two four-week sessions. At Bluffton College (Ohio), students are exposed to a 1-3-1-3-1 calendar; at Colgate University (N.Y.), to a 1-3-1-4-3 system. One of the most widely studied calendars that modify the 4-1-4 system is found at Austin College (Texas) and is described as follows:

The fall term is divided into two seven-week sessions in which the student has the option of taking two courses each session. Alternately, the student may choose to take four fourteen-week courses during the fall term or take an appropriate mix of seven-week and fourteen-week courses. The four-week January term, in which the student gains one course credit, provides a change of pace through its unique opportunities for special intensive courses, independent study, and off-campus study. In the spring term, the student usually takes four courses, each of which lasts fourteen weeks. There is also an optional eleven-week summer term which has a seven-week session followed by a four-week session. This yearly calendar provides different time lengths for various courses, making for a greater variety of approaches and a more interesting year of learning [Austin College, 1980, p. 145].

One of the most complex, yet manageable, calendars is provided by Ottawa University (Kans.). As described in Ottawa's 1976 catalogue:

The Ottawa University calendar is unique in the flexibility it offers students and the opportunity it provides for concentration on a limited number of courses each session. The calendar is divided into five periods of 7-7-4-7-7 weeks each [refer to the diagram]. The student may take only two courses in each of the seven-week sessions and only one course in the four-week winter term. Student evaluations of the Ottawa calendar have been overwhelmingly favorable. The most often heard comment from students is that the calendar permits them to concentrate intensively on two courses without having to juggle two or three others at the same time. There are two regular summer terms of four weeks each in June and July [during each of] which students may take one course. . . . Students may enroll for independent studies in August for one course credit. The Ottawa calendar is often called the 2-2-1-2-2 calendar in obvious reference to the number and sequence of courses offered [Ottawa University, 1976, p. 3].

Sept.-Oct.	Nov.-Dec.	Jan.	Feb.-March	April-May	June	July
Session One TWO COURSES	Session Two TWO COURSES	Winter Term ONE COURSE	Session Three TWO COURSES	Session Four TWO COURSES	June Term ONE COURSE	July Term ONE COURSE

A similar 2-2-1-2-2 calendar is found at Eckerd College (Fla.), the original architect of the 4-1-4 calendar. During the last several years, Ottawa University has revised its calendar. These changes and the rationale for them are described by Keith Shumway (1980), the academic vice-president at Ottawa:

In the nine years the [2-2-1-2-2] calendar was in effect, and during which time it served to help shape the calendar changes that occurred at Austin College and elsewhere, increasing pressures were felt in some disciplines for courses that ran longer than seven weeks. There was a decline in enrollment patterns and student interest in the use of the winter term for January. The calendar had been internally studied a number of times by students, staff, and faculty. This data was of value to a new calendar study process that occurred in 1978-79. As a result of that process, it was decided effective in the fall of 1979 to drop the winter term and to retain the shorter sessions for as many courses as possible while encouraging certain departments to explore parallel use of semester-length courses. As a result, starting with the 1979-80 year, we introduced what we refer to as the "flexible" calendar. Approximately 50 percent of the courses remain in the shorter design of the 2-2-1-2-2 mode, and another 50 percent have a semester format. Students choosing to stay with the shorter design generally can do so, and departments needing a longer design for a specific learning experience have that option. The modified calendar seems to be working and has been generally accepted as a solution to the problems that we had identified.

Antioch College (Ohio) offers a complex calendar, diagramed in Figure 3, that builds on the interplay at Antioch between work experiences and academic preparation (Antioch College, 1977, p. 52).

Figure 3. Sequence of Study and Work Quarters, Showing Options for Entering Students at Antioch College.

options	Year 1				Year 2			
	summer	fall	winter	spring	summer	fall	winter	spring
option A	study	study	work	work	study	work	study	work
option B	study	work	study	work	work	study	work	study
option C	—	study	study	work	study	work	study	work
option D	—	study	work	study	study	work	work	work

‖ = 1 week division break   ‖ = 2 weeks division break   ‖ = 3 weeks division break

Note: Subsequent years normally begin with the same activity as in the spring quarter of the second year.

Whereas the calendars just described have been made more complex in response to increased diversification in student and institutional needs and interests, other calendars have been simplified so that they require a student to participate in only one educational program at a time or so that the amount of structure in the calendar has been reduced. We turn now to these simpler calendar systems.

Multiple Instructional Units of Constant Length with a Single Course per Unit. The first college to make use of a "block system" was Colorado College, which introduced basic instructional units ("modules") of three-and-a-half weeks, followed by four-and-a-half-day breaks. Each academic year consists of nine modules. Students take a single course during each module and in this way are able to concentrate on one course at a time. Concentrated learning, in turn, "fosters seminar-type teaching rather than traditional lectures, allows for extensive fieldwork in a subject area, and enables the institution to engage prominent visiting teachers who would not be available for a conventional semester-long course" (Chickering and others, 1977, p. 255).

The Colorado College plan (in 1973) "provides for three types of courses: the single course that lasts three-and-a-half weeks, the extended course that lasts either seven or ten-and-a-half weeks, and adjunct courses in music or dance that meet in the late afternoon or evening and extend over a full semester. Students may be involved in two extended courses and an adjunct course, or a single course and an adjunct course. A classroom is assigned for the exclusive use of each course, and professors and students are free to work out arrangements for the best use of their time. Periods of suitable length can be adapted to the requirements of the particular subject matter of the course and to variations in teaching style" (Heiss, 1973, p. 48).

A modularized program is also provided at Monterey Peninsula College (Calif.) in its interdisciplinary humanities program (GENTRAIN). Students study Western civilization from prehistory to the present in fifteen independent modules, each lasting two weeks:

Within this structure . . . the GENTRAIN system offers students a uniquely flexible mode of education. They may take as many of the units as they like, receiving one semester unit of credit for each whether they enroll for one or all fifteen. They may take each unit for a letter grade (necessary for transfer to the University of California system), for "credit" (sufficient for a transfer in the state college system), or for no credit, as an adult education course. And they can take the course over and over again if they like, with no risk of boredom or a feeling of déjà vu; for while the syllabus remains a constant, the lectures are continually changing.

The four instructors who run GENTRAIN are highly qualified educators (one in philosophy, one in art history, one in literature, and one in history and political science), but even they cannot present a detailed review of all of civilization in thirty weeks. Rather, each year they meet to determine a "theme" for each of the units they will present, a focus about which the fifteen hours of class time will revolve. The syllabus for each unit, ranging from fifty to eighty pages of notably cogent prose, is distributed before the unit begins, to serve as background and bibliography for the lecture; the lectures take off where the syllabus ends.

The result is, in the words of Philip Nash, MPC's dean of instructional planning, "a series of snapshots of global history." Each year the GENTRAIN camera pans across the timeline of Western civilization and stops to click at slightly different scenes.

The year begins with two weeks devoted to prehistory, the early civilizations that flourished before 1200 B.C. The eighty-page syllabus provides a quick glimpse of man's evolutionary journey to the Bronze Age, and then an overview of Bronze Age cultures and their religions, art, language, and literature. A bibliography at the end of each chapter steers inquisitive students to more detailed sources.

In class each instructor has three or four lectures in which to expand on particular aspects of the theme that has been chosen to bring the unit into focus. Throughout all lectures, students, as well as other instructors, are encouraged to interrupt with questions or comments.

The sixteenth and last hour of the unit is devoted to testing for those students who are taking the course for a grade or for credit. Students desiring a grade are also required to submit a short essay on a given topic ["Tracking Civilization . . . ," 1978, p. 38].

The modularized system, as used at Colorado College and Monterey Peninsula College, is not now in widespread use. Within the context of more traditional calendars, however, several colleges have offered single-course programming for many years. Two experimental colleges, Raymond College at the University of the Pacific (Calif.) and Evergreen State College (Wash.), have given students the opportunity to work on a single project at any one time during the academic year. The "Embryo" program at Raymond encourages "the spontaneous formation of study groups which . . . grow out of the first few days of faculty-student interaction" (Lyon, 1979, p. 33). Students spend all or part of each semester working with these study groups. Similarly, at Evergreen, most students enroll in a single program each quarter, working either alone or in a study group.

Thus, a "block system" can be built around a modularized system, as at Colorado and Monterey Peninsula, or built around a traditional semester or quarter calendar, as at Raymond and Evergreen. As noted by Levine (1978, p. 24), the block system holds several advantages and disadvantages:

Advantages

1. Studies are deeper and less fragmented than in concurrent course calendars.
2. Block-long field trips and fieldwork can be undertaken easily.
3. Daily schedules can be left to the discretion of the faculty members and students in terms of the particular nature of the day's studies.
4. Prominent scholars who might otherwise be unavailable can be brought to campus to teach for a block (less than one month).
5. Students are quite enthusiastic about the calendar.
6. Students reportedly work hard.
7. Faculty have to prepare for only one course at a time.
8. Acceleration of studies is possible.
9. Faculty feel they accomplish more than in conventional calendar systems.
10. Attendance and teaching patterns can be more flexible.

Disadvantages

1. More classrooms are necessary.
2. Faculty are required to teach more courses per year and become fatigued by the pressure.
3. Students are required to work harder.
4. The intensive format is not suited to all courses.
5. Classroom friendships are more difficult for students to sustain because classes change every few weeks.

6. The intensive format may discourage students from experimenting with unfamiliar courses.
7. Registration, bookkeeping, and grading occur up to nine or ten times per year.

Single-Event Programming. The block system allows the student to concentrate on a single topic but still operates within specific calendar constraints. Some colleges are exploring the use of single-event programming. They offer workshops, institutes, and/or short courses for academic credit that are specifically tailored, in duration and location, to the unique learning goals of the instructional unit being offered and the available time of the potential student population (often adults).

Intensive short-term workshops and institutes have been used frequently for freshman orientation at the start of the fall term. One of the most notable and dramatic orientation workshops was conducted by Prescott College (Ariz.; now the Prescott Center for Alternative Education) during the 1960s and early 1970s. Before each academic year, students and faculty members jointly participated in a wilderness-survival experience that not only highlighted the emphasis in the Prescott curriculum on personal growth and ecological education but also promoted the formation of meaningful student-faculty relationships. A comparable orientation experience of a somewhat more cultural nature has been offered in the Humanities Cluster College at Bowling Green State University (Ohio). Faculty members and students participate in two "blitz weeks" during which they tackle several major themes (such as "success") from an interdisciplinary perspective, working with a variety of media and art forms throughout the week (Magada and Moore, 1976).

Extended orientation programs are being offered currently at Eckerd College (Fla.) and the College of the Atlantic (Maine). At Eckerd, all freshmen attend an "autumn term." Students take a course taught by their mentor and engage in one academic project for credit (Chickering and others, 1977, p. 259): "This project is stimulating in content, teaches basic academic skills, and focuses on the interdisciplinary nature of learning." The orientation program at the College of the Atlantic (COA) blends many features of both Prescott's wilderness

and Eckerd's academic orientation programs. Following is an
excerpt from a recent COA catalogue:

> *Outdoor Orientation.* A strong community spirit is one of COA's
> distinguishing features, and the Outdoor Orientation helps to nourish this
> feeling of shared enterprise and interreliance. The Orientation precedes the
> opening of school each fall and provides the opportunity for entering and
> older students to get to know one another through the experience of
> wilderness travel. The Outdoor Orientation is five days long and serves as
> an introduction to both the college and some of Maine's true wildlands.
>
> The Orientation trips are planned and led in small groups by ex-
> perienced students and faculty members. These trips are not a test of en-
> durance. They simply present an opportunity to camp and sharpen skills
> and at the same time to form the judgments and friendships that will be
> the basis of the coming term.
>
> Recent Orientations have taken people down the Allagash River in
> northern Maine. Future trips will include backpacking in interior Maine
> and canoeing on the St. Croix River, the Machias River, and rivers in Nova
> Scotia.
>
> *Academic Orientation:* Following the Outdoor Orientation, all stu-
> dents and faculty members gather at the college for a three-day weekend.
> Mornings and afternoons are devoted to reviewing the academic program,
> explaining degree requirements, and discussing the college's various re-
> sources; evenings are spent in such activities as films, a cookout, and a
> dance. There is also time during academic orientation for students to meet
> with their advisers and to become acquainted with the resources of the Bar
> Harbor area [College of the Atlantic, 1978, p. 9].

Another way in which workshops and other single-event
programs have been used extensively is through the cultural activities of the campus. Virtually all colleges offer a variety of
concerts, exhibitions, and visiting lectureships; several have attempted to systematize these offerings and apply them more
directly to the central academic goals of the college as well as to
other academic activities. In many instances, these cultural
events are also transformed from single, one-day events to more
extended workshops or institutes.

At Davis and Elkins College (W. Va.), cultural activities
are coordinated under the "IMPACT" program, while at Ottawa
University (Kans.), not only are various cultural events coordinated under the institution's "University Program Series," but
each student is required to participate in the series. The follow-

ing description of the 1976 Ottawa program conveys the essence
of this rather distinctive academic requirement:

Each full-time student, during each seven-week session of residency
in the university, will participate in the University Program Series. Individual programs within the series provide a platform for the concerns of university students and faculty; create interest in important public and intellectual issues; encourage appreciation of the arts through performance and
discussion; ensure continuing confrontation with the claims of Christian
faith outside of formal study; and in general provide for the gathering of
substantial portions of the university community around a series of common experiences as a means of overcoming fragmentation of ideas and relationships and of serving the broader purposes of general education for
all members of the university.

Included in the series are religious services, convocations, concerts,
lectures, productions of the drama department, and other special programs
as announced. Recent campus appearances have been made by the City
Center Acting Company presenting "Three Sisters" and "She Stoops To
Conquer," author Elizabeth Janeway, the Newport Jazz Festival featuring
Clark Terry, Max Roach, and Bill Evans, *Time* editor Marshall Loeb, the
American Chamber Ballet, and composer Aaron Copland. Programs will be
held in certain daytime hours kept open in the weekly class schedule for
this purpose and also some evenings and Sunday afternoons.

Beginning in February of 1977, nine programs will be available in
each seven-week session, and each full-time student is required to attend
any five of the programs. He may choose the five (and more, if he desires)
in terms of those programs that interest him most and at times that best
suit his convenience. It is also hoped that student choice will be made with
a view to expanding interests and becoming exposed to areas insufficiently
known or appreciated as a means of enriching the total educational experience.

The total programs available for on-campus students and the community of the university are intended to enhance the total educational,
cultural, and religious environment of the university and strengthen its
community. For that reason, substitution of programs elsewhere to meet
the requirement is not fully consonant with the purposes of the university
although off-campus students are expected to attend such programs as are
available to them wherever they may be.

However, in order to allow greater choice for each on-campus student to choose programs from such resources as Kansas City and the University of Kansas in Lawrence, one of the five required programs may be
chosen from similar off-campus opportunities. In case the student elects to
attend an off-campus program, he must have the approval of his adviser before the event occurs. The full list of nine programs will be published at

the beginning of each seven-week session and given to each student so that he will have an opportunity in advance to determine the programs likely to be of greatest interest in meeting the overall requirement [Ottawa University, 1976, p. 23].

Single-event programming has taken on a slightly different emphasis at Northern Illinois University (Keating, Cervi, and Cypert, 1978). There the program, a weekend residential experience, is designed to facilitate social and emotional growth in an outdoor education program. Problem-solving activities that require both physical and intellectual cooperation make up part of a two-and-a-half-day weekend to develop strengths in four dimensions: interpersonal, intrapersonal, intellectual, and physical. Formal evaluations of this program have shown an increase in participants' positive self-concept and identity with a corresponding decline in self-criticism.

Extended workshops are used frequently at Fairhaven College (part of Western Washington State University) and at the College of the Atlantic (Maine). The Fairhaven workshops

are a collection of art/craft facilities, programs, and student activities. Among the workshops, there is a ceramic studio, a darkroom, a stained glass workshop, a textiles workshop, a woodshop, a women's center and gallery, a media center, a Fairhaven community newspaper (*Tuna Gas News*), a student "Vocations for Social Change" work/study office, and an organic gardening/alternative energy/alternative life-style program called Outback. Each of the programs was initiated by students and exists in the context of the Fairhaven living-learning program. Each provides facilities adequate to work in the medium; however, they are not professional studios. Many workshops are run cooperatively with participants sharing some of their tools and materials.

The workshops exist both for casual pursuit of crafts [and] for academic work. Students who are serious about a particular workshop may arrange to get credit for their work either through participation in classes or through independent study projects with a Fairhaven faculty member [Western Washington State University, 1977, p. 56].

At COA, workshops are a vital part of the problem-solving, ecologically oriented curriculum. Workshops are generated by either students or faculty members and focus on such topics as whales, alternative energy, subdivision law, and homesteading. "Workshops are intended to develop students' ability to deal with concrete problems. They often contribute productively to the community beyond the college. In addition, they aid students in learning how to work cooperatively and effectively in a team effort" (College of the Atlantic, 1978, p. 44).

By combining extended workshops with traditional academic programs and by linking "extracurricular" cultural activities of the college more closely with the formal curriculum, a college can respond to a more diverse set of needs and can significantly enrich its academic program, not by adding new activities but by making better use of existing programs.

Unspecified Duration of Instructional Units. Several colleges have recently explored, and several educational theorists have advocated, the use of unstructured calendars. Heiss (1973) notes that Friends World College (N.Y.) uses "only the base skeleton of a calendar because [its] programs demand minimum restraint on year-long operations" (p. 47) and that "some colleges such as Leeward Community College in Honolulu, Hawaii, admit students at almost any time during the year" (p. 49), operating on short-term intensive course plans or time blocks. College IV (now Kirkhof College) of the Grand Valley State Colleges (Mich.) used to offer both a regular calendar, registration being held before the beginning of each term, and an open-ended calendar, with continuous registration, which may take place any time after the fifth day of the term (Grand Valley State Colleges, 1977). Students at College IV who participated in the open calendar were enrolled exclusively in "self-paced" courses. Currently, students in self-paced classes must begin at the start of each semester with the assumption that they will finish; if they do not, one additional semester is open to them (R. Holland, personal communication, 1980).

One of the most articulate arguments for flexible, non-structured calendars has been presented by Richmond (1977, p. 135): "The amount of time needed to adequately present the content of a course should determine neither the duration of a student's tenure in a course nor the duration of the course. Competency assessment of the skills required to successfully complete a course and of the course content should become the determining factors." According to Richmond (pp. 136-137):

In a flexible all-year curriculum, the concept of continuous student progress through the curriculum sequence would become a reality because students would be permitted to enroll in more advanced courses of a curriculum sequence or in other courses immediately upon completion of one course. Provisions could also be made for any student or faculty member to take an extended leave from school at any time during the calendar year, and the duration of the leave and the reason for the leave could be determined by the individual requesting the leave. Such a curriculum design has the natural flexibility to adjust to the normal needs of acceleration and remediation that permit each student to work at a pace comfortable to his learning style. . . .

In a flexible curriculum, the number of students enrolled in a course would become insignificant to the decision to offer or not to offer a particular course during any given school term. Numerous students could be enrolled in any given course during any point in time. The electronic production of lectures and demonstrations for courses would be advantageous to the personalized approach to the teaching-learning process because of the replay and personalized potential of the videotaped process. The availability of the professor as a resource person in the personalized atmosphere would be an added dimension to the self-directed learning situation.

In the flexible all-year curriculum design, the academic year would have neither an ending nor a beginning. Consequently, a student would not be able to fail at the end of a school term. A student would not have to wait until the beginning of a semester, a quarter, or a trimester to matriculate as students have traditionally been forced to do. College instructional facilities would be conducted around the year like a bank, the local supermarket, or the corner drugstore. Unwarranted postponements of the implementation of the decision to enroll in college can often lead to an eternal delay in the matriculation at a postsecondary institution for some potential students. . . .

The flexible curriculum would permit postsecondary institutions the option of eliminating the use of failing grades in the assessment of a student's lack of progress. No student would even fail a course: he could return to school after an extended absence and pick up his academic progress where he left off. The opportunity would also be provided for a student to work at a particular course as long as it required to successfully complete the course. An "I" grade would be assigned to all incomplete courses, and passing grades would be assigned only when performance assessment justified such action.

As Richmond (1977) has noted, a flexible, nonstructured calendar is dependent on the use of specific instructional technologies (for example, videotapes, programmed instruction, computer-assisted instruction) or new instructional methods (for example, self-paced instruction, audiotutorial instruction).

Unlimited Duration of Instructional Units. Up to the present, the dominant assumption in American higher education has been that a student is buying instructional services for a specified period of time. In undergraduate institutions, this duration is usually two or four years. These services are being employed primarily so that the student can obtain a degree or certificate. Thus, a calendar is appropriate to describe the scheduling and duration of particular instructional events (courses, modules, workshops, and so on). Even colleges offering external degree programs, such as Empire State College (N.Y.), provide services for a limited period of time until the student has obtained a particular degree.

Only when we look outside the higher education community do we begin to find educational programs that serve learners over an unspecified period of time. Many corporations, for instance, offer management development, career planning, and even liberal arts programs over an employee's entire working life. One prominent corporation estimates that its midlevel managers who receive educational services over a period of thirty to forty years will obtain the equivalent of three or four master's degrees in business administration.

A collegiate institution could provide similar lifelong learning services. A student might, for instance, sign a contract with a college at an early age which would enable him or her to make periodic use of educational counseling services at the college (helping the student clarify learning needs, identify appropriate community resources, and evaluate progress toward specific educational objectives); take courses or workshops offered by the college (or other cooperating institutions if the student moves); receive appropriate degrees, credentials, or academic credits; "stop out" periodically for educational sabbaticals or leaves; and couple personal learning experiences with family "educational vacations."

The lifelong learning contract might be made with the college by the individual learner, by a corporation, or even by a union. New collective bargaining agreements might begin to include educational as well as medical, dental, and mental health benefits. Payment for services could be made in a lump sum (to hedge against inflation), through a monthly or yearly payment plan, or on a per-hour-of-service basis.

In providing lifelong services, a college would undoubtedly need to shift its emphasis from classroom instruction for eighteen- to twenty-two-year-old learners to educational counseling with mature adult learners. Although such a transition may be painful, it is certainly not impossible, as witnessed by the extraordinary transformation of Marylhurst College (a traditional four-year liberal arts college) to the Marylhurst Center for Lifelong Learning (Ore.). Marylhurst still provides liberal arts programs that lead primarily to a degree, but the center could readily modify its program to accommodate a lifelong learning contract system.

A somewhat less profound change is incurred if the lifelong learning contract is given to graduates of the institution. Such a program is offered by Ottawa University (Kans.) in its Contract Assurance Program. This program is described in the 1976 catalogue (Ottawa University, 1976, p. 19) and has been only slightly modified by 1980:

> All graduates of the Ottawa University residential campus in 1973 and thereafter will receive a "contract assurance bond" at the time of graduation that entitles them to enroll for up to ten regular credit courses at reduced rates, or in many cases at no charge, during the ten-year period following the first anniversary of their graduation. A regular credit course is defined as a course offered in the Registrar's listing of on-campus courses for each session, and that, apart from graduates wishing to utilize the "contract assurance bond" option, has sufficient minimum enrollment. Independent studies are not included under the contract assurance bond program. Graduates of Ottawa prior to 1973 also are eligible to participate in the program beginning in the summer of 1974.
> The contract assurance bond is nontransferable and offers benefits according to the following schedule:

Tuition free if Bachelor of Arts degree earned at Ottawa University with at least thirty course units of credit (or less if under accelerated graduation program) completed at Ottawa;

Tuition reduction of 75 percent if Bachelor of Arts degree earned at Ottawa University with nineteen to twenty-nine course units of credit completed at Ottawa;

Tuition reduction of 50 percent if Bachelor of Arts degree earned at Ottawa University prior to 1973 or if Bachelor of Arts degree earned at Ottawa University with eight to eighteen course units of credit being completed at Ottawa.

On the basis of the schedule above, Ottawa graduates may enroll in ten regular credit courses of the university to improve previous skills or to gain new skills and knowledge.

Although this program does not provide educational resources that are specifically tailored for the adult learner, it does represent a major new step for liberal arts colleges that wish to continue to be of educational value to their graduates. Such a program not only keeps alumni interested in (and supportive of) the college, it also enables the college to make a tangible commitment to lifelong learning: "Ottawa graduates can be secure in the knowledge that a continuing partnership has been formed between them and their alma mater to guarantee that the information and skills needed to help them keep pace in a rapidly changing world are available" (Ottawa University, 1976, p. 19). Such a program shatters the traditional concepts about the yearlong college calendar and the exclusive commitment of a college to the learning of students for only four years.

Wheaton College (Mass.) similarly has moved toward a lifelong learning commitment to its students through a Career Assistance Program (CAP) for alumni. A range of services are offered to the established professional graduate who may want career updating, the reentering graduate who wishes assistance in becoming oriented or reoriented to the job market, and the recent graduate who wishes assistance in finding a job or changing careers. CAP activities provided to alumni of Wheaton include (1) the "Wheaton Network," a national network of alumni who represent a wide range of occupational areas and are available to assist fellow alumni with career advice, information, and employment contacts, (2) individual career counseling, including skills assessment, résumé preparation, and job-hunting strategy information, (3) a computer-based career exploration and decision-making program (SIGI, developed by the Educational Testing Service of New Jersey), (4) regional programs and workshops on such topics as "mentoring" and "dual-career couples," as well as specific occupational concerns, and (5) resource files on employment agencies, support groups, and career-counseling organizations. Much as Ottawa University provides its alumni with continuing liberal education, Wheaton College provides its alumni with continuing career assistance, thereby making good on its claim (and the claim of most colleges) of concern with its students' long-term welfare.

Concluding Comments: Individualizing the Calendar for Adults. Common sense and experience have long indicated that a virtually infinite mix of time uses and responsibilities constrains adults' participation in colleges and degree programs. As innovative programs in the late 1960s and early 1970s sought to serve an increasingly broader age range of learners, the implications for altering the academic calendar to meet the needs of midlife and older adult students became clearer.

In stimulating the development of University Without Walls programs in twenty public and private member institutions in 1971, the Union for Experimenting Colleges and Universities (UECU; Ohio) included a statement about time as one of its "eight organizing concepts": "Employment of flexible time units so that a student could spend varying periods of time in a particular kind of program experience. Programs were to be individually tailored by the student and adviser. There would be no fixed curriculum and no uniform time schedule for the award of the degree" (Greenberg, 1972, p. 12). Each UECU member institution adapted this concept to its own circumstances and needs.

At Loretto Heights College in Denver (Colo.), the concept of a "learning segment" was established to provide for individualization within the regular semester system. A "learning segment" is a period that begins on the day of registration and extends for exactly sixteen weeks without reference to the traditional Christmas, spring, and summer breaks. The full twelve-month calendar is utilized. Tuition is paid for a period of time equivalent to the regular semester, and services are rendered within the sixteen-week segments of active enrollment.

Short courses, seminars, media presentations, independent studies, and field projects can be completed, using learning contracts, for brief periods within the learning segment. Learning experiences can also be continued beyond the sixteen-week period by learning-contract agreement between the student and the faculty adviser. Extending the segment requires reregistration and additional payment of tuition. Special extensions must be approved by the faculty adviser and program administrator. Courses taken at other accredited colleges which can be included in UWW degree programs and which may be offered on the quarter system, on different semester schedules, or on an intensive or modularized basis can be accommodated. In this way, students can make full use of a wide variety of course offerings at many convenient accredited institutions. This design extends curricular choices and widens the range of learning resources that a small college can offer far beyond its own limited curricular resources.

Registration is conducted nine times a year (excluding the busy months of May, August, and December) on the first Friday of the month. Each registration is followed by intensive weekend orientation workshops. Admissions, enrollment, special workshops, and faculty-adviser assignments cycle throughout the year. The peak registrations tend to occur in September, January, and June, but the multiple enrollment options can accommodate a wide variety of adult students' individual, family, and work patterns and recognize the pressures and demands of adults' lives.

"Stopout" periods are common for catching up, taking a breather, accumulating tuition funds, varying the pace, synthesizing ideas and directions, or responding to the various crises and emergencies in the role-complex lives of adult learners. Students are held in inactive status ("stopout") for a reasonable period (often one year) before being considered a "dropout," officially withdrawing from the program, reapplying, or being taken off the active roster.

During demanding times, as when the student is preparing a proposal for academic credit for prior noncollege learning (advanced-standing credit) or synthesizing theoretical and experiential learning for the required major work and degree review before graduation, a student can register part-time, or for a few credits within a full load, for "educational planning." This registration provides for the time the student often needs to spend with the faculty adviser. It also supplies needed tuition revenue to support advisement and evaluation services rendered by the institution and the program staff.

More frequent registrations such as "learning segments" make significant demands on faculty and administrative staff while seeking to respond to adult students' needs for time flexibility. A reasonable balance between learner-centered responsiveness and institution-centered convenience and feasibility must be maintained if such individualized approaches to time use are to be successful.

During the 1970s, extensive research and growing experience with enrolled and potential adult students made it clear to colleges that time constraints are one of the most significant barriers to adults returning to college. Cross (1979, p. 106) describes "lack of time due to home and job responsibilities" as a "situational barrier" and "inconvenient schedules and full-time fees for part-time study" as an "institutional barrier" to adults' pursuit of higher education.

Charland (1976) has emphasized the role-complex, resource-constrained, vocationally motivated, and present-oriented characteristics of the adult learner. Greenberg (1980) has described the sense of urgency that adults bring to their decisions to return to college—decisions that are often years in the making. Women's lives, especially, are characterized by this sense of urgency at various times in the life cycle, as when reentry women strive to "make up for lost time" spent in child rearing and homemaking or when working women try to juggle their multiple roles as mothers, wives, employees, citizens, and students.

Time is viewed by older adults as a precious resource, often being ranked as important as money. Therefore, colleges that hope to attract, serve, and meet the real needs of adult learners should carefully consider the multiple time demands in older adults' lives. Academic calendars are usually designed for young adults whose primary role is that of student and for traditional faculty habits and preferences. These calendars are often not appropriate for adult learners.

The curricular dimension of time is within the control of the institution. Its importance cannot be overemphasized. The principle of flexibility in structuring time is particularly essential now that colleges serve increasingly diverse learner populations.

Curricular Clock

Weekday/Daytime Instruction. At present most colleges offer a large majority of courses during the standard academic "workday": 8 A.M. to 5 P.M. According to Levine (1978), 59 percent of undergraduates take all their courses during the day, and at selective liberal arts colleges, the percentage is even higher—73 percent (Levine, 1978, p. 241). Although these hours are usually convenient for full-time faculty members and for students who reside on campus and go to school full-time, other times of day may be more convenient for part-time faculty members and for the increasing number of students who commute to school, work part- or full-time, and/or are raising children. For these latter students, alternative times must be found for counseling, classes, modules, workshops, and so on.

Honolulu Community College has made an innovative attempt to meet the needs of a group of people whose schedules differ from the traditional college student's (Cox, 1969). Three plans were devised for firefighters who have an on-again, off-again duty schedule. Plan 1 involved one hour of class attendance during normal class hours on Monday-Wednesday-Friday. The firefighters skipped class entirely the following week, making up material with class notes and the instructor's aid. Plan 2 was a class composed solely of firefighters in two-hour sessions Monday-Wednesday-Friday. The class met only on alternate weeks. Plan 3 duplicated Plan 1 except that the firefighters attended ninety-minute classes on Tuesday and Thursday on alternate weeks.

Weekday/Evening Instruction. Courses are now more frequently being offered in the evening, though a very small percentage (0.4 percent) of students in selective liberal arts colleges take all their classes at night (Levine, 1978). Generally, those liberal arts colleges that have moved to evening classes have shifted their primary mission to include the provision of academic services for adults. A classic example of this movement is the Marylhurst Center for Lifelong Learning (Ore.). Most of the Marylhurst courses are now offered during weekday evenings or during one of the other nontraditional times described in the following pages. William Paterson College (N.J.) has similarly accommodated adult learners by scheduling many of its courses and programs in the evening and on weekends. Twenty-eight major programs are now being held during these nontraditional times at William Paterson. The Lindenwood Colleges (Mo.) established an Evening College in 1972 that provides a full set of courses in the evenings in such areas as the humanities, natural sciences, social sciences, and business. Fontbonne College (Mo.) expanded its course offerings during the evening hours and on Saturday to meet the needs of the older, part-time student (Freidman, 1979). In addition to expanding both the number and variety of course offerings, Fontbonne College has experimented with increasingly longer class meetings on a concentrated eight-week basis.

Weekday/Marginal-Time Instruction. Several colleges are exploring the use of "marginal" time for course offerings. Levine (1978, p. 242) has noted that "early morning classes, scheduled to meet before working hours, and weekend colleges are recent phenomena that seem to be gaining in popularity if a growing number of advertisements in the *New York Times Education Supplement* is any indication. Between 7 A.M. and 9 A.M., the University of Santa Clara offers what it calls 'Early Bird classes' leading to an engineering degree. And Long Island University has a degree in management that includes classes offered to suburbanites on their way to work in New York City by commuter train."

Other colleges offer special workshops for businesspersons and for homemakers during breakfast or lunch hours. The New

School for Social Research (N.Y.), for instance, offers a "Language at Lunchtime" program of short-term, intensive courses to help New York City residents acquire rapid fluency in a language. Making use of public and closed-circuit television, many colleges now offer courses for credit at an early hour (usually 5 A.M. to 8 A.M.). Perhaps the boldest venture in this regard is the late-night (after midnight) courses offered via radio by Mercy College of New York.

Weekend Instruction. Weekend courses are offered currently at a variety of colleges and universities, including Carlow College (Pa.), College of Mount St. Joseph (Ohio), Mercy College (Mich.), Mercyhurst College (Pa.), St. Thomas Aquinas College (N.Y.), Wayne State University (Mich.), the University of Southern California (Berk, 1979), Queens College (N.Y.; Resnick and Kaplan, 1971), and Winthrop College (S.C.; Jenkins, 1978).

In the future, we are likely to find many more colleges and universities adopting a weekend college system for undergraduate education and inviting entire families to participate in what might be described as brief "educational vacations." Such educational vacations are already a reality at Rockland Community College (N.Y.; Fey, 1977). This institution offers a lifelong educational program that seeks to respond to the needs and interests of a variety of age groups found within the typical family unit. The "Family College" is a weekend program at Rockland that targets specific learning opportunities to each age group within the family as well as educational experiences for the entire family (such as visits to museums, cultural centers, parks, and historic sites). For adults in the family, a mix of courses, both graduate and undergraduate, are offered in the arts, humanities, sciences, and business administration. Personal enrichment, recreation, and leisure activities are also available. For elementary school-age children, learning activities are offered in languages and science; crafts, singing, and magic are provided to further artistic and creative interests. In addition, the "Education for Living Institute" offers a variety of courses, workshops, and growth experiences that address critical transition periods in changing family-life patterns, such as divorce, death of spouse or child, and changes accompanying adolescence or the birth of a child. The Rockland "Family College" extends the role of colleges and universities and challenges us to rethink our traditional assumptions about the purposes of postsecondary education.

Extended-Time Instruction. For a long time, colleges have offered condensed courses during summer school that require full-time participation of students for several weeks. Recently, several colleges have attempted variations on this model. Goddard College (Vt.), for instance, offers an "adult degree program" (ADP) that builds on a series of intensive twelve-day residential programs:

> The idea of the educational community is basic to residential adult education. An ADP group—usually about fifty students and six to eight faculty—is very much a community during its twelve-day resident periods (Sunday through the second Thursday). The scheduled parts of the residency are short courses on topics of current and continuing concern, orientation, and evaluation sessions about the what, why, and how of ADP, lecture-discussions by and with faculty and others, presentations of culminating work by students who will graduate at the end of the residency, and a number of communal bread-breakings and celebrations. . . . Students and teachers are together a great deal, at these times and in the individual or small-group conferences at which last term's work is discussed and next term's work is planned.
>
> Beyond these scheduled events—somewhat formal in this basically informal two weeks—there is the life of the college houses: late-night discussions that take middle-aged people back to the passionate intensity of their teens and twenties, the continual exchange of ideas and interests and experiences [Goddard College, 1978, p. 31].

An adult participant in Goddard's ADP is able to complete a six-month semester by participating in two residential programs at a six-month interval:

> At the opening residency, a student chooses or is assigned a faculty supervisor for the coming term and spends a number of hours with that person making detailed plans for study. To be considered are previous learnings, interests, needs, the resources the student will have available at home and at work. The plan states what is to be read, what is to be written and by what deadlines, what research or observation or interviewing may

be necessary, what form reports to the faculty member will take, and how the project will be brought to a close.

The study is planned to be comparable in the amount of work to be done to a full semester of study in a traditional college or university, work for which the college may grant . . . the equivalent of fifteen semester hours of academic credit. . . .

The work at home is likely to consist largely of reading and writing, though it may involve practicum experience too. . . . Reports to the supervising faculty member are posted off periodically, usually every three weeks. They take many shapes: formal essays, annotated bibliographies, pages from journals, sample of work done, chatty letters full of questions. Faculty responses are equally varied: criticism and comments, suggestions for additional reading, new ideas or information, a paper returned with a lot of marginal comments, a list of questions raised by the work the student has submitted.

The semester ends at the next residence. The six or eight or ten students who have been working with the same faculty member meet to talk about what they have been working on as they met six months before to share their plans. Each student has an extensive evaluation conference with the faculty member. Student and faculty member each make written evaluations of the semester's work. The ending of one term merges into the beginning of the next [Goddard College, 1978, pp. 32-33].

Goddard also offers a summer-based degree program "for persons—particularly younger adults—who want more interaction with faculty than ADP's twice-a-year residencies and dialogue by mail provides" (Goddard College, 1978, p. 57). By offering these special adult degree programs, Goddard is able to blend the rich experience of residential education with the flexibility of part-time attendance and is able to overcome the problem of being located in an area (Plainfield, Vermont) that, though attractive, is not immediately accessible. More colleges can be expected to explore variations on this extended-time model in the near future.

A variation of this pattern is used in the Loretto Heights College (Colo.) University Without Walls/Students-at-a-Distance project. Adult learners who live outside the Denver metropolitan area are required to spend three intensive four-day periods in Denver, at the beginning, middle, and end of their individualized degree programs. Workshops are conducted over the weekend between Friday and Monday. A student meets with his or her faculty adviser for planning and evaluation. Often, assessment of prior noncollege learning (advanced-standing proposals) takes place during these times, and predegree review sessions are held to review the student's entire degree program before graduation. These intensive periods also provide time for personal reflection and study as well as interaction with other, distant students. The results are often a reduced sense of isolation and heightened personal renewal in addition to clarification of program processes and requirements.

Concluding Comments: Individualizing the Clock for Adults. As varied as different people's use of the calendar may be, uses of each twenty-four-hour day may be even more diverse. Most people are aware of their own habits of being primarily "morning people" or "night people." Class schedules arranged for the "morning" faculty member may not accommodate the needs of the "night owl" student. Faculty office hours held between 9 A.M. and 3 P.M. are likely to miss the student employed full-time. Late afternoon and early evening classes are often difficult for mothers of young children. Weekend schedules for male or female heads of household may be tolerable for short periods but are likely to give rise to family conflict if continued long. These "secondary" social impacts of institutional decisions deserve consideration as curricular schedules are rearranged.

In recognition of the wide diversity of uses of the daily clock, many colleges have increased their use of self-directed, independent curricular options. These methods of learning also recognize the self-directed nature of adult learning styles and preferences, so convincingly described by Tough (1979) and Knowles (1975).

Control of one's own use of time is seen by adult students as a central condition of adulthood. In research done in Project Transition, a special project of the University Without Walls at Loretto Heights College (Colo.), students aged twenty to sixty-five frequently mentioned "making my own decisions," "giving myself permission," "being internally motivated," and "prioritizing" as keys to their definitions of adulthood (Greenberg and Charland, 1980, pp. 63-70). In addition, when asked

"What do you most need to learn next?," a significant number of the more than 200 adults in the project identified these same adult-defining items as the things they also most needed to learn. In other words, by ordering the ways people use their time, colleges may indeed be contributing to dependency and infantilization and may inadvertently supply disincentives to the expressed goal of helping students take responsibility for their own lives.

This phenomenon may be true for younger and older adult learners alike. Examples of young adult graduates who become disoriented and confused during the period after commencement are common. One wonders whether colleges too often overschedule for students. When the structure of class schedules is removed, many graduates feel lost and anxious. Rigid schedules may negatively affect older adult students also. After being responsible for their own decisions and priorities in time use, adults often resist giving up their autonomy to institutional schedules that reduce their freedom and treat them like children.

Programs that provide for increasingly independent and self-directed uses of time, however, can help people learn how to manage the limited resource of time, how to judge what can realistically be accomplished in a given period, and how to make decisions about priorities in their uses of time. These approaches encourage maturity and responsible adult behavior patterns.

Curriculum designs that place minimal or no restrictions on the amount of independent study, independent field projects, or self-directed learning that is permitted can help remove some of the barriers imposed by the varied pressures and uses of time and can promote skills in organizing and managing time, so necessary to successful adult life.

It should also be recognized that some students need assistance in learning how to structure their time use. Class schedules may have this positive effect. Individualization of degree programs and academic advising that goes beyond the mere signing of a student's schedule card can assist students, both young and old, to learn time management. Curricular designs that incrementally move from highly structured time sequences at the freshman level to increasingly self-directed, independent learning experiences at the senior level can provide an appropriate mix of support and independence as students proceed through a degree program. And, in recognition of older adults' capacities and needs for defining their own uses of time, programs that serve older learners can often confidently place unusual amounts of responsibility on the learner to read, write, study, work, and synthesize his or her own learning if they provide simultaneously for periodic discussion, advisement, and interactive support with faculty and institutional staff.

In the final analysis, the clock belongs to the learner. It is the institution's responsibility to value the limited resource of time that students have to give to the educational process while making it clear to the student what the expected outcomes of a particular set of learning experiences are. The curricular clock that balances structured group learning opportunities with self-directed, flexible alternatives can meet both the institution's and the learner's needs for control and for appropriate use of the limited resource of time.

— II —

SPACE

Maximizing the Use
of Instructional Settings
On- and Off-Campus

Hall (1966) has written about space as the "hidden dimension" in interpersonal relations. Space also appears to be the "hidden dimension" in the curriculum of American colleges and universities. Very little has been written about the uses of instructional or noninstructional space in collegiate institutions or about the implications of these uses for teaching, learning, and the collegiate curriculum. Even Heiss (1973) and Levine (1978), in their extensive surveys of curricular innovations, give relatively little attention to the innovative use of space. The collegiate catalogues, in which most colleges and universities try to identify everything that is even remotely interesting about their curriculum, rarely mention space and its use for instructional purposes other than to show the customary pictures and brief descriptions of a new classroom building, a new library annex, or a laboratory. More recently, catalogues have begun to include pictures of students working and learning in community settings.

In part, this neglect may result from the widespread dis illusionment during the 1970s regarding funds spent for capital improvements during the 1960s. New buildings were constructed during the enrollment boom of the 1960s not only to accommodate more students but also to improve the quality of instruction. Unfortunately, as with the purchase of new audiovisual equipment, this capital investment rarely paid off in the improvement of instruction.

Typical of most colleges and universities is a story about the use of a new instructional facility on the campus of a university in the Pacific Northwest. A new building was constructed with a circular, multilevel amphitheater, fully equipped with the newest audiovisual equipment. Courses could be conducted in the round; chairs were not bolted to the floor, thereby allowing for flexibility in the layout of the room; the floor was carpeted for a more relaxed atmosphere; students and faculty members could even abandon the chairs and sit on the three tiers. Within the first two years, the audiovisual equipment was returned to the A-V center because of infrequent use. The circular space was being used exclusively as a semicircular, traditional classroom. Faculty members and students were explicitly told not to move the chairs (it is harder to clean up when chairs are moved about), and the abandonment of chairs was strongly discouraged. This scenario has been repeated at many colleges and universities. Leading advocates of curricular change in American higher education tend to ignore the spatial dimension.

Recognizing that spatial reconfiguration must be coupled with other curricular changes, one should consider the vital role played by space in all aspects of teaching and learning. As Sommer (1969, p. 98) has noted, instructional space "is all too frequently taken for granted by those who plan educational facilities as well as those who use them." Sommer has persuasively shown that the design of instructional space and the arrangement of objects occupying this space significantly influence the amount and type of student participation, the nature of student-

faculty relationships, and the attitudes of students toward learning. Although he focused primarily on the use of space in a traditional classroom, Sommer notes that in the near future much
of our attention will necessarily be shifted to the use of noninstructional space for learning. Following is a description of alternative uses of space to facilitate student learning both within
and outside the classroom.

Instructional Space

On Campus. Most collegiate instruction now takes place
in a formally designated classroom, laboratory, or studio, though
much of what a student learns occurs outside these formal environments: in the dormitory, at the student union, in the hallways between classes, or on the job. Formal instructional space
can be arranged, of course, in a variety of patterns, depending
on the nature of the topic being discussed and the type of interaction desired. Typical alternatives to the standard straight-row
classroom are the arrangement of chairs in a semicircle or complete circle, the arrangement of chairs around one or more sides
of worktables, and the free and changing arrangement of chairs
and tables in an open space.

Recently, many colleges and universities have explored
the use of circular, multitiered classrooms; freeform, multitiered
classrooms; and "modularized" classrooms in which walls can
be moved easily to establish new configurations of space that
are appropriate to changing uses of the room. Although the
third design is found much more frequently in elementary and
secondary schools than in collegiate institutions, it is becoming
increasingly attractive as colleges and universities face the prospect of doing increasingly diversified instruction in the space
available. No longer can many colleges afford the luxury of
space that is designed inflexibly for a single purpose.

On Campus/Quasi-Instructional. Traditionally, most colleges have decided that several noninstructional areas on campus
(such as the library, auditorium, or chapel) will serve instructional purposes some of the time. The instructional role to be
played by the library is obvious. In recent years, however, with

the advent of "learning centers," the use of the library space for instructional purposes has become even more direct.

> In addition to the traditional libraries that store printed materials and offer quiet rooms for reading, a growing number of institutions now operate learning centers or workshop areas for the storage, retrieval, and use of knowledge recorded in audio or visual forms other than print. In most instances, the activities of the center involve students, faculty, and center personnel in experiences that make teaching and learning interchangeable. In many cases, the center serves as a means through which the student can use programmed materials at his own pace. Some centers are equipped with dial-access systems that allow students in the dormitory to tie in with materials on file at the resource center [Heiss, 1973, p. 109].

Off Campus. Some colleges now own or lease edge-of-campus or off-campus conference facilities that are used for instruction. Allegheny State University (N.C.) owns such a center, as do Bethany College (W. Va.), the Ponoma campus of California State Polytechnic College, and the University of New Hampshire. In general, these institutions receive income from their centers through rental to outside organizations, but they also make the facilities available to their own faculty members and students. These conference centers generally provide instructional facilities that are more flexible, comfortable, and attractive than the facilities available on campus. The conference centers are particularly appropriate for intensive, short-term residential programs, as the centers generally provide housing and meals for off-campus visitors. Most of these centers were funded through foundation grants or alumni gifts.

Other collegiate institutions (for example, Washington State University) have chosen to purchase or lease more rustic retreat centers, usually located in a nearby mountain region, or to use corporate training facilities, local schools, or church camps for special programs. Schools and church camps can often be used at very low cost, and corporations are often willing to provide their facilities at no cost or low cost to a college, writing off excess expenses as tax-deductible contributions.

Noninstructional Space

On Campus. For several reasons, college administrators and faculty members should give serious thought to more extensive use of on-campus space that is not formally designated for instruction. First, because such space is already available, it can be used at no (or little) additional cost, this benefit being of particular value to a growing college that needs more instructional space. Second, noninstructional space is often more conducive to certain types of learning than space that is formally designated for instruction. Students are often more relaxed, more receptive to learning, and more willing to participate in discussions in "nontraditional" settings. Third, noninstructional space often involves the cooperation or even active participation of noninstructional staff members, thereby increasing their knowledge of, and sense of involvement in, the academic program of the college. Fourth, noninstructional space on campus often seems more like the "real world" than a classroom does. What students learn in nontraditional settings is often more readily transferable to noncollegiate settings.

What are the noninstructional settings in which teaching and learning can take place? Student living quarters (dormitories, apartments, fraternities, and sororities) are an obvious choice. For many years, faculty members and administrators have recognized the value of convening courses, workshops, meetings, and advisement on the student's "home turf," thereby enabling the student to feel less defensive and more open to exploring new ideas.

This concept has been significantly expanded in the establishment of "living-learning" centers. As of 1973, Heiss (1973, p. 35) was able to account for more than 250 colleges and universities that had "extended teaching-learning discourse beyond the classroom by using student residence halls for learning as well as for living space." Heiss (p. 35) notes:

The placement of small classrooms, study units, faculty offices, and advisory services in freshman and sophomore residence halls has been

fairly successful in mitigating the impersonal quality and attendant alienation of large institutions. Usually the living-learning space is used for
teaching those segments of the general education program that lend them
selves to small-group discussion, but in some cases other facilities are also
available for instruction or self-instruction. These may include closed-
circuit television systems, playback screens that enable students to review
parts or all of a demonstration or lecture, language laboratories, record libraries, dial-access services to the library, and other "packaged" learning
materials. . . .

  In an effort to provide facilities for deep immersion in a particular
area, some colleges operate theme houses where students working in the
same area of concentration or freshmen studying the same general education option live together for some part of their college program.

  One of the first and most successful of these latter theme
houses was established at Stephens College (Mo.) in the 1960s
under a grant from the Ford Foundation. According to a recent
Stephens College catalogue, the Stephens House Plan "is a liberal arts program for freshmen who are interested in taking
basic, related courses in the liberal arts with a team of teacher-
advisers. . . . The plan is limited to 80 students who are invited
on the basis of interest and academic achievement. . . . The
House Plan academic program is built on three basic, required
courses from the departments of English, Religion and Philosophy, and General Humanities" (Stephens College, 1979, p. 66).

  Noninstructional areas other than the dormitory are also
appropriate for teaching and learning. At the University of Vic-
toria (B.C.), comfortable sitting areas have been set up outside
the classrooms, thereby transforming hallways and courtyards
from just places through which students and faculty members
travel to places where they can continue discussions begun during the formal class period. Such discussion can continue, of
course, at the student union or the professor's office; however,
it is perhaps more likely to continue if begun in a comfortable
space immediately adjacent to the classroom, rather than in the
classroom.

  Classes can also be taught effectively in various service
centers of the college, especially "after hours." One enterpris-
ing young professor obtained the use of the president's office
for an evening seminar. Not only did the students taking this

seminar feel "special," they also tended to be more serious in their preparation for the seminar (even though the president did not attend any of the sessions). In other instances, career-preparation courses have been held in an appropriate on-campus office; design courses in the public relations, publications, or graphic arts office; accounting courses in the business office. Not only are these spaces available at certain times of the day, they also lend realism (and hence encourage a seriousness of purpose) and provide tools (calculators, computers, drafting tables, and so on) and illustrative materials (such as layouts and budget sheets).

The outdoors is an excellent instructional space and, as faculty members know, is often favored by students on a balmy spring or autumn day. Although holding a course out on the lawn can be distracting at times, it also can be relaxing and conducive to personal reflection and small-group conversation. A typical classroom often does not provide sufficient space for a large number of students to be organized into small groups for discussion. If the class were to move outdoors, these small groups might be managed rather easily, the groups located far enough apart so as not to be distracting or overheard.

On-campus noninstructional space can be used in a quite different manner by a college that makes full use of itself as a location for work experiences and internships. Frequently, faculty members and administrators are likely to ignore the college campus as an appropriate field setting. It is often assumed that a student must be placed in an off-campus setting to learn about the "real" world and that a student cannot gain a sense of detachment from an on-campus placement and hence will not learn as much or perform as well. Both arguments are specious. The problems of colleges are just as real as those of noncollegiate institutions, involving such "realistic" concerns as money, personnel, energy, and politics. A business major can learn a great deal about small-business management and public administration from serving as an administrative assistant to an academic department head. A political science major can receive valuable insights and experience serving as a staff aide to the faculty senate of his or her college, as can a sociology, psychology, or education major who serves as a staff aide to a faculty or curriculum development committee or a teaching-improvement center.

The "detachment" argument is also questionable, for a student will often be in a position later in life when the outcomes of the organization with which he or she is working will be directly relevant to strongly held values or aspirations. Learning how to work within a highly involving context early in one's professional career is valuable.

While many colleges may wish to place their students in on-campus internship positions that are directly relevant to future career positions, others may wish to use the student-labor model of Berea College (Ky.) and Warren Wilson College (N.C.). Since 1859, Berea has required all students to work ten to fifteen hours a week.

Students work in more than 100 different labor departments. Of the 1,400 students, approximately 300 work to meet basic needs of the college community for food, cleanliness, and building maintenance. Another 450 students work directly in relation to the academic program in assignments ranging from secretarial duties in various departments to providing assistance as teaching associates, tutors, or laboratory technicians in educational areas. Other college offices and services are also staffed primarily by students. Two hundred students work in the offices of admissions, registrar, labor, and accounting as well as in the library and the health service.

The labor program is probably best known outside the college for its student craft industries where 350 students work as general laborers, craftsmen, and managers. Student industry products in weaving, woodcraft, needlecraft, ceramics, lapidary, and broommaking are marketed through a sales operation on campus, by mail order, and by distribution to stores in urban centers. Students also help to staff the Boone Tavern Hotel, the Berea College Press, and the laundry.

Further, Berea has a strong commitment to its Appalachian area, and the labor program helps to fulfill this commitment by cooperating in community service programs in which approximately 100 students work. Over 300 students are employed in summer campus programs. Others are assisted in finding summer employment elsewhere with private business or working under cooperative arrangements with community service agencies such as preschools, hospitals, and recreation and forestry programs [Laramee and Spears, 1978, p. 321].

In return for this work, students receive financial aid amounting to from one fourth to three fourths of the cost of term bills for a student carrying a normal academic load. In addition, "Through the fellowship of meaningful work experiences, an atmosphere of democratic living obviates social and economic distinctions and instills an awareness of social responsibility. As an educational tool, the labor program provides opportunities for acquiring skills, applying learning, exploring areas of knowledge, and developing creativity and personal abilities" (Laramee and Spears, 1978, p. 321). The student-labor program at Berea is essential to virtually every operation of the college and enables the college to make each of these operations a rich resource for the learning of all Berea College students. In this way, the college is able to make efficient use of the noninstructional space on campus.

Warren Wilson College operates a similar on-campus work program. The college runs a cattle and hog operation and asks for student assistance with this and other on-campus operations. A Work Council at Warren Wilson consisting of one faculty member, one work supervisor, and six students coordinates the work program. All resident students work fifteen hours a week to earn room and board expenses. Thus, as at Berea, students at Warren Wilson are exposed to a wide variety of work experiences and learn how to assume responsibility for real jobs without having to leave the college. The entire campus, in this way, becomes a learning environment.

Colleges that intend to serve older adult students must consider how the physical environment of the campus and the spaces used for instruction affect the adult returning to college. Although formal classrooms with armrests for writing may be necessary for some instructional purposes, they are reminiscent of childhood for most adults. Adultlike environments that promote participation and provide a welcoming, comfortable atmosphere are relatively informal. Lounges, living rooms, and conference rooms with a large table around which to gather are usually more appropriate to adult learning styles than chairs placed in rows facing a lectern.

Mary Baldwin College's (Va.) Adult Degree Program is housed in a lovely, refurbished old home. Offices are decorated tastefully and efficiently and communicate a friendly, adult atmosphere. Stephens College (Mo.) provided space in a comfortably furnished building for its College Without Walls program. Students gather in a living-room setting for seminars and class discussions.

At Loretto Heights College (Colo.), the University Without Walls program office provides a small, informal drop-in office area. A coffeepot is always plugged in. Mailboxes bear both faculty members' and students' names to encourage easy and efficient communication, especially when students are on campus and faculty advisers may not be available for conversation. A phone is available for local student use. A small resource library, bulletin boards on which dozens of events and brochures are posted, a table at which students can work, and informal "director's chairs" invite older adult students to sit around and chat, relax, or take care of on-campus business. Direct entrance to the program office from the outside campus as well as from the hall provides for a busy but convenient traffic pattern. Pencils and message pads are available; and, when possible. a typewriter is free for occasional student use. Files of program guidelines, forms, and announcements are set out for easy student access. A place on campus where the adult student can come invites participation and informality and gives a message of "welcome."

One of the most difficult adjustments to returning to college for many adults is the lack of space at home in which to study quietly. Special efforts are often needed to provide library-carrel or lounge space on weekends and in the evenings for working adult students. At Colorado Women's College, a special project has been developed to provide a few community women who were not necessarily enrolled students with small office spaces in which to pursue creative, independent projects. A special place in which to work alone with one's own key and belongings can be a precious gift for adult students who are accustomed to having to share their homes with family members and their offices with colleagues. Sometimes unused dormitory space can be converted to such creative uses.

Space can welcome, and space can repel. Adults' creative and flexible uses of college-campus spaces can serve important needs for privacy, reflection, and study. In many ways, learning is a solitary activity. Moreover, informal uses of campus spaces can induce participatory learning in small groups and can most appropriately provide adultlike settings for the free exchange of ideas in seminars and classes. Space often defines the nature of activity. Creative nontraditional uses of space can increase the quality of learning and add new and fresh dimensions to many learners' space-confined lives.

Off Campus. Space in the local community can be used in two quite different ways. First, space can be used for courses conducted by the college. Flathead Valley College (Mont.), for instance, conducts virtually all its courses at various off-campus facilities: storefronts, government buildings, and so forth. More frequently, off-campus space is used by conducting courses at the home of a faculty member (or student) or at a field location (for example, conducting a geology course at the site of a major faultline).

Increasingly, the wilderness is being chosen as an appropriate site for collegiate instruction. Building on the experiences and successes of the Outward Bound program and Prescott College (Ariz.), several colleges now offer courses in the wilderness. Davis & Elkins College (W. Va.) conducts one of the more extensive of these programs through a private, nonprofit educational institute, Woodlands, which is formally affiliated with the college. This institute offers mountain climbing and whitewater boating in conjunction with Davis and Elkins courses.

Any academic subjects are possible study topics for the whitewater trips. Particularly exciting are sociology, chemistry, American history, geography, literature, geology, and human ecology. On a given trip, several topics are selected from which each student chooses one for concentrated study. Students are supervised in making systematic investigations and preparing reports in the chosen areas.

Lessons are numerous for every subject. In sociology, we start with Appalachia, then travel amidst Virginia and Maryland farm communities, past Thornton Wilder–type small towns, float through suburbia, then between Washington's juxtaposed wealthy urban and Black communities, and end with Chesapeake Bay fisherfolk. American history begins along the Potomac with our Indian and Revolutionary legacies, is abundant with Civil War battles, and continues, into today, even to Watergate. For chemistry, the river's transect provides an opportunity for sampling and analyzing water and air and determining the causes and consequences of pollutants [Davis and Elkins College, 1977, p. 7].

The institute provides all technical equipment as well as food and special clothing. Wilderness trips are conducted throughout the Appalachian region as well as at a 400-acre "wilderness campus." The College of the Atlantic (Maine) and Carleton College (Minn.), among others, offer similar wilderness experiences. The *Journal of Experiential Education* (Association for Experiential Education, 1979) lists more than 100 colleges, universities, and associations offering academic programs that utilize the outdoors in a wide variety of ways.

Several colleges are fortunate to own or lease field stations that are located off campus or even in another country. A consortium of colleges in upper New York State (the College Center of the Finger Lakes) operated a marine-ecology field station on Lake Seneca for many years. It now runs a successful international field station on San Salvador Island in the Bahamas. At this field station, students study archeology, anthropology, sociology, political science, and health care as well as biology, astronomy, and marine ecology. The Bahamian program now runs for more than six months each year and involves students from many colleges and universities throughout the United States.

Field studies have also been conducted in urban settings. Many rural or suburban colleges provide their students with an opportunity to experience and work with urban problems and people. Davis and Elkins College (W. Va.), for instance, provides a "Washington Study Center" for students from the college who are working on a variety of projects in Washington, D.C. The study center includes kitchen facilities and an on-site faculty coordinator. Along with approximately 100 other colleges in the United States, Davis and Elkins also participates in the Washington Semester Program directed by the School of Government and Public Administration of American University in Washington, D.C.

Virtually all colleges and universities now offer some form of off-campus, credit-generating experience that exposes students to realistic work experiences and contemporary problems, this approach to higher education having been spearheaded by Antioch College (Ohio) in the early part of this century. Duley (1974, pp. vii-viii) identifies and briefly describes eight types of off-campus experiential programs:

Cross-Cultural Experience. A student involves himself in another culture or subculture of his own society in a deep and significant way, either as a temporary member of a family, a worker in that society, or as a volunteer in a social agency with the intention, as a participant observer, of learning as much as he can about that culture and his own.

Preprofessional Training. A student serves in assigned responsibilities under the supervision of a professional in the field of education, medicine, law, social work, nursing, or ministry, putting the theory he has learned into practice, gaining skills in the profession, and being evaluated by his supervisor.

Institutional Analysis/Career Exploration. A student has a temporary period of supervised work that provides opportunities to develop skills, to test abilities and career interests, and to systematically examine institutional cultures in light of the central theoretical notions in a chosen academic field of study.

Work Experience (Cooperative Education). Cooperative Education is that education plan which integrates classroom experience and practical work experience in industrial, business, government, or service-type work situations in the community. The work experience constitutes a regular and essential element in the educative process, and some minimum amount of work experience and minimum standard of successful performance on the job are included in the requirements of the institution for a degree.

Service-Learning Internship. Service-learning has been defined as: the integration of the accomplishment of a task that meets human need with conscious educational growth. A service-learning internship is designed to provide students responsibility to meet a public need and a significant learning experience within a public or private institution for a specified period of time, usually ten to fifteen weeks.

Social/Political Action. A student secures a placement, under faculty sponsorship, which gives him the opportunity to be directly engaged in working for social change either through community organizing, political activity, research/action projects, or work with organizations seeking to bring about changes in the social order. He also usually fulfills a learning contract made with his faculty sponsor.

Personal Growth and Development. A student undertakes a program in an off-campus setting that is designed to further his personal

growth and development such as the wilderness survival programs of the
Outward Bound Schools, or an apprenticeship to an artist or a craftsman,
or residence in a monastery for the development of his spiritual life, or
participation in an established group psychological or human relations program.

     Field Research. A student undertakes an independent or group re-
search project in the field under the supervision of a faculty member, applying the concepts and methods of an academic discipline such as geology, archeology, geography, or sociology.

     Interesting examples of several of these types of field ex-
periences are found in a series of articles on the integration of
internships and the liberal arts in a 1978 issue of *Liberal Education.* In one of these articles, the "Career Awareness Micro-
Internship Program" at Augustana College (S. Dak.) is described.
This program has been designed "to use exploratory internships
to demonstrate the career potential of liberal arts education to
both students and prospective employers. These internships are
intended to help students become more knowledgeable and informed about possible career options and to help them develop
greater personal confidence in their own abilities and greater regard for the usefulness of their liberal arts education. It is also a
basic premise of the program that the business and professional
community will become more aware of the career potential of
the liberally educated person as prospective employers and students are brought together within the internship format"
(McCart, 1978, pp. 331-332). Another of these articles (Dye
and Stephenson, 1978, p. 343) describes a University of Ken-
tucky program on ethics that "combines the experience of a
public-policy-oriented internship with the reflection afforded
by common readings and discussion of ethical issues in a seminar format."

     Critical to the spatial dimension is our recognition that an
internship or work-study program provides not only the resources of off-campus personnel and equipment but also the
space (environment) in which students can learn about themselves (values, attitudes, skills, knowledge), about various careers,
about contemporary problems, and about the probable nature
of their future lives. One collegiate institution in San Francisco

recently placed a map of the city on the cover of its catalogue and declared that this was "a map of our campus," implying that this institution makes full use of its urban location. Other colleges might be committed similarly to the removal of artificial boundaries between campus and community.

Mobile Instructional Space

Personally Defined. When planning for a curricular innovation, it is usually necessary to acknowledge and promote the existence of personally defined space—that is, study space. Typically, this study area is found in the student's residence. Commuter students, however, who cannot always find quiet places to study and work at home, may need study areas on campus. The college library usually provides ample study areas, but these areas often are not attractive to students, do not provide comfortable seating, or are closed during late night hours, when many students do most of their studying.

College libraries that do provide attractive and comfortable study areas, as at the University of California at San Diego and Mercy College of Detroit, seem to be used frequently for studying. Colleges that provide areas where students can bring food (such as the student union or dormitory), listen to music through headphones or in special listening areas, sit in lounging chairs, and/or enter and exit at any time of the day or night are also likely to be successful in promoting on-campus studying.

If the security guard insists on closing college offices at 6 P.M., the children are studying or watching TV until 10 P.M., and the college library closes at 9 P.M., where can the employed adult student study? Perhaps an underutilized alumni building could be opened to adult students late into the night. Individual keys could even be supplied. The faculty lounge may not be in use in the evenings and is comfortable and safe. Arrangements might be made with a community organization, church, or public agency for the use of a room, library, or lounge not often occupied in the evening or on weekends. A business executive on the board of trustees might arrange for the local bank community room to become a learning center in the evening. An under-

utilized apartment-complex social room might be used one
night a week for classes or designated as a quiet "learning room"
for study and informal off campus student gatherings. Some
students might share the rental of a small apartment, furnished
with study tables, chairs, a typewriter, and a small resource library to be used by a number of persons on different schedules
throughout the day and evening.

Few colleges have taken responsibility for the personal
study-space needs of older adult students. And yet, finding adequate, quiet study space is noted by many adult students as a
significant barrier to effective learning and college enrollment.
It is less expensive to supply a coffeepot, a few comfortable
chairs, and a place to read and write than to equip a laboratory
or a library or to build a dormitory. Consideration of the basic,
pragmatic needs of adult nonresidential students will be necessary if colleges are to move beyond their orientation to the
dormitory and the fraternity house as they seek to serve the
needs of increasingly diverse students.

Mobile Classroom Laboratory. In several ways, colleges
and universities have recently begun to make use of various
vehicles (usually buses or trailers) to provide educational programs to student populations for which the campus is inaccessible or to students who are in transit to the campus. College IV
of the Grand Valley State Colleges (Mich.) has offered a module-mobile program to residents of Grand Rapids, Michigan
("Stop, Shop, and Learn," 1975). Housed in a mobile unit that
is a cross between a bookmobile and a trailer, this program incorporates more than 250 minicourses that local residents can
take for academic credit. Module-mobile students pick up instructional materials for a particular course when the mobile
unit visits their neighborhood once a week. These materials are
designed for home study. Students return to the mobile unit to
take tests that indicate whether they have mastered the material
(a score of 90 percent or better). If not mastered, the material is
studied again, or the student meets with a College IV instructor
or tutor/counselor, or both. After mastery of ten modules in a
subject area, a student receives five hours of academic credit. As
of 1975, ninety-five students, ranging in age from seventeen to
sixty-five, had taken modules.

In contrast to the module mobile offered by College IV, Cornell University (N.Y.) offers a "Peoplemobile" (a used school bus) staffed by college-age summer assistants. The students provide information on social and educational services in a local county to low-income residents. The students help these persons solve specific problems that are defined by the residents by referring them to appropriate agencies or seeking help in other ways (Farley, 1971). Similarly, a mobile counseling unit has been provided by the Metropolitan Junior College District of Kansas City, Missouri, which assists youth in the inner city by providing vocational-education information and counseling (Stitt, 1976).

The most extensive use of mobile instructional units has been made by in-service education programs. The Oklahoma Department of Vocational and Technical Education equipped a tractor-trailer with data-processing equipment that is provided to teachers for their own updating as well as the education of students ("Data Processing on the Move," 1975). The Atomic Energy Commission (now the Nuclear Regulatory Commission) provided a mobile laboratory for training in the use of equipment that is not readily available in most colleges and universities.

In-service information on career education has been provided to elementary and secondary education teachers by Rhode Island College through its Mobile Career Education Resource Unit (Zajano and Arnoff, 1976-77). A twenty-three-foot mobile van was stocked with materials on career education, with specific emphasis on nonconventional career opportunities for women and bilingual or non-English-speaking students. Teachers were exposed to the materials and instructed in their use. Mobile in-service units have been used for work with administrators of nursing homes, extended-care facilities, and small hospitals in Arizona (Newby and Harker, 1976) and the education of nurses in remote areas of Pennsylvania (Hall, 1976).

The use of mobile classrooms and laboratories for educational purposes holds great promise in many fields. One might envision a mobile ecology laboratory, for instance, that would be used not only for field research but also for teaching students in the field and making off-campus presentations to community groups. Mobile classrooms and laboratories would be equally appropriate in a variety of other fields, such as teaching set theory to elementary school children, studying the oral-cultural history of a region, or learning about astronomy.

While mobile classrooms and laboratories have been used most extensively in bringing higher education to people who usually do not have access to this resource, one mobile-classroom program has reversed the process and is now providing traditional students with instruction while they are traveling to campus. The administration and faculty at Mountain Empire Community College (Va.) have recognized the "wasted" travel time (averaging fifteen hours a week) of many of the college's commuting students; they have provided five buses that contain thirty-two student stations equipped with flip-down desks, reading lamps, earphones, cassette recorders, cassette recorders with a filmstrip viewer, AC outlets, and storage compartments (Vaughn, 1974a, 1974b). The buses also contain projection systems (slide, film, overhead transparencies, screen), video receivers and recorders, cassette playback systems, a control panel, AM/FM radio, toilet, refrigerator, heating units for hot drinks, and a luggage compartment. The buses are carpeted, air-conditioned, and heated. Learning packages have been prepared for many courses so that students can study on the way to school. Even without the learning packages, students can use the study areas and resources to prepare for class.

One could envision the two types of mobile instructional programs being combined. A bus or van could transport students to and from campus, providing study space and audiovisual equipment en route. During two- to three-hour layovers off campus, the vehicle could be available for media-based and self-paced short courses such as those provided at College IV.

On a somewhat grander scale is the campus-at-sea ("World Campus Afloat") program started by Chapman College (Calif.) and now conducted by the International Association of Shipboard Education, with the University of Colorado providing academic credit. Students take undergraduate courses on board a ship en route to various parts of the world. The on-board academic program is amplified by various on-shore field trips. The

campus-at-sea program is appropriate for students who can afford, in terms of time and money, a long overseas experience
and who wish to couple traditional classroom experiences with
travel.

Similarly, the schooner *Westward* is an oceanographic
ship used for college credit courses in nautical and marine science ("Going to School at Sea," 1980). The courses are offered
by the nonprofit Sea Education Association, Inc., of Woods
Hole, Massachusetts. Though students are drawn from two
dozen United States colleges, this sixteen-credit program is
listed in the catalogues of Boston University, Cornell University,
the College of Charleston, Colgate University, American University, and the University of Pennsylvania. The vessel *Westward* is
a minicollege offering one-semester courses for liberal arts majors and others interested in learning about the oceans. There
are guest lecturers from the Marine Biological Laboratory at
Woods Hole before departure. While at sea, students pick a research topic to pursue.

Anne Arundel Community College (Md.), one of the first
colleges to offer a course in estuarine biology, offers a flexible
program of marine studies for students who will transfer to
four-year colleges and universities (Philp, 1978). Biological
interrelationships of organisms and estuarine principles are covered in extensive weekend field trips on the Chesapeake Bay, followed by six to eight hours of laboratory work. Anne Arundel
Community College sponsors many "floating workshops" on its
own research vessels. Courses are offered on such topics as water quality, celestial navigation, boatbuilding, and marine biology.

Travel. Most college students can now receive academic
credit for certain educationally planned trips to other countries
(or even other regions of the United States). At least 600 colleges and universities now offer some type of study-abroad program (Heiss, 1973). In many instances, this travel occurs through
a college-sponsored tour conducted by a faculty member during
an intersession or summer term. In other instances, students attend one of the overseas campuses of an American university,
such as the University of Maryland or Stanford University (Calif.),

or participate in a cooperative interinstitutional program, such as the European Study Program conducted jointly by Central College (Iowa) and Davis and Elkins College (W. Va.). A third alternative is the more intensive, living-learning program in which students live with a family and attend a nearby university, usually taking courses in the native language. The Experiment in International Living (Maine) has been a pioneer in such living-learning programs.

Many colleges and universities encourage students of traditional college age (eighteen to twenty-two) to participate in a study-abroad program during their junior year. Kalamazoo College (Mich.), which makes extensive use of off-campus experiences, provides on-campus course work for students during their freshman year, off-campus career-service experiences during their sophomore year, study-abroad experiences during their junior year, and a senior thesis experience during their senior year.

Friends World College (N.Y.) has made extensive use of study-abroad experiences that involve students throughout their tenure at the institution. Heiss (1973, p. 8) describes this college's program as it existed in 1973:

> Friends World College was founded in 1965 to provide students with in-depth knowledge and firsthand experiences in a culture other than their own as well as to promote an understanding of several other cultures and developing regions. The college is committed to developing change agents whose work might help create a better world. To this end, the entire world is treated as a classroom, students study problems in their actual social setting, and the curriculum revolves around the emerging concepts that are shaping the future of mankind.
>
> The college has seven fixed centers to which students are rotated every six months. These are in North America, Latin America, Africa, West Asia, South Asia, East Asia, and Europe. When seniors return to the North American Center in Westbury from their various overseas assignments, they take an orientation seminar in which they pool their experiences, and they also conduct and lead the senior seminar. . . . The faculty serve essentially as resource persons, consultants, and contact personnel.

Media-Based. We will consider four media that are being used with increasing frequency for instructional purposes: television, radio, telephones, and newspapers. For an increasing number of undergraduate colleges and universities, television has become an effective tool for expanding access for nontraditional student populations or for increasing the flexibility of the instructional program being offered to traditional students. The City College of Chicago (Ill.) has offered televised courses for credit through its TV College since 1956. This TV College now enrolls over 100,000 credit students (Zigerell and Luskin, 1978). Students view programs on their home television sets, using a study guide or suggested readings and assignments. Midterm and final exams are written at one of four academic centers. Two hours each week are set aside for students to converse with the TV instructor by telephone.

Perhaps the most fully developed program using television is offered by the University of Mid-America (UMA; Neb.; Walton, 1975). Books, cassettes, and study guides supplement television-based courses. Weekly overviews and cumulative course summaries, lesson by lesson, are often carried in newspapers distributed statewide. Study centers and WATS telephone-line networks enable students to interact with instructors if clarification is needed. Modeled after the British Open University, the University of Mid-America does not restrict admissions, offers home-based courses, and operates regionally located learning centers. UMA was formed as a consortium of state universities located in Nebraska, Kansas, Iowa, South Dakota, and Missouri (Hurt, 1977).

In several regions of the country and in some states (for example, Connecticut and California), collegiate institutions have joined together to pool instructional television resources and have founded various interinstitutional consortia. At least seven instructional television consortia now exist in California (Warner, 1976). Connecticut Regional Community College has similarly been established as a consortium of state institutions. This college offers televised instruction over the Connecticut Public Television Network (McAnliffe, 1978). As of 1978, over 1,000 students were enrolled in three courses being offered through seven participating colleges in this consortium.

Under a grant from the Fund for the Improvement of

Postsecondary Education (FIPSE), a television consortium has been established by the Archdiocese of San Francisco to create a "Senior University," which will provide interactive closed-circuit television programs to older adults in the San Francisco Bay area. Many community colleges are also making extensive use of televised instruction in urban areas—for example, Dallas Community College District (Texas) and Miami-Dade Community College (Fla.; Luskin and Zigerell, 1978).

Even more sophisticated use of televised instruction is now evident. Increasingly, colleges and universities are making use of community antenna television and master antenna television (Miles, 1972). Case Western Reserve University's Schools of Engineering and Management (Ohio) serve a thirty-mile radius in northern Ohio through a two-channel Instructional Television Network (ITN; Walton, 1975). The programs are broadcast from two classroom studios (where class is conducted in a "business as usual" fashion) with links to distant classrooms—typically, corporate facilities. Companies outside the ITN broadcast area are served through the circulation of videotapes. Stanford University (Calif.) similarly offers courses through a four-channel, one-way video, two-way audio, instructional television network. Eighty participating industries give their employees an opportunity to earn up to six credits per quarter.

The University of South Carolina serves nineteen learning centers throughout the state with a closed-circuit educational television system. Programs are beamed to regional campuses of the university, technical educational centers, and secondary schools. Each course is telecast two evenings a week to these learning centers. Students are required to attend five meetings near campus each semester in addition to receiving instruction at one of these learning centers. During these meetings, students interact with the instructor and make use of campus facilities.

Using somewhat more sophisticated equipment, the Federation of Rocky Mountain States more than ten years ago employed a communication satellite to beam televised education programs to health professionals in remote areas of the West. The scientists and educators who were involved in early communication satellite operations continue to provide more closed-circuit programming at the elementary and secondary school level than at the collegiate level.

Serving their current students more effectively, several collegiate institutions now provide extensive closed-circuit television communication systems that enable students to watch and listen to lectures or seminar discussions from another room or at another time. Oral Roberts University (Okla.), for instance, provides an audiotutorial, dial-access information-retrieval system that relies heavily on closed-circuit television as well as more traditional media. Comparable resources are available at Florida Atlantic University for use in individualized instruction programs. In the late 1960s at the University of Oregon, Dr. Arthur Perls effectively conducted a "seminar" on alienation through the use of closed-circuit television and teaching assistants, with a course enrollment of over 2,000 students. As of 1978, 9 percent of undergraduates had taken courses using live television lectures, and 35 percent had taken courses using prerecorded television lectures or demonstrations (Levine, 1978). It is to be expected that instruction utilizing television will increase markedly in the years ahead. Even the Public Broadcasting System is now involved in producing televised courses for use by colleges and universities.

Numerous other examples of instructional innovations using television could be offered (Walton, 1975). The range of these innovations is witnessed by the following sample of programs: (1) a video series for college credit being offered nationwide by member stations of the Public Broadcasting System with comprehensive study guides and examinations developed by the Coast Community College District (Calif.; Watson and Luskin, 1975), (2) an experimental program in remedial English being offered over open-circuit TV devices by American River College (Calif.; Boettcher, 1968), (3) a freshman-level course in general psychology being offered through television instruction, with tests also being administered by TV, at the Department of Psychology of the University of Akron (Ohio; Dambrot, 1972), (4) the use of scripts and an "integration leader" to encourage student discussion at the end of each period of instructional television for an introductory biology course at Rhode Island

College (Keogh, 1970), (5) a fifty-four-program series on international relations being offered on television by Berger Community College (N.J.; Luskin and Zigerell, 1978); and (6) a humanities course adapted from the University of the Air, sponsored by the City University of New York and the State University of New York, and being offered by Geneseo State College (N.Y.; Moss, 1970).

Levine (1978, p. 186) reports nine ways in which television can be used to instruct undergraduates, relying in part on a book written by Brown and Thornton (1971):

1. A substitute for live faculty lectures on campus.
2. An enlarger of slides, documents, pictures, or even faculty in large lecture rooms.
3. A way to offer instruction off campus, to geographically distant locations, to other colleges, and so on.
4. A means of permitting the repeated and convenient observation of an event.
5. A means of encouraging faculty and students to observe their own behavior; for example, teaching.
6. A means of sharing with many others such experiences as childbirth or field behavior.
7. A way of videotaping short demonstrations or creating a continuous tape of instructional resources that can be shown at strategic times during class.
8. A means of dramatizing or bringing information to life.
9. A means of making excellent learning opportunities such as *Roots, Civilization,* and *The Ascent of Man* available to audiences across the nation or world.

Televised instruction offers several important advantages over most other modes of instruction. Levine (1978, p. 187) identifies the following:

1. Television permits education to reach large numbers of people who might be unable to attend classes at college.
2. College students prefer television classes to lecture instruction.

3. Unlike radio, television is employable in all subject matter.
4. The quality of recorded broadcasts is more even than that of live classes.
5. Television broadcasts can be aired repeatedly at locations and times convenient to the audience.
6. Television is a familiar medium associated with recreation rather than work.

Dallas Community College (Texas) has found that its telecourses increase enrollment, reach students who would not otherwise attend regular classroom instruction, and stimulate community interest in certain subject areas (Mittelstet, 1978). Colorado State University has been able to use instructional television to accelerate the learning of engineering transfer students (Churchill, Lord, and Maxwell, 1971).

Several disadvantages can also be noted concerning the use of instructional television. Levine (1978, p. 187) suggests the following:

1. Television requires a large audience to be cost-efficient.
2. Radio or tape is an instructional medium superior to television for music.
3. Teachers and students are less favorable to the use of television in college than in the lower grades.
4. College students prefer small discussion classes to television courses.
5. Television is essentially a one-way medium even though it has been adapted to two-way communication via telephones.
6. College faculty feel threatened by television.

Clearly, television as an instructional resource and as a vehicle for extending instructional space must be taken seriously in the 1980s. A "University of North America" that would build on television as a teaching medium was seriously proposed at a national higher education conference (Dennis, 1971). Given the disadvantages of television, it is also clear that this medium is not a panacea but is an important tool to be used alongside other instructional tools in the enrichment of instructional offerings for an increasingly diverse and demanding student population.

Radio is being used by some colleges, such as Purdue University (Ind.), the University of South Florida, Cosumnes River College (Calif.), and Mercy College (N.Y.), to reach nontraditional populations. Between 1979 and 1981, the Fund for the Improvement of Postsecondary Education (FIPSE) supported a number of innovative uses of radio through its "Special Focus Program: Better Strategies for Educating Adults." National Public Radio (D.C.), along with West Virginia Wesleyan College, collaborated on an instructional/audio program for adults, offering the program in Newark, New Jersey, New York City, Norfolk, Virginia, and San Diego, California. Greenville Technical College (S.C.) was funded to implement Home College with the local library system to provide educational radio services for blind, aged, disadvantaged, and handicapped citizens.

According to Levine (1978, p. 185), radio holds the following advantages and disadvantages:

Advantages

1. Radio reduces the unit cost of instruction and thereby tuition.
2. It is cheaper than television.
3. It eliminates visual images which distract students and reduce learning in some subject areas.
4. It enables a teacher to reach more people than can be accommodated in a single classroom.
5. It may be a more effective medium for learning than print or lecture (however, there is conflicting evidence on this point).
6. It permits instructional outreach to homes at convenient audience listening times.

Disadvantages

1. Radio is not as effective as instruction by television when used alone, particularly in teaching manual tasks, but also in subject areas where visual images improve the association process.

2. It does not accommodate student questions and feedback except by phone hookups to the studio or periodic class sessions run by the instructor or section leaders.
3. It requires a relatively large audience to be cost-effective.

The telephone is another nonvisual medium that can be used to extend instruction to learners who are off-site. At the University of Michigan, skills training in mathematics, language, logic, scientific method, and reasoning is provided through a classroom-telephone-computer (CTC) network. This network makes instructional simulations available through minicomputers and telephones located in remote locations that are used as terminals to access computers at the university. Telephones are also being used to transmit lectures and discussion to remote locations through the use of conference-call and closed-circuit facilities. The University of Illinois, the University of Wisconsin, and several military education centers are now enriching telephone lectures with remote-controlled visual displays (for example, 35-mm slides), which are activated over the telephone by the lecturer, and with electronic blackboards that transmit an instructor's writings and drawings on a "blackboard" by telephone to the remote location, where the words and patterns are reproduced on a TV screen. Queensborough Community College (N.Y.) has invented a telephone conferencing instructional system for homebound handicapped students and has linked its efforts with those of National Public Radio (D.C.) and Greenville Technical College (S.C.) (Fund for the Improvement of Postsecondary Education, 1978). Finally, telephones are being used for tutorial assistance at Foothill College (Calif.) and in conjunction with a radio talk show sponsored by Cosumnes River College (Calif.).

Another medium, the newspaper, has been used sparingly by colleges and universities. A college-level newspaper course on the theme "America and the Future of Man" was first offered in 1973 at the University of California at San Diego. More than 250 newspapers throughout the country printed weekly 1,400-word lectures prepared by nationally known experts. Credit for the course was given by 180 participating colleges and universities; students submitted assignments to a designated instructor at one of these institutions and participated in two in-class sessions. The *Chronicle of Higher Education* reports that 30,000 people had received academic credit through this program as of 1977.

Levine (1978, pp. 188-189) identifies the following advantages and disadvantages in using newspaper courses:

Advantages

1. Courses by newspaper are cheap for sponsors and may attract students to college who would not otherwise attend.
2. Scheduling is entirely up to the student.
3. The cost to the student is minimal, and there are no start-up costs, such as buying a television set.
4. Such courses can provide continuing education as well as college-level study for people not interested in earning a degree.
5. Great teachers who could not collectively be brought to a campus or community can teach together.

Disadvantages

1. Relatively short, weekly lectures are not a sufficiently substantial base for an entire course.
2. Many of the benefits of convenience and accessibility are lost if newspaper courses are not fully self-contained.
3. The print medium, especially poor-quality newsprint, is of limited value in the study of certain aspects of art, music, and natural science.
4. The slow pace of such instruction means that it would take an interminable period to earn a degree by newspaper. (Newspaper courses are seldom the only way degree candidates earn credit, however, and degree granting is not their purpose.)

Simulated Environments. One of the potentially most profound forms of mobile space that can be used by a college or university is the simulated environment. Temporary simulated environments can be created in which students (and faculty members) can live for short periods and engage in intensive learning experiences. A typical and modest form of a simulated environment is the "language table," which for many years has been set up at student cafeterias. A certain table is designated for a particular language (for example, German), and only that language may be spoken there. Entire dormitories have also been used as "language houses," in which students speak the foreign language and simulate daily living patterns of another culture.

More complex and ambitious examples of simulated environments can often be found outside (and even in opposition to) the formal curriculum of the institution. At many colleges and universities, a yearly festival, carnival, or homecoming celebration is held, during which students expend an enormous amount of energy, time, and even money in designing and building booths, exhibits, floats—even entire buildings. They transform their residences into castles, famous buildings, or other fanciful structures, and they prepare major theatrical productions. Although these activities are often viewed with disdain by some faculty members and administrators, for students they can be valuable sources of learning about problem solving, cooperative behavior, principles of design, needs assessment, and so forth.

At California State University in Chico, the yearly "Frontier Days" involves construction of a Western village on the university's quad. Each year, an entirely new village is constructed over a two-day period. The village may contain a functioning flour mill, a store in which homemade goods are sold, a music pavilion, or a solar greenhouse. Although the Chico Frontier Days are viewed as anti-intellectual and distracting by some academicians at the university, one can readily identify a number of important lessons that can be learned from constructing and living in this simulated village.

Without trampling on the spontaneity and even antiestablishment character of such temporary simulated environments, the faculty members and administrators of a collegiate institution might wish to enrich these activities by offering short courses related to the theme of the event or to the tasks that need to be performed to create the temporary environment.

At an even more ambitious level, we can identify attempts

to create entire colleges on a simulated or temporary basis. During the late 1960s and early 1970s, many student demonstrations culminated in creation of temporary colleges ("teach-ins") or establishment of longer-term "free universities." According to Lichtman (1973), some of the free universities served primarily as focal points for educational and political revolution, while others acted like community centers that matched people with common interests and resources. Although many of these "temporary systems" have ceased to exist, much can be learned from their remarkable success during the early 1970s, especially from those free universities that linked interests and resources.

Some "free universities" which have prospered and expanded and which now have a strong community base are the Denver Free University (Colo.), the University of Man (Manhattan, Kans.), and the Learning Exchange (Evanston, Ill.). We should come to realize from the history of this movement that some colleges must be prepared to set up short-term alternative educational systems periodically that will immediately address a set of emerging needs that cannot be met through traditional institutional structures. Business and industry are beginning to make use of "collateral" organizations that are set up temporarily alongside regular organizations to address specific and unique programs (Zand, 1974). Colleges can create similar collateral organizations that will respond to unique short-term problems and needs.

The Council of Independent Colleges has begun to use temporary educational simulations in its "College 1" program (Bergquist, Lounibos, and Langfitt, 1980) and in its current Quality Undergraduate Education (QUE) project. The short-term (one month) College 1 program was held during the summers of 1978 and 1979 at Bowdoin College (Maine). During each of the two summers, a group of ten faculty members and twenty to thirty students from small liberal arts colleges created from scratch a temporary college that focused on the theme "Passages: Planning for Work, Leisure, and Service." At College 1, the learning of faculty members was considered as important as the learning of students. Instructors used this opportunity to explore new teaching methods, different relationships with students, and even new modes of integrating work and family. In Project QUE, more than sixty small liberal arts colleges have selected a single "target academic program" for extensive development or refinement. One of the central steps in this program development or refinement initiative is pilot testing of the target academic program design, primarily through the use of temporary educational simulations. A survey of the different ways temporary educational simulations are used by these colleges will be included in a formal report to be prepared by the fall of 1983.

A mediocre Hollywood western of several years ago, titled *Westworld,* was based on the intriguing concept of an adult theme park (in the mode of Disneyland). An educational simulation could be constructed similarly. A college could focus on a particular theme (perhaps "Toward the Year 2000," "New Perspectives on China," or "The American Depression") and create a simulated environment related to this theme in which students (and faculty members) would live and work temporarily. Food could be prepared that reflects this theme—as it was at Whitworth College (Wash.) when students taking a course on futuristics were served at the cafeteria food that could be expected in the future. Students could be involved actively in the design and creation of this simulated environment and afterward could participate in a critical analysis of its accuracy and impact. A simulated environment (for example, on Japanese society) might even precede and help prepare students for the real environment (a trip to Japan). This simulated environment also could be used as a "halfway house" for students to readjust to the college environment on returning from the trip.

Temporary environments, along with the wide variety of other spaces that have been identified, should be challenging and expansive for the college faculty member or administrator who has viewed the traditional college classroom, laboratory, or studio as the only appropriate—or available—space in which teaching and learning take place. We are all aware that many of

the most important learning experiences for students occur outside formal instructional spaces. We can either lament this fact
or choose to move beyond (but not abandon) these formal settings to meet the students and their learnings on the student's
home turf or on a turf that is new and rich with learning for
both the student and teacher.

— III —

RESOURCES

Achieving Optimal Use of People, Situations, and Materials

Daily, the curriculum of a college or university is defined by the people who carry it out and by the materials and equipment that are used in support of these people. The resources of a curriculum are central to its character. A faculty member at a private university in the Northeast recently stated, in an interview, that the curriculum of a college or university is defined by the nature of its resources—particularly by its faculty: "The curriculum is not only (or even primarily) a list of requirements and sources that are offered. The . . . curriculum can be more closely equated with the attitudes, knowledge, and skills of the faculty as they are conveyed to students on a daily basis inside and outside the classroom" (Bergquist, 1979, pp. 15-16).

Although a strong argument could also be made that the

curriculum is defined by the learning outcomes of students, the roles of faculty members and other personnel and the resources of the college or university are critical. Following is a description of several ways in which people, materials, equipment, and learning environments have been used by colleges and universities for instructional purposes.

People

Faculty Member as Instructor. The primary instructional resource in any traditional college or university is the faculty. Even in nontraditional settings, the "mentor" or "educational adviser" role played by faculty members is central to the success of the college and its curriculum. Usually, instruction is provided by a full-time or part-time faculty member who has expertise in the area being covered by the instructional unit in question. The most common alternative to this use of instructional personnel is the undergraduate or graduate teaching assistant. Usually, an undergraduate teaching assistant will assist a regular faculty member rather than teaching a course alone. Graduate teaching assistants (GTAs), however, often teach courses (or at least sections of courses), especially at large, research-oriented universities. According to Levine (1978, p. 178), GTAs are employed by 22 percent of college and university faculty members in some or most of their undergraduate courses. At small, independent liberal arts colleges, however, only 3 percent of faculty members make use of GTAs, largely because these institutions lack graduate-level programs.

Arrangements are sometimes made for the use of GTAs at liberal arts colleges through exchange programs with graduate-level universities. Western Washington State University (WWSU), for instance, recently initiated a program whereby a graduate student from a Third World studies program at the University of Chicago serves in a one-year teaching internship at WWSU. One faculty member from WWSU, in turn, spends a year at the University of Chicago in a postdoctoral program on Third World studies. Both institutions benefit from this arrangement. WWSU can begin a new Third World studies program through the use of advanced graduate students in the area and through the opportunity to expose current WWSU faculty members to the field during a postdoctoral leave. The University of Chicago benefits from the opportunity to provide its graduate students with teaching experiences that will increase their "marketability" after they obtain doctorates.

Another on-campus instructional resource person is the faculty member from elsewhere in the institution who is brought in once or twice to teach a particular segment of a course. An extended version of this procedure is team teaching, which is found at virtually all colleges and universities. According to Levine (1978), 47 percent of undergraduates have taken one or more team-taught courses. Levine (p. 181) notes several of the advantages and disadvantages of this approach:

> When team teaching works well, it is highly rated by students and faculty; however, it usually doesn't work well. Faculty [members in] instructional teams generally are used to working alone, are unfamiliar with subject matter outside their specialty, and tend to treat their teammates' specialty areas as sacrosanct. As a consequence, team teaching is often fragmented, becoming little more than several faculty sharing a common classroom. The larger the team, the more often there tends to be discontinuity or lack of integration between individual faculty presentations. Furthermore, when team size increases, faculty attendance tends to drop off and a sense of responsibility for the course decreases. These are not insuperable obstacles but rather problems that must be dealt with in planning team-taught courses.

An alternative use of on-campus faculty members as instructional resources has been initiated at the State University of New York, Stony Brook. Faculty members and students work together in a particular interdisciplinary area (for example, world hunger) through Federated Learning Communities (FLCs). One member of an FLC is a tenured faculty member who is relatively inexperienced in the area. This person serves as a "master learner" for two years and "acts as a 'model' student for the other students, a discussion leader, and an internal evaluator and liaison between faculty members and students in the program" (Wood and Davis, 1978, p. 37). The master learner's only teaching activity is in a "meta-seminar," where students are assisted in learning how to learn, in integrating the material of other courses, and in developing confidence in their own ability to think and write creatively A comparable Master Learner Program has been initiated at William Paterson College (N.J.).

In addition to teaching classes, most faculty members function as tutors for students in a wide variety of independent studies. One of the difficult tasks in allocating faculty resources is to find a common measure for the number of independent studies that faculty members may supervise and time spent in group instruction, such as courses and seminars. The more committed an institution is to learner self-direction, the greater the encouragement and incentive system for such tutorial activity must be.

When a regular faculty member is asked to function as an evaluator of experiential learning, either prior noncollege learning or sponsored field-based learning, the faculty role shifts from instructor to assessor of learning outcomes. This role shift often requires additional faculty time and training. As student populations become increasingly diverse and older, more faculty time is being required for assessment functions. Recently, the American Council on Education (ACE) Office on Educational Credit and Credentials reported that 97.5 percent of academic institutions responding to a survey (2,162) award credit for extrainstitutional learning (American Council on Education, 1980). Although the ACE Military Guide, National Guide, and various examination programs accounted for a large proportion of these credit awards, portfolio assessments of prior noncollege learning can be found in hundreds of public and private institutions. These new assessment roles for faculty members require that institutions find new ways to account for and reward faculty time and effort spent on these innovative efforts if they are to be considered part of the mainstream activities of the institution.

Finally, faculty members from other colleges and universities are valuable instructional resources. They visit an institution for a short or long period and assist with or conduct an instructional unit (single course session, segment of a course, entire course). Most colleges and universities occasionally invite faculty

members from other colleges, host a visiting scholar, or participate in an interinstitutional faculty exchange program; several
make particularly extensive or unique use of visiting faculty
members. A formal visiting program has been initiated at Fairhaven College (Western Washington State University) that brings
in faculty members from diverse fields. These visiting faculty
members meet with classes, offer workshops, join students for
informal discussions and meals, and frequently live in the residence halls. At Thomas Jefferson College (Grand Valley State
College, Mich.), distinguished visiting faculty members are invited to the campus through its biennial National Poetry Festival. Both Fairhaven and Thomas Jefferson are able to remain
small, yet provide diverse and changing faculty perspectives to
their students through the use of visiting faculty members.

Faculty Member as Adviser/Mentor. Most collegiate institutions give formal recognition to the role of the adviser or
mentor as a valuable instructional resource and contributor to
the curriculum. There is much less agreement among colleges
and universities, however, about which type of advisement or
mentorship is considered instructional in nature and an integral
part of the curriculum. Academic advising is usually included,
but advising that relates to personal issues or career planning is
often excluded. Advising done by faculty members is considered
part of the instructional process, whereas advising done by
counselors or other student-services personnel is often considered extracurricular. There are signs, however, that this dichotomy is changing as the diversity of the student population increases.

Typically, a faculty member assumes the role of academic
adviser. He or she works alone and helps a student select a major area of study and individual courses. The faculty member
often serves only as a bureaucratic checkpoint for students who
must get the faculty adviser's approval and signature for a course
of study that they have already chosen independently (often in
consultation with peers, family, counselors, or other faculty
members). A faculty member may be assigned to students in a
particular class (for example, as adviser to senior students) or
may be assigned to an entering class to work with this class until

it graduates. In most instances, these traditional modes of academic advisement have not been very successful in contributing to a student's overall education. In their study of twenty-six colleges, Levine and Weingart (1973, p. 18) found academic advising to be "uniformly unsuccessful" at all institutions except Sarah Lawrence (N.Y.), where faculty members expend a considerable amount of time in an advising role.

Several colleges have recently attempted to improve academic advising by including people who are not members of the faculty on advising teams and/or by changing the role the faculty member plays in the advising process. The College of the Atlantic (COA; Maine) assigns a two-member team of advisers to each entering student, selecting from among staff, students, and faculty in an advising pool. By the end of the second year, each COA student chooses a permanent advising team composed of one faculty member, one student, and one nondesignated community member. Both advising teams help the student plan a program of study directed toward his or her educational or occupational goals. The team members also approve independent studies and the fulfillment of degree requirements. William Jewell College (Mo.) also provides students with an advising team if the student chooses to use this advising format rather than an individual faculty adviser.

At Eckerd College (Fla.), each entering student selects a faculty member as a mentor, having been given a descriptive list of mentors and projects. During the freshman year, the student takes at least one course from this mentor, and the mentor serves in an advising role for the student as he or she works out an academic program for the first year. Another Eckerd College faculty member in the student's area of specialization is selected as the mentor for upper-division work. In the paracollege at St. Olaf College (Minn.), each faculty member serves as a "tutor" to a small group of students for an academic year. The tutor meets with the students either individually or in small tutorial groups at least once every two weeks. At Bradford College (Mass.), faculty members in all fields teach English composition in a tutorial format through topics in their areas of knowledge. They also serve as advisers to the students they tutor who are freshmen and sophomores.

Mentors are probably used most extensively in external degree programs specifically oriented to adult learners, such as Empire State College (N.Y.) and the Vermont External Degree Program, and in various experimental, adult, or individualized programs (such as New College at the University of Alabama and the University Without Walls programs) that make extensive use of student learning contracts (see the description of learning contracts in Chapter Five). At these institutions, a faculty member serves in a variety of mentoring and advising roles that take the faculty member well beyond the traditional role of "knowledge dispenser" or "judge." These more nontraditional roles call for the faculty member or mentor to function as a generalist rather than a specialist. Attention is centered as much on the learner and the learning process as on the subject matter. It is difficult, if not impossible, to separate personal concerns from typically academic concerns. The relationship between student and faculty adviser in these nontraditional settings is a peer-learning partnership. The traditional, hierarchal relationship between faculty member and student is replaced by a more equal, adult/adult relationship. A learner-centered attitude often replaces a curriculum-centered approach, echoing the research of Carl Rogers and Barry Stevens (1971), Erich Fromm (1956), and Abraham Maslow (1970). Persons who are skilled in such adviser/mentor roles are able to provide learners with a careful mix of challenge and support, leading students to the "growth edges" of their learning without overwhelming them with information or harshly judging them.

From a developmental point of view, such as that indicated by Daniel Levinson's (1978) research, this kind of adviser/mentor relationship may be one of the most critical components of an effective, learning resource system. Levinson's study of forty adult males points to the mentor relationship as a necessary ingredient in the development of men's goals. Levinson (1978) calls this goal-setting activity of early adulthood "forming and living out the Dream." For women, the absence of role models and mentors has been thought to be a potential retardant to career goal setting and realistic life planning. Programs that serve adults typically serve large numbers of reentry and working adult women. Providing opportunities for close relationships with adviser/mentors appears to be a major factor in the quality of college programs for adult women. Some colleges that have recognized this phenomenon and designed programs to provide for such relationships are Goddard College (Vt.), Clark University (Mass.), Mary Baldwin College (Va.), the Vermont External Degree Program, and Empire State College (N.Y.; Fund for the Improvement of Postsecondary Education, 1979b).

Tom Clark and his colleagues at the Center for Individualized Education at Empire State College (Clark, 1978b, pp. 176-178) have identified eight roles that are assumed in these nontraditional settings:

1. *Facilitator-Counselor.* Because professors in individualized education often shift from teaching subjects to helping learners, they must learn to be learning facilitators and, on occasion, counselors of individuals or small groups. Although this less directive and more personal role seemed awkward at first, faculty members began to discover its merits, as these quotations indicate: "I found that it was difficult, awkward, to lecture when I was working with students one-to-one, or in small groups, so I gradually learned to become a facilitator of the learning process." "It is difficult to escape being a counselor when working in an individualized program because many things which are going on in an individual's life such as change in marital status, change in value system, a change in perspective are brought into conversations about the learning process and have to be discussed."

2. *Broker-Negotiator.* Faculty members indicated that the change in authority relationships engendered by their nontraditional program necessitated their learning how to negotiate with students rather than dictate to them. Also, because a wide range of learning resources besides the teacher are used in individualized education, the faculty member needed to become a broker for the student in obtaining the learning experiences the student needed.

3. *Instructor-Tutor.* Professors in nontraditional programs do teach, of course, but they often do it in nontraditional ways, such as one-to-one; in intensive weekend residences; by computer or programmed instruction; in interdisciplinary, thematic, or problem-oriented ways; in short modules. These variations very often are new to the teacher who has been taught by more traditional means.

4. *Evaluator.* All professors must evaluate, but faculty members in nontraditional programs said that new skills had to be learned to shift from letter-grading schemes to approaches that required much greater explicitness regarding the criteria, the indicators, and the methods of

evaluation. Written evaluations or learning contracts, evaluations of experiential learning or "portfolios" of prior learning, and competency testing are three examples of the nontraditional approaches to evaluation required of these faculty.

5. *Administrator.* Nontraditional teachers often must develop, organize, and coordinate a wide range of learning resources, such as tutors, field supervisors, peer teachers, student task groups, and mediated materials. Because each student may be doing something somewhat different from any others, this becomes quite a chore. The administrative and paperwork demands of nontraditional teaching leave little room for the absent-minded professor.

6. *Developer and Coordinator of Learning Resources.* When the teacher in class and the textbook at home are not the only vehicles for learning, the professor must be able to find, develop, and coordinate various other learning resources, such as field placements, internships, peer teachers, counselors, community faculty, tutors, museums, and libraries. In effect, the professor must create a "stable," or "pool," of people and places which offer a wide range of learning opportunities for diverse students.

7. *Creator and User of Instructional Materials.* All professors use instructional materials, mainly books and articles; but the nontraditional teacher also must learn to use programmed learning guides, computer-assisted instruction, audiovisual materials, PSI modules, educational television. Moreover, because many nontraditional programs do not have instructional materials readily available, professors must learn how to create materials appropriate to their students' learning needs and situations.

8. *Planner of Individualized Programs.* Few faculty members in traditional programs must think through, with a student, an entire degree program that reflects that particular student's prior learning and learning objectives. The closest most of us get to that situation is academic advising, which usually is constricted by prescribed courses and requirements. In individualized programs, the prescription is in the hands of the professor and student, within general institutional parameters. Nontraditional professors, therefore, must learn how to design not just a course but meaningful degree programs for and with their advisees.

By broadening the range of roles played and functions served by a faculty member, a college can make more effective and efficient use of its valuable and expensive faculty resources. In broadening the instructional role, one also comes to recognize the value of nonfaculty personnel, for many of the skills needed in a facilitative-counselor, broker-negotiator, administrative, developer, coordinator, creator, and/or planner role are not held exclusively (or even primarily) by faculty members. We turn now to these alternative human resources.

Instructional Support Staff. One usually thinks of the instructional support staff as a group of people who handle the "nuts and bolts" of the instructional program (for example, clerical staff, registrar), provide quasi-instructional services (for example, counselor, librarian), or meet "extracurricular" needs (for example, dormitory personnel, student-union personnel). In some instances, however, these people are used creatively and efficiently in the provision of direct instructional services and in the design and planning of more effective instructional programs.

Noninstructional personnel can be supervisors for on-campus student interns or participants in work-study programs such as those offered at Berea College (Ky.) and Warren Wilson College (N.C.). A secretary in the history department can assist a student on a work-study assignment who wishes to learn about office management. An assistant dean can be a mentor to an undergraduate major in public administration. The director of the computer center can offer an advanced-level course in systems programming. A clerk in the business office can instruct a group of first-year accounting students on the way books are kept at the college. The president of the college or university—in keeping with a three-century-old tradition in American colleges and universities—can offer a seminar on leadership or contemporary social values (Rudolph, 1962).

One of the most frequently overlooked resources is the student-counseling and career-placement personnel. Not only can (and do) these people assist in the advising and mentoring functions of the institution, they often teach in one or more of the behavioral sciences. If student counselors (as well as faculty members and administrators) conceive of the student-personnel function as incorporating elements of prevention as well as remediation and treatment, it is appropriate also for these counselors to work closely with the faculty on the design and implementation of a curriculum that is both academically and developmentally sound. During the early 1970s, the Mental Health Division of the Western Interstate Commission for Higher Education (Boulder, Colorado) provided a training program on institutional research and planning for counselors who were assigned or wished to assume this expanded role. In 1980, a new project was begun at Memphis State University (Tenn.) under the direction of Arthur Chickering to more fully explore the relation between student services and academic programs as they impinge on the mental health of diverse learners.

Noninstructional/Off-Campus Personnel. To expand the perspectives and expertise available to students as well as reduce instructional costs, some colleges and universities have begun to make extensive use of community resource people. A surprisingly small number of collegiate institutions, however, have availed themselves of this type of rich human resource.

"Thirty percent of the seminars offered in the Tufts Experimental College," Levine (1978, p. 180) finds, "are taught by community resource people," and Metropolitan State University (Minn.) "supplements its core faculty with several hundred community resource people who work full- or part-time in noncollege jobs in the St. Paul/Minneapolis community." The School of Continuing Studies at the University of New Hampshire and the Marylhurst Center for Lifelong Learning (Ore.) similarly make extensive use of part-time, nonacademic personnel in their adult-oriented programs.

At more traditional colleges, which are directed mainly toward young adults, community resource people are occasionally employed to assist students in planning their academic program (College of the Atlantic, Maine) and to assist in the evaluation of competencies (Alverno College, Wisc.). Several colleges also involve community members in teaching assignments. At Antioch College (Ohio), distinguished alumni are invited to visit the college during the summer to lecture and teach. Bard College (N.Y.) offers cross-generational seminars attended by students and members of the community that are addressed to problems of mutual concern.

Throughout the seventies, the use of community resource persons and adjunct faculty by colleges and universities increased considerably. The most extensive use of noninstructional off-campus personnel has occurred in programs that serve adult learners, are highly individualized, and make extensive use of off-campus, experiential learning. Traditionally, colleges have used public school classroom teachers as critic teachers to supervise the work of student teachers. Practicing physicians commonly supervise medical interns and residents, in cooperation with university medical schools. Social workers regularly supervise social work students. Law students are often placed in practicum situations as law clerks, researchers, and legislative aides. It is not surprising, then, that practicing professional artists, musicians, businesspersons, government-agency personnel, social service workers, accountants, computer specialists, journalists, and others are more and more frequently enlisted by college programs to supervise and evaluate the field experiences of both younger and older adult learners.

The assessment of prior noncollege learning has expanded greatly throughout the 1970s and is offered at the more than 350 colleges that hold membership in the Council for the Advancement of Experiential Learning (Council for the Advancement of Experiential Learning, 1979-80). The entrance of increasing numbers of older adults into institutions of higher education has stimulated the need to expand employment and volunteer-related, sponsored, experiential learning. Eldred and Marienau (1979) have identified more than 130 baccalaureate programs for adults, available in forty states in both public and private institutions, most of which utilize learning resources beyond the campus. These cooperative designs serve to link colleges with communities and provide the rationale to include both faculty and nonfaculty professional adjuncts in students' resource networks.

The use of community professionals in partnership with college faculty members has been particularly extensive in the more than thirty University Without Walls programs in both private and public institutions, at Empire State College (N.Y.), and in programs that have developed off-campus centers, often located far from the home campus, such as Goddard College (Vt.), Nova University (Fla.), Pepperdine University (Calif.), the

University of Redlands/Whitehead College (Calif.), and the University of Northern Colorado. Antioch College (Ohio) has been a leader in alternative work-study patterns since the 1930s. Thomas Edison College (N.J.) has no instructional faculty, but utilizes a wide variety of learning resources from throughout the state for instruction and evaluation.

As we enter the 1980s, we find that collegiate instruction is rarely confined to the resources of the institution's campus. Linkages between faculty and off-campus resource persons have widened the sources of learning for students of all ages and clearly have moved the higher education curriculum into fuller partnership with the worlds of work and community service. This linkage has the potential to strengthen career planning, preparation, and mobility and to provide a desirable balance between theoretical and experiential learning for both younger and older learners.

Peer Students. Bruffee (1978, p. 449) has noted, in his description of a peer-tutoring program for writing, that:

> In 1963, Theodore M. Newcomb reported research demonstrating that although the single most powerful force in undergraduate education is peer-group influence, and although in large American colleges undergraduate peer groups profoundly affect most changes which students undergo in values and attitudes—especially those related to social development and self-understanding—undergraduate institutions had at that time not found ways to turn peer-group influence to account in achieving academic educational objectives. They had failed so far to provide what Newcomb called "the essential conditions for mobilizing peer-group influence around intellectual concerns." In 1966, Burton R. Clark and Martin Trow reasserted the importance of Newcomb's study. "The central problems of mass higher education," they said, "are students' indifference to ideas and the irrelevance to their education of their associations and relationships with other students." The seemingly vast changes in student values during the past ten years—from heady social protest to slogging vocationalism—have not changed this fundamental fact.

Several colleges have recently attempted to make more extensive use of peer tutoring. Students at the New College of Hofstra University (N.Y.) can participate in a Peer Group Teaching program for which they receive credit. Levine and Weingart (1973) have found that Antioch (Ohio), Santa Cruz (Calif.),

Sarah Lawrence (N.Y.), Stanford (Calif.), Tufts (Mass.), and Trinity (Conn.) all offer peer-teaching opportunities, though few of these collegiate institutions have offered many of these courses. At several other experimental colleges, such as Raymond College of the University of the Pacific (Calif.), students and faculty members serve as both learners and tutors in jointly planned seminars. Peer-tutoring projects at the City University of New York, the University of California, and Brooklyn College (N.Y.), identified by Bruffee (1978), each make use of more experienced and highly motivated students to assist in the instruction of poorly prepared students.

In a summary description of their Facilitation of Learning Project (Fund for the Improvement of Postsecondary Education, 1979b, p. 51), Webb and Shaw of the University of Florida distinguish between peer tutoring and peer teaching-learning. The peer tutor is placed in a superordinate teaching role with reference to the other student(s) with whom he or she is working. Peer teaching-learning, in contrast, "places students at the same level of academic development in situations in which they must work together, teach each other, and learn from each other, constantly exchanging roles as teachers and learners." The Facilitation Project places students in this peer teacher-learner role in mathematics and chemistry courses.

Levine (1978) finds that peer teaching is offered at only 5 percent of four-year colleges. Levine and Weingart (1973, p. 108) previously found peer teaching to be the "weakest student-centered program" that they had examined in their study of twenty-eight college curriculums, in large part because students have been taught to regard the faculty as the primary source of knowledge. Nevertheless, Levine and Weingart (1973, p. 98) identify several positive (and negative) aspects of peer teaching:

Student teachers universally found teaching to be difficult but worthwhile. While there was some disappointment expressed because of unanticipated problems and an inability to achieve all course goals, on balance every instructor interviewed was glad to have taught a course. Appraisals by the student participants and faculty sponsors were less positive. Most of the students were disappointed in the student-led courses and considered them worse than a faculty-led course. Nevertheless, enthusiasm did exist both for specific courses and for the concept of peer teaching. Some faculty sponsors and student participants praised the quality of the material, the flexibility, and informality and occasional liveliness of the class, and the obvious enthusiasm of the teacher; but most respondents complained of poor structure and the teacher's lack of classroom leadership and lack of knowledge—although the faculty were generally more charitable than the students, recognizing that the courses are "more exploratory than a professor's" and "a joint effort of all in the room."

In a number of programs that serve older adult learners, peer advising and counseling has proved effective. Examples of such programs are the University of Kansas's Adult Life Cycle Workshop, Indiana University's Adult Learning Services, Syracuse University's (N.Y.) peer-counseling service, and the University of Rhode Island's Division of University Extension. The Rhode Island program uses peer counseling to help meet the needs of adult, part-time students in community-based continuing education centers around the state.

Family/Friends/Relatives. Although one does not usually conceive of family, friends, or relatives as valuable resources for learning at the postsecondary level, there is no clear reason for believing that these people cease to be important sources of not only inspiration and encouragement but also personal and professional insight, knowledge, and skills. The challenge is to integrate these resources into the formal educational program of the student's college or university.

Institutions of higher education might begin to offer courses specifically designed for couples or offer couples a special tuition reduction for attending the same courses. Even more ambitiously, a college might offer a program (such as weekend or vacation college) for an entire family. By offering the same program to more than one member of the family, a college can increase the probability that a student will continue to work on the content of the course outside the classroom—this being particularly important for the commuting student.

Friends can be valuable sources of inspiration and learning for students and can be linked formally to a college's instructional program. In addition to serving as peer teachers, friends can be given tuition reductions if they take a course together or participate in a joint project. As with couples and families, this inducement could be of particular value to commuting students, who tend to make friends off campus. The "car pool" idea might be borrowed by commuter colleges: an "educational pool" or "neighborhood educational program" might be constituted of students living in one neighborhood or section of a city. These students would attend class and study together and possibly even share transportation to the college. The course instructor or a teaching assistant might visit the neighborhood occasionally, or an arrangement might be made with a nearby public library to provide the students with textbooks (obtained from the college) and/or library research assistance.

A program of this sort is being conducted by the National Congress of Neighborhood Women (located in Brooklyn, N.Y.) in two locations (Brooklyn and Pittsburgh, Pa.), through cooperative arrangements with several collegiate institutions. Cosumnes River College (Calif.) also embraces part of this model in its use of neighborhood libraries. The college has located "Telebrary" units in the public libraries, allowing residents in the area to play television materials developed by the college specifically for senior citizens, the disadvantaged, and special-interest groups. The libraries provide supportive materials for reading after viewing.

Public libraries are playing an increasingly vital role for adult learners in the United States today. The Library Independent Study and Guidance Project is a federally funded program to encourage libraries to set up instructional support services for adult learners (Walton, 1975). Nine public library systems throughout the nation cooperate with the project and receive funds to support their efforts. The libraries are developing services to assess the needs of self-directed adult learners, training staff members in the delivery of these new services, attracting people to use these newly available resources, and evaluating their effort as they proceed. Learner consultants assist the learner in educational planning; serve as a referral service to educational institutions for lifelong learning; identify contacts at each institution; accumulate collections of resource material; compile subject bibliographies, reading lists, and study guides; and help the independent learner outline a special independent learning project. For those who cannot come to the library, guidance is provided through telephone and correspondence, and books are also mailed.

Two programs are notable in their effort to facilitate the independent adult learner (Walton, 1975). In 1974, the Free Public Library of Woodbridge, New Jersey, developed a detailed plan for introducing three services to the independent learner: (1) advisory services, offering assistance to learners in planning and carrying out their educational goals; (2) informational services, supplying in-depth and up-to-date descriptive materials of nontraditional programs of study at traditional institutions; (3) referral services, contacting agencies to which a referral is appropriate and interceding if a problem arises. The Atlanta Public Library features two major components in its Independent Learning Program Services: (1) The advisory service involves a one-to-one interaction between a specially trained learner adviser and a patron. Learner advisers help individuals define their learning needs, formulate intermediate and long-range objectives, locate materials and learning tools, and guide evaluation efforts. (2) The clearinghouse information service focuses on referral to learning resources outside the library: community-resource files (listing activities at such institutions as the YMCA or area churches) are kept current, as are schedules of classes and seminars at colleges and universities, theater schedules, correspondence school catalogues, and information about external degree programs, credit by examination, testing programs, and so forth. Libraries, in playing such an active role, become more than the repository of knowledge by facilitating the adult learner's participation in community programs and actively engaging adults in the pursuit of their own learning goals.

Relying on the printed media, a group of friends, couples, or families might participate in a program of the "Great Books" type that is sponsored by the college or university. The study group would receive the college's assistance in identifying appropriate books, in preparing study guides, and even in arranging occasional visits from a faculty member. Members of the study group might receive academic credit for the course by successfully completing a test or project that demonstrates content mastery.

Collegiate programs that build on existing interpersonal relationships may soon become prevalent as colleges and universities increasingly address the needs of the adult learner and commuter student. Many colleges will no longer be able to rely on the campus itself as a foundation for building a "community of learners." They will have to build on the foundation of the learner's existing relationships with family, friends, and relatives.

Simulated Persons. This category includes the use of role playing, historical re-creations, and other quasi-dramatic modes of instruction. Most educators are familiar with the occasional use of theatrical devices by faculty members who dress up and impersonate a particular historical, literary, or scientific figure. Yet, a faculty member need not engage in such elaborate role playing to be effective in conveying the essence of a particular person's ideas or perspectives or the stance of a particular school of thought. The faculty member need only indicate to the students that for a specified period of time (for example, one class period), he or she will be speaking from the perspective of this person or as a representative of a particular point of view. The instructor then lectures, leads discussion, or solves problems, answers questions, or asks questions from this perspective. (Chapter Six contains a fuller description of this method.)

The Student Himself/Herself. The learner is himself or herself a resource that must be not only acknowledged but also built into the design of all instructional units and curriculums. How are the student's past experiences and present knowledge, skills, and expertise used to complement and accelerate his or her learning? Many colleges and universities tend to be oriented toward the weaknesses and inexperience of the student: the primary assessment task is to determine where knowledge gaps exist and to fill these gaps with the knowledge of faculty members, books, peers and/or field experiences. Alternatively, a college or university can be oriented to the student's strengths and experience, assessing and building an instructional program around those areas in which the student has already been learning and growing. Many of the learning-contract systems (which will be described in Chapter Four) emphasize the assessment of strengths rather than weaknesses. Particularly in working with adult students who have extensive resources and experiences, college and university faculty members must focus on strengths and resources rather than weaknesses and deficits.

The student also can be a resource to himself or herself in an instructional context that encourages the learner to be his or her own teacher. One of the most widely known and studied of such efforts at instructorless or leaderless education was initiated by Joseph Tussman at the University of California during the early 1960s. Building on the innovative work of Meiklejohn at the University of Wisconsin in the 1920s, Tussman conceived of his Experimental Program as a blending of classical and innovative education. Although the Tussman program was initiated before the Berkeley Free Speech Movement in 1964, his program is associated with this movement in the minds of many educators.

Tussman was concerned primarily with creating a program that exemplifies and serves freedom in all its aspects. Tussman (1969, p. 30) did not equate freedom with a laissez-faire model of education: "To turn children loose is not to make them free. One is free to swim only if one knows how." Tussman believed that freedom comes with expansion in the areas of intellectual interest for a student; with intellectual habits, power, and self-discipline; with individuality; and with relevance. His Experimental Program focused on ancient Greece, seventeenth-century England, and America. All entering freshmen studied the same material and were involved in rather traditional activities: lectures, writing, and faculty/student conferences. In addition, however, all students participated in seminars that met twice a week, once with a faculty member present and the second time without a faculty member present. Thus, students were frequently required to rely on their own resources and guidance as well as those of their peers. A number of problems arose in the implementation of the Experimental Program at

Berkeley, as Tussman (1969, pp. 62-130) has candidly noted and as Levine and Weingart (1973, pp. 40-44) have documented. The student-led seminars, in particular, suffered from low attendance and a lack of direction, even though these seminars were supported enthusiastically by most students and faculty members.

Recently, the lifetime work of William Perry (1968) of Harvard has been seen as supporting the notion of students' relying on themselves as learning resources. Perry's studies show that students' intellectual and ethical development progresses from reliance on the teacher as the authority to increasing autonomy as the learner matures intellectually. These studies suggest that colleges that encourage students to trust themselves as learning resources are most likely to support and enhance intellectual development. Conversely, academic programs that assume that the teacher will maintain control and authority over the students' learning may, indeed, work against student development and self-reliance.

Before moving on to consider nonhuman resources, we will review the way people are identified and used as educational resources at one other college. Lindenwood 4 (Mo.), an experimental college in the Lindenwood Colleges complex, makes use of a learning community consisting of several resources described above, which the colleges places in four categories: students, faculty administrators, faculty sponsors, and resource persons.

> The first citizens of the learning community are the students themselves. Their competence and imagination are the most vital resources of Lindenwood 4.
>
> Other citizens of the community are faculty administrators, faculty sponsors, and resource persons. . . .
>
> Faculty administrators serve a nucleus of thirty students as advisors, mentors, and academic and career counselors. They act as general administrators of the Lindenwood program in the regional center and serve as the students' main avenue of communications with the colleges.
>
> Faculty sponsors work with no more than ten students, and are chosen for each trimester by the student and the faculty administrator. Interacting with students on a one-to-one basis, the faculty sponsors assist students in developing their program of studies and work substantively with individuals through a regular schedule of meetings. Faculty sponsors may be independent psychologists, physicians, artists, scientists, writers,

community organizers, other professional persons, or professors employed at the Lindenwood Colleges or other institutions.

At the graduate level, a student may nominate his or her own faculty sponsor in the student's area of concentration, subject to approval by the faculty administrator. In the M.A. program, faculty sponsors must be able to work at a level of considerable specialization.

Resource persons provide the student with a broad range of expertise and help integrate Lindenwood 4 into the larger community. Regional centers maintain long-term relations with individuals and groups at various institutions such as mental health facilities, hospitals, video centers, business and government agencies, and other colleges and universities. These provide a permanent resource for Lindenwood 4 in career counseling, internships, job placement, and setting academic perspectives. Reciprocally, the regional centers contribute services and provide programs for their communities.

Students, faculty, and resource persons work for mutual reinforcement, critique, and development. All are teachers, all are learners contributing to the community, opening up new avenues of awareness and developing new skills [Lindenwood Colleges, 1976, pp. 178-179].

More than most colleges and universities, Lindenwood 4 has made effective use of available human resources and has planned for the student use of these resources so that they will not be forgotten or used sporadically, as nontraditional resources so often are.

Materials, Equipment, and Environments

Print. Whether speaking of the library holdings of a college or of the books students buy from college or off-campus bookstores, one usually turns first to books when describing the nonhuman resources of a collegiate institution. In addition to books, colleges and universities provide such print materials as journals, magazines, newspapers, packaged instructional programs, simulations, and games. As noted in our discussion of the spatial dimension of the curriculum, the University of California at San Diego has conducted an entire course through one print medium, the newspaper. The "Great Books" course that was first offered at the University of Chicago and is now being offered at St. John's College (Md.) is based on the primacy of another print medium, the book.

In spite of technological advances and increased media diversity, both learners and institutions continue to rely on the printed word in the form of books more than any other material resource for learning.

Nonprint. Although books and other print media remain the primary instructional materials for most colleges and universities, various nonprint media are becoming increasingly prevalent—though our colleges have not been transformed into McLuhanesque, nonliterate enterprises as some critics in the late 1960s predicted. Many faculty members are still wary of making extensive use of any nonprint medium other than the blackboard. As most audiovisual-center directors will attest, even the overhead and opaque projectors are viewed with suspicion by many faculty members. The hesitancy of some instructors to use these audiovisual devices may be attributed in part to their lack of knowledge and skill in using the equipment and preparing the appropriate materials (such as transparencies). The audiovisual-center director often must also be faulted, however, for insensitivity to the instructor's intentions for the course and overall educational philosophy and teaching style. A-V assistance is often offered in an indiscriminate manner by technicians who want to be overly helpful and/or want to record yet another hour of faculty contact for which they will be credited when budget or salary time comes around.

For many years, faculty members in the visual arts, history, and foreign languages have made extensive use of 35-mm slides, motion pictures, and audiotapes. As noted in our discussion about the spatial dimension, a few colleges and universities now make use of videotape. With technical advances (and significantly reduced costs) in half-inch and three-fourths-inch videotape recording and playback equipment and with the introduction of videodisc playback units, one can expect more extensive use of video equipment in the near future. If nothing else, faculty members who now make extensive use of 35-mm slides may find it worthwhile to transfer these slides (and even their slide narratives) to color videotape. In the near future, holography (the projection of three-dimensional figures) undoubtedly will become another valuable and widely used instructional tool, as will other laser-mediated technologies.

Computer. Increasingly, computers are assuming a vital role in the instructional life of American colleges and universities. Computers are now being used in instructional settings in at least four ways: (1) to convey, and to test for comprehension of, new instructional material (computer-assisted instruction), (2) to simulate complex physical or social systems, (3) to assist the instructor in recordkeeping and grading of objective tests, and (4) as a topic for study and a vehicle for the student's acquisition of knowledge about computer systems programming. The first two of these functions are served less frequently by computers at most colleges and universities than are the third and fourth and are given further consideration in Chapter Five.

As a vehicle for recordkeeping and test scoring, computers are being used most frequently in large universities and, in particular, in courses with large student enrollments. With the increased use of complex instructional planning and testing systems, such as the Personalized System of Instruction (see Chapter Five), however, even small colleges will benefit from a computer that keeps track of student activities and accomplishments.

In using the computer to expose students to the computer sciences, Dartmouth College (N.H.) has led the way. All students at Dartmouth are given a share of computer time, take a basic computer programming course, and have access to computer terminals throughout the campus. Over 90 percent of the students at Dartmouth will have made use of the computer before graduation. It is likely that "computer literacy" will be included in many general education programs and liberal arts sequences in the coming decade. The rapid growth of computer use in all areas of life and their decreasing size and cost clearly demonstrate that the use of computers is fast becoming a prerequisite for study in other fields as well as a necessary skill for all educated persons.

A more recent development in the use of computers is in the area of counseling and advising and is exemplified by such systems as System of Interactive Guidance and Information (SIGI), a computer-based aid to career decision making. SIGI is a project of the Educational Testing Service (Princeton, N.J.), which has been joined by CAEL (the Council for the Advancement of Experiential Learning) in Project LEARN, to adapt the guidance system for use by older adults. Adaptations are also being developed for such systems as DISCOVER and EXPLORE. EDUNET is a national computing network of colleges and universities that makes possible the sharing of computer-based resources in higher education and research.

Developments in the area of computer-assisted instruction and counseling have become so rapid that it has become necessary for academic administrators and faculty members to take special training workshops in order to keep up with the field. The business and commercial world is far ahead of higher education in this area. However, it is rapidly becoming clear that as costs decrease, equipment becomes miniaturized, and software becomes more sophisticated, institutions of higher education will be making increasing use of computers for both educational and advising purposes as well as for data-keeping and information-storage purposes. It is also to be expected that other agencies in the community (libraries, government agencies, private consulting firms, and even supermarkets) will soon be making interactive computerized services available to the public in potential competition with colleges and universities unless cooperative linkages are established over the next few years.

Laboratory/Studio Equipment and Supplies. Little need be said about this essential instructional resource other than to note that laboratories are often thought to be the exclusive domain of the physical, biological, and behavioral sciences, while the studio is thought to be the exclusive domain of the visual and performing arts. As a result, little money is allocated for, or encouragement given to, the provision of laboratory or studio equipment and supplies in other fields of study. A laboratory in history or philosophy is conceivable, as is a studio for creative design and problem solving in schools of urban studies and education. Some of the most innovative and productive instructional practices involve the simple transplantation of an instructional method that is traditionally used in one field to another, quite different field.

Altered Environments. What may seem like science fiction or fantasy today very probably will be established instructional practice before the end of the twentieth century. Learning-enhancing drugs, meditation, biofeedback, or reliance on various extrasensory abilities may become acceptable in many colleges and universities. We have only begun to appreciate the potential of various resources to increase our capacity to learn significantly, to relax while learning, or to retain material already learned.

Some resources for the enhancement of learning are destructive, dehumanizing, or illegal. We must address many ethical problems associated with these resources. Yet, when the ethical, social, and technical problems associated with the use of learning-enhancement resources have been addressed (if not solved), we can expect to find that one or more of these resources will be deemed appropriate for collegiate education. At present, meditation has gained credibility as a learning resource. Its acceptance is evidenced by the proliferation of courses on meditation, by the establishment of a collegiate institution, Maharishi University (Iowa), that is specifically dedicated to the promotion of one form of meditation (transcendental meditation), and by the widespread use of this technique in business, industry, and social service agencies as well as schools and colleges.

Learning Environments. In Chapter Two, we described the use of nontraditional environments both on and off campus for instructional purposes. In each of these cases, one also might speak of the environment as a learning resource that can be just as valuable and academically respectable as a book or piece of laboratory equipment. Just as the capacity of a college or university to meet its students' learning needs can be measured in part by the number of volumes in its library, by the size of its computer, or by the size and design of its art studio, so might its capacity be measured by its access to a rich and diverse set of learning environments. The undergraduate liberal arts college might not be able to compete with the large research university in library size, computer size, or studio resources (unless consortial or other cooperative arrangements are established); however, with some imagination and initiative, it should be able to provide students with an impressive variety of resources to meet their learning needs and interests. All resources—people, materials, and equipment are acquired for instructional use by a college not just through the expenditure of money but also through the expenditure of time and creative energy. Often a collegiate institution can be best served through effective resource management—that is, through locating and efficiently using existing on-campus and off-campus resources. In particular, a college can be served effectively if resources are used that have been overlooked or undervalued in the past. Collaboration with other agencies extends a small institution's resource capacity. Many of the alternative resources just described can be used to increase both efficiency and effectiveness in the instructional domain. Of particular note is the continual value of personal interaction among students and institutional personnel. Without this critical element, learning resources, however exotic, are likely to be cold and ineffective.

By using the entire community as a learning resource, small colleges can extend the range of their curricular offerings and provide rich and useful learning opportunities to students, well beyond the capacity of their small faculty resources. Greenberg (1978) has "mapped" the community learning-resource system on which learning-resource inventories can be organized. She has also identified seven "learning levels," the roles they imply, and the kinds of behaviors that result. Through an analysis of community resources and understanding of various learning levels, explicit and systematic use can be made of varied learning environments, appropriate to meet the needs of diverse learners.

As student populations become increasingly older and diverse, the necessity and opportunity to use employment and community volunteer activities within the context of degree programs will increase. And as the connections between theoretical campus-based learning and experiential community-based learning become more logical and necessary, the quality of the curriculum is likely to be enhanced as learners of all ages participate in lifelong education in both collegiate and community settings from their youth to their senior years.

— IV —

ORGANIZATION

Arranging Instructional and Administrative Units Effectively

As noted in the introduction to CASC's *Developing the College Curriculum* (Chickering and others, 1977, p. xiv), the "curriculum" of a college is traditionally defined by the set of courses being taught at the college or university or by a particular course of study. The term *curriculum* is derived from the Latin *currere* (to run), carrying the sense of a process or route of academic travel. Thus, the way a college's academic offerings are organized constitutes, or at least is a vital dimension in, the curriculum of the institution.

In at least three ways, organization determines or influences the route of academic travel. First, the college or university must organize its instructional offerings in a way that constitutes one or more degree-granting programs. Second, the institution must determine how to sequence the curricular elements that constitute the degree program. Third, the people in

101

the institution must be organized in a certain manner in order to provide these curricular elements. Following are descriptions of alternative approaches that have been taken in the organization of the curriculum from each of these three perspectives.

Organization of Degree Program

Single Unified Program. The first colleges in America offered a single academic program to all students based on a curricular model that had been developed at Cambridge University. Only in the middle of the nineteenth century did some colleges and universities begin to provide students with alternative courses of study (called majors) and with alternative individual course offerings (called electives). Very few colleges in the United States now require all students to take the same course of study, and until the late 1970s there was a trend away from required courses and toward an increased number of electives.

Those institutions that have retained or established a single, unified curriculum generally have tried to accomplish one of three curricular goals: (1) to provide students with a classical liberal education, (2) to help students prepare for a particular career or profession, or (3) to enable students to design a completely individualized program that is responsive to unique needs and interests.

The best-known example of an institution that provides students with a classical liberal education is St. John's College (Md.). All students attending St. John's participate in the same program, involving a twice-weekly seminar in which the Great Books of Western civilization are discussed, a preceptorial (for juniors and seniors), foreign language tutorials, mathematics tutorials, a music tutorial, specific laboratory experiences, yearly lecture series, and yearly "don-rag" meetings (assessment by the tutors of the student's progress for the year).

The St. John's curriculum centers on a list of Great Books that changes little. During the past thirty years, St. John's has made only minor changes in its curriculum. If one begins with the assumption that the list of Great Books has been selected thoughtfully as a compendium of human knowl-

edge in the Western world, there is little need for majors, electives, or other options among students who wish to obtain a
broad liberal education. There also is little need for curricular
change.

Just as St. John's College organizes its liberal learning curriculum around a relatively constant and comprehensive input
base, the Great Books, the liberal learning curriculums of several
other colleges are organized around a relatively constant and
comprehensive output base: competencies. Alverno College
(Wisc.), Sterling College (Kans.), and Mars Hill College (N.C.),
among others, have identified the competencies that seem to be
associated with a liberally educated person and then built their
curriculums and student-assessment procedures around these
competencies. These colleges differ significantly from St. John's
in the diverse and elective nature of the inputs into their curriculums. Like St. John's, however, these colleges provide a single,
unified academic focus: in this case, all students are working
toward achievement of a specific set of competencies. These
colleges believe that their carefully selected competencies (like
the Great Books of St. John's) provide sufficient scope to meet
a wide variety of student needs and interests. One similarly
might envision a single, unified curriculum for a college that focuses on a particular societal or regional problem, the curriculum revolving around either a common set of inputs (books,
experiences, or resource people) or outcomes (competencies,
knowledge, skills, and/or attitudes).

A single, unified curriculum is also being offered by many
colleges that train students for a particular career or profession.
Most proprietary schools, for instance, offer a standard curriculum for students who wish to become bookkeepers, beauticians,
or electricians. Similarly, many collegiate institutions (especially
two-year community colleges and technical schools) specifically
prepare students for certain vocations and professions by offering a single, all-encompassing curriculum for all their students.
Some of these colleges are moving in the same direction as Alverno, Sterling, and Mars Hill by defining basic competencies
and organizing their curriculums around these competencies—
for example, the nursing program at Mount Hood Community

College (Ore.) and the College for Human Services (N.Y.; Grant and others, 1979).

Finally, some colleges have preserved a unified curriculum by abandoning a common content and, instead, embracing a common process or procedure. One example of a common process that can be used to design degree programs in any and all subject areas has been developed by the University Without Walls program at Loretto Heights College (Colo.). Greenberg (1980) identifies as follows the twelve unifying processes that are used by every UWW student: (1) individualization, (2) one-to-one faculty adviser/student relationship, (3) degree plans, (4) learning contracts, (5) learning stipends (a portion of paid tuition available to cover off-campus learning-resource expenses), (6) use of the community as a learning resource, (7) use of adjunct faculty and resource persons, (8) personalized evaluation, (9) transcript supplements, (10) advanced-standing credit evaluation, (11) predegree review, and (12) degree review.

In addition to providing consistency and coherence in this process-oriented approach to curriculum organization, these procedures have been linked with specific developmental needs or "tasks" as identified in the research and literature on adult development by such writers as Havighurst (1948), Loevinger (1976), and Weathersby (1977). The average UWW student's age is thirty-six, and the range of persons who have been in the program since 1971 is from sixteen to seventy-four. A wide variety of developmental needs are served.

Particular "intended outcomes" of a generic nature also flow from these processes, such as oral and written communication skills and goal setting, planning, coordinating, and self-evaluation skills. When the curriculum is organized through these processes, the sequences and mix of each student's program are unique. Individual needs of learners from a wide variety of backgrounds and experiences can be met, and degree programs can parallel traditional predesigned majors and general education designs or can deviate from these designs to meet more current, rapidly changing career and personal needs. This approach is particularly appropriate in serving diverse adult students.

Several experimental colleges (such as New College at the University of Alabama and Johnston College at the University of Redlands, Calif.—neither of which now exists) require that each student negotiate and periodically review an individual curriculum "contract" with the college. As with the Great Books, competency-based curriculums, and common-process curriculums, an assumption is made that one curricular procedure (in this case, contracting) is of sufficient complexity or flexibility to meet the learning needs of all or most students. Thus, although St. John's, Alverno, the College of Human Services, Johnston College, and Loretto Heights College look quite different as institutions of higher learning, they share the strength—and risk—of committing themselves to a particular educational philosophy or purpose and of asking all students to work within the context of this philosophy or purpose. To the extent that American higher education can sustain and make effective use of diversity, those collegiate institutions with single, unified curriculum concepts are desirable and viable.

Concentration/General Education/Elective Programs. Most colleges and universities are unwilling to limit themselves to a single course of study that is required of all students. However, they do want all students to take certain courses or cover certain subject matter, and they believe that the student should be able to choose an area in which to concentrate his or her study (major), with possibly a second area of lesser concentration (minor). They also believe that students should be free to pick and choose among other courses (electives) offered elsewhere in the institution. This model has prevailed in American higher education for at least a century and continues to be the dominant model, with periodic shifts in the relative emphasis on the general education, concentration, and elective elements.

As reported in *Missions of the College Curriculum* (Carnegie Foundation for the Advancement of Teaching, 1977), Robert Blackburn and his associates at the University of Michigan found that in both 1967 and 1974, 33 percent of the curriculum in four-year collegiate institutions was devoted to courses in the student's area of concentration. With all the changes in the character of collegiate institutions and the needs and demands of students, the proportion of courses taken in the area of concentration remained unchanged. This was not the case for the general education and elective course elements. In 1967, 13 percent of the curriculum at four-year institutions was devoted to general education and 24 percent to electives, whereas in 1974 the percentages had evened out, 34 percent of the curriculum being devoted to general education and 33 percent to electives. Variability in the relative emphasis placed on general education and electives may be continued into the early 1980s, while many colleges and universities increase the size of their general education program and decrease the number of electives students could take.

There seems to be general agreement among traditional institutions that about one third of the student's collegiate education should be devoted to an area of concentration, the remainder being devoted to broadening experiences through either a prescribed general education program or student-selected electives. Although there is general agreement about the desired extent of concentrated studies in the curriculum, there is significant disagreement about the form this concentration should take.

Many colleges and universities equate the area of concentration with a major field of study. The student selects one discipline and takes all of his or her concentration in this discipline. Other collegiate institutions or individual departments may supplement the major field (for example, chemistry) with a cognate field (for example, mathematics) in which the student is to take certain courses or a certain number of courses. Alternatively, or in addition, a student may select a minor area of concentration in which he or she moves beyond an introductory or survey level, usually taking at least two upper-division courses in the discipline.

Another variation on the traditional model is the trial major offered at Bard College (N.Y.): "All freshmen must select a major and take two of their four courses in that field. A student may change majors as often as desired; however, several departments require a basic background obtainable through specified courses to be taken prior to a student's acceptance as a major in the sophomore year" (Levine and Weingart, 1973, p. 65). Levine and Weingart report, however, that though the trial major "was intended to quickly expose students to both breadth and depth," it has become "only 'the fossilized remains of a program' " (p. 65) and may be a needless formalization of a typical search process in which most students engage. Nonetheless, as the authors acknowledge, the formalized trial major may have saved some students from majoring in an area they would have disliked.

In some instances, a college or university has retained the traditional concentration/general education/elective elements of the curriculum but has modified or expanded on these elements, giving them new life and relevance for the contemporary student. We will examine the curricular organization at two such collegiate institutions: Ottawa University (Kans.) and Emory and Henry College (Va.). At Ottawa University, the general education program consists of seven basic core seminars, seven physical-activity courses, and a cultural/educational-activity requirement:

There are seven basic *core seminars* in the general education program. The content of these seminars examines the persistent questions facing mankind from the perspectives of the past, the present, and the future. Among the questions considered are man's understanding of himself, man's relation to the world, and man's collective problems in society. The seminars offer many learning experiences and settings. In each core seminar there are a variety of learning modes, such as small-group discussions, media presentations, field trips, large-group presentations, and individually designed instructional modules.

Two of the core seminars are normally undertaken in the freshman year, followed by three additional seminars in the second year. The final two core seminars are scheduled in the senior year of study. The senior core seminars are regarded as culminating learning experiences that require the advanced student to utilize the skills of inquiry, problem solving, and expression developed during his previous college years. . . .

Physical activities are considered an integral part of the general education program. Seven required activity courses are to be completed during the course of the undergraduate program.

Cultural and educational activities offered through the University Program Series provide opportunities each session for students to enrich formal learning experiences with lectures, concerts, drama, films, religious presentations, and discussions with outstanding individuals. Students are required to attend seven events of their own choosing from among the twelve or more university program events offered in each seven-week session.

Cross-cultural living and study opportunities may be planned as an important element in the overall educational plan. Each student is encouraged to take part in a cross-cultural learning experience designed to complement his total educational program. The experience may be completed in this country or in a foreign country. It may be taken for college credit, with specific study requirements, or without credit. The basic purpose of the cross-cultural experience is to introduce the student to a culture other than his own with the objective of broadening his understanding of himself, of the world in which he lives, and of people of other cultures. Students may participate in this program individually through programs such as the Experiment in International Living, as a member of a student group from Ottawa, or in a group sponsored by another accredited college or university [Ottawa University, 1976, pp. 10-11].

The area of concentration at Ottawa is not defined by an individual discipline or even a combination of major and minor fields, but rather by individualized depth preparation for a particular career:

The distinct advantage of the depth study approach over the traditional "major" offered by many institutions is its extensive flexibility. No two students' goals are alike in every detail, and therefore the educational experiences needed to help them achieve their unique goals should not be identical. The concept of the depth study permits the student to draw upon a wide range of academic departments and educational experiences in designing the individualized depth study plan he needs to achieve his own goals.

The specification of precisely which learning experiences and academic courses [compose] the depth study grows out of the planning of the student's educational contract. The crucial criterion for evaluating the adequacy of a depth study proposed by a student is whether it is deemed to have significant potential for helping him achieve his goals as outlined in the educational contract. . . .

The flexibility of the depth study approach allows students to include practical, nonclassroom experiences in their programs. For example, internships in banks, corporations, governmental agencies, schools, and hospitals have provided students with valuable career-oriented knowledge and skills. Special independent study activities conducted off campus provide another important alternative to the more formal course work. The Ottawa calendar is especially suited to the inclusion of brief, concentrated learning experiences in a variety of actual field settings [Ottawa University, 1976, p. 11].

The elective program at Ottawa also extends the usual boundaries of this curricular element:

College years are not only a time for setting career goals and working toward those goals, but they are also a time for exploring a variety of areas of learning in which the student may have an interest. These explorations are encouraged at Ottawa through its approach to elective courses. Electives serve the purposes of broadening the general education of the student and also of enriching his depth study. Prerequisites are not a barrier to participation in a large number of the courses in the Ottawa curriculum as they are in many colleges. Elective experiences may take the form of unusual credit courses, such as the program in volunteer services established in 1972 to develop the skills and knowledge needed by students to become effective citizens in their communities. A wide range of elective course options are available to the student in the regular academic sessions and especially in the winter term, in which many of the courses offered are of a nontraditional nature [Ottawa University, 1976, p. 12].

Emory and Henry College offers a general education program, an area of concentration, and elective courses, as do Ottawa University and many other collegiate institutions. The general education element at Emory and Henry is composed of eight components:

The Writing Program. The Emory and Henry writing program is based on the premise that effective writing is one of the essential components of a liberal education and is part of almost every aspect of each individual's educational experience. It also is an important tool used in many professions. Emory and Henry offers a basic writing course, English 101, in which all freshmen enroll unless placed into an advanced course through departmental testing. The course brings together a small group of students (twelve to seventeen persons) to write and study the processes of writing. To complement the basic course, a writing assistance laboratory offers individualized or small-group instruction to students needing review work or tutorial aid.

Freshman Studies. Courses in the freshman studies program engage students in the consideration of questions concerning self, society, and human values. The distinctiveness of these courses is that they are humanistic rather than disciplinary and frequently cross departmental lines. Each class enrolls a small number of students, ensuring an individualized and personalized approach. Freshman studies complement disciplinary studies, and together they urge the student toward recognizing the use, responsibility, and interconnectedness of all human knowledge. Freshman studies are offered by departments from all divisions within the college, making available a wide variety of subjects and methods of approach.

Disciplinary Studies. Disciplinary studies are intended to allow the student to discover that the world of intellectual endeavors is a many-faceted world, presenting an array of challenges. Their aim is the acquisition of knowledge within limited areas of inquiry, the development of skills and methods peculiar to these areas, the fostering of intellectual judgment, the cultivation of critical thinking, and the appreciation of human action and achievement.

Great Books. The purpose of the Great Books course is to study some of those works of the human imagination and spirit that are recognizably great because they have helped shape the intellectual tradition to which we are heirs. These are the works that have become part of our language of image and idea and that continue to speak significantly to our time and place. Every sophomore student takes the Great Books course, which features team teaching and use of special programs including movies and guest lectures.

Religion Course. Through the course in religion, students consider the roots, teachings, and contemporary understandings of the Christian faith, using the Bible as a basic source. This particular element of the curriculum stems from Emory and Henry's role as a church-related college and also from the college's belief that every educated person should be aware of religious issues and questions. In the course, students are encouraged to understand sacred writings in a historical context and to appreciate their contemporary relevance. Students typically take the religion course during the junior year.

Value Inquiry Studies. Value concerns are intrinsic in every area of learning because of the application of knowledge to actual situations, individual and social. A liberal arts college must accept the dual task of helping students in the acquisition of knowledge and helping them make informed decisions about those moral and ethical issues that are part of the consequence of knowing. Several departments will be involved in the offering of value inquiry studies, giving students the opportunity to explore ethical issues related to their own concentrations.

Global Studies. The people of the world have been increasingly linked in recent years due to modern communication and transportation systems, and responsible members of society cannot ignore these global interdependencies. Emory and Henry seeks to encourage students to investigate seriously matters of global significance, define their relevant components, and defend value decisions. Global studies will be available through several E&H departments, and every senior student will take one of the studies. Each course will focus on some region or worldwide topic, encouraging an appreciation for global concerns that transcend Western culture.

Divisional Seminar. Every senior student will take a divisional seminar designed to enhance the integration of knowledge by exploring the interrelationships between the various disciplines within a division. The seminar will bring together students from a variety of departments within the division, focusing on a problem or topic which is common to all their areas. By working and discussing together, the students will learn to recognize the interdependence of various fields and the limitations of each one alone [Emory and Henry College, 1978, pp. 2-3].

The major and minor fields of study at Emory and Henry have been combined into a single area of concentration and, like the Ottawa University program, blend academic and career preparation in a five-component program:

Primary Discipline. The primary discipline is that field of study or group of courses most directly related to the student's professional career goals. Normally, it consists of eight to ten courses, including core courses which cover the foundations, principles, and theories of the field along with advanced courses that permit specialization in some branch or track within the field.

Contextual and Support Areas. The support areas include courses taken outside the primary discipline, selected from fields which relate to that discipline. These courses are chosen to complement and enrich the primary area, increase the student's depth and breadth of knowledge, and illustrate the interrelatedness of various typs of knowledge.

Foreign Language and Quantitative Methods. One aspect of the contextual and support areas is the development of skills in foreign language or in quantitative methods, important in the communication process of many contemporary professional fields. The catalogue description of each area of concentration indicates the minimum courses necessary to meet the skill requirement appropriate to that program of study.

Development of Historical Perspective. Since all human beings are by nature historians, the proper study of history is essential to a liberal education. Each area of concentration includes courses that foster a sense of historical perspective by emphasizing both the concreteness of history and the conceptual framework through which we view the facts of history to give them meaning.

Senior Project. Each senior has the opportunity to work on a one-to-one basis with a faculty member on a project that helps bring into a single focus the knowledge acquired from various disciplines studied in college. The area of concentration describes acceptable types of projects, with options ranging from independent study and research to internships and applied experiences [1978, p. 3].

The electives program at Emory and Henry constitutes about 20 percent of the curriculum (six to eight courses out of a total of thirty-eight courses), compared with the 24 and 33 percent averages reported by Blackburn. Given the diversity of experiences and number of options within the general education element and area of concentration at Emory and Henry, a large proportion of electives may not be necessary.

Ottawa University and Emory and Henry College are not alone in giving new life to the traditional organization of a degree program. They illustrate the type of thoughtful modification that has been made at a number of liberal arts colleges throughout the United States that serve primarily the eighteen-to twenty-two-year-old student.

A number of other new liberal studies programs have been developed with the older adult student in mind. At the College of Professional and Continuing Education at Clark University (Mass.), a common liberal studies seminar setting is provided for returning adult students that leads to the preparation of a portfolio for the assessment of prior noncollege learning (Fund for the Improvement of Postsecondary Education, 1979a). Project Transition, a six-credit, one-semester series of seminars and life/career-planning activities, a project of the University Without Walls at Loretto Heights College (Colo.), reintroduces the traditional liberal arts disciplines to returning mid-life and older adults through four one-month-long seminars: "The Psychology of Adulthood," "Values in Human Experience," "Perspectives on the Future," and "Learning as Adults" (Fund for the Improvement of Post-Secondary Education, 1979a; Greenberg and Charland, 1980). Elements common to these innovative approaches for adult learners are use of traditional liberal learning disciplines and materials, focus on the adult student himself or herself as the object of study, beginning where the student is before moving forward into institutional agendas, and small-group support environments coupled with individual counseling and advisement. Some institutions require particular reentry general education seminars for all returning adult students; others make them available as elective opportunities.

Multiple-Major and Interdisciplinary-Major Programs. To add greater breadth to students' educational experiences and to avoid the excessive specialization that pervades many single-major programs, some colleges and universities encourage or require students to major in two or more areas. Haverford College (Pa.) and the University of California at Santa Cruz offer a double-major option, though because of the heavy workload, not many students avail themselves of it—9 percent at Haverford and 7 percent at Santa Cruz (Levine and Weingart, 1973).

Other colleges avoid the problem of overloading students with too many courses in a double major by offering interdisciplinary majors that fully (or partly) integrate two or more major fields of study. The College of the Atlantic (Maine) is organized entirely around interdisciplinary programs (environmental design, environmental sciences, social and cultural studies, and values and consciousness) and requires that students engage in a significant activity in each of these four areas while concentrating on one. Bradford College (Mass.) offers only integrated interdisciplinary majors. Students major in administration and management, American culture, creative arts, humanities, human studies, or international studies or may design an individual major that incorporates integrated work in at least two disciplines.

Reed College (Ore.) offers interdisciplinary majors in such areas as American studies, international studies, history/literature, mathematics/economics, mathematics/sociology, philosophy/literature, and philosophy/religion. Similarly, Brown University (R.I.) offers fourteen interdisciplinary majors, Trinity College (Conn.) offers three, and Yale University (Conn.) offers special interdisciplinary majors in history and the arts and letters, social sciences, culture and behavior, and combined sciences (Levine and Weingart, 1973). Interdisciplinary majors are also found in colleges that are specifically oriented to certain societal problems, such as the College of Human Services (N.Y.).

Two of the most far-reaching attempts to provide a double-major option arise from the environmentally oriented curriculum of the University of Wisconsin at Green Bay (UWGB) and the interdisciplinary, liberal arts curriculum of the New College at Hofstra University (N.Y.). The UWGB curriculum is organized around four colleges (Community Sciences, Creative Communication, Environmental Sciences, and Human Biology). Each student at UWGB selects a particular environmental theme to study in depth. This concentration, or major, crosses disciplinary and college lines. The student also has the opportunity to study a second, more focused (usually disciplinary) field. Thus, a student may select urban analysis as the broad field of study and sociology as the more narrowly defined disciplinary field. A student at UWGB also has a third option, a collateral major, which focuses on preparation for a particular profession or graduate program. Other colleges, even without an environmental emphasis, could readily adopt this integration of problem, disciplinary, and career foci. For example, a student could major in urban studies (problem focus), history (disciplinary focus), and business (career focus) to prepare for work in public administration.

The New College of Hofstra University builds on the classical individualized apprenticeship model at Oxford University by offering a multitiered organization of its degree program. At the most general level, the New College curriculum is organized around four programs of study: area studies, creative studies, applied programs, and interdisciplinary studies. Each of these four programs (with the exception of interdisciplinary), in turn, contains a series of concentrations (for example, humanities, social sciences, fine arts, premedical, women's studies), which students elect as a focus for their baccalaureate study. In interdisciplinary studies, a student designs his or her own program of study. Most of the concentrations also can be subdivided into emphases. An emphasis may be a discipline, a cluster of disciplines, or an interdisciplinary theme. Students wishing a more precise focus for their studies often select one of these emphases:

As an illustration, one student may wish to enter the Area Studies Program as a freshman; after a year's experience, this student may elect the humanities *concentration* within the Area Studies Program; and after another year, this student may exercise the option for a literature *emphasis* as the student's particular interest in the humanities becomes clearer through experience.

As another example, a student may begin work in the social sciences *concentration* of the Area Studies Program with an initial interest in psychology. After experiences in faculty-offered courses and student-initiated projects, the student may wish to enter the Applied Program in Psychology for a more discipline-based approach. As still another example, a student may begin work in the Applied Program of Premedical Studies, later determining that the Natural Sciences *concentration* of Area Studies is more appropriate to the student's individual interests; this student might also be able to develop an *emphasis* in community services, including an off-campus education field placement in an environmental agency [Hofstra University, 1978, p. 53].

Following is a list of the concentrations and optional emphases that are affiliated with each of the four programs of study at New College:

Area Studies: concentrations in humanities, social sciences, and natural sciences.

Optional Humanities Emphases include philosophy, literature, dramatic literature, art history, anthropology.

Optional Natural Science Emphases include biology, chemistry, mathematics.

Optional Social Science Emphases include history, economics, political science, sociology, psychology.

In addition, Area Studies students may complement their concentrations in the humanities, social sciences, and natural sciences by completing an interdisciplinary emphasis in the Applied Programs of either education or community services.

Creative Studies: concentrations in fine arts and/or theater arts and/or writing arts.

Optional Fine Arts Emphases include graphics, printmaking, painting, design, illustration.

Optional Theater Arts Emphases include community theater, theater arts service, theater performance.

Optional Writing Arts Emphases include poetry, fiction, and nonfiction.

In addition, some students may be able to complement their concentrations in the Creative Studies Program by completing an interdisciplinary emphasis in the Applied Programs of either education or community services.

Applied Programs: concentrations in premedical, prelegal, and psychology; emphases within education, community services, and business services.

Premedical Emphases include biology or chemistry.

Prelegal Emphases may include one of the Area Studies disciplines or a community services emphasis.

Psychological Emphases include clinical, social, developmental, or experimental. Some students may also be able to include a community services emphasis.

Education Emphases are elementary education, teacher training, and child study.

Community Services Emphases include the theoretical, historical, and experiential study of community services and community service institutions.

Business Services Emphases include courses and projects of a pre-professional nature.

Interdisciplinary Studies: individually designed thematic or problem-centered concentrations; optional emphasis in Women's Studies.

Within the Interdisciplinary Studies Program, students have the opportunity to design their own nondiscipline-based, thematic concentration, which may also include the Applied Program emphases of either education or community services [Hofstra University, 1978, pp. 53-54].

We see at both UWGB and New College of Hofstra an attempt to maximize curricular flexibility and the individualization of degree programs for students. Other organizational strategies have also been used with this goal in mind: (1) optional degree tracks and (2) student-created degree programs. We turn now to a brief description of these approaches.

Optional Degree Tracks. Given that some students may wish to proceed with degree planning in one way (for example, individualized contracting) while others may prefer a second way (for example, working in a major and minor area), several colleges have tried to individualize the degree-granting procedure by offering students a choice of two or more degree tracks. At Vassar College (N.Y.), students have been offered three paths to a baccalaureate degree: the Independent Program, the Concentration in a Discipline, and the Multidisciplinary Concentration. According to Heiss (1973), students who choose the Independent Program "select and combine their courses on the basis of their own goals. This program is designed both for those who seek breadth rather than specialization and for those who wish to specialize heavily in one problem or period" (p. 65). Students who choose instead to concentrate in a discipline at Vassar "follow a more controlled path to their degree, but departmental majors have been revised to provide new opportunities for students to work at their own pace and follow their own interests. Broad guidelines have replaced the former distribution requirements, and at least one fourth of the student's work must be taken outside of her major field" (pp. 65-66). The multidisciplinary concentration builds on regular courses in the curriculum as well as interdisciplinary courses: "These latter courses focus on contemporary problems or issues, applying different concepts and methods of inquiry, and on the study of the past as it relates to present-day problems. Seminars and lectures are offered at ascending levels of complexity to provide for integration and coherence in the student's program" (p. 66).

Three degree-planning options are also available to students at Austin College (Texas): the Basic Program, the Special Program, and the College Honors Program. Nearly all students begin in the Basic Program, and most remain in this program until graduation. Students wishing to design a nontraditional concentration select the Special Program. The College Honors Program is made available to those students who exhibit exceptional academic skills, need exceptional flexibility, and are willing to assume additional responsibility for program design.

The Basic Program at Austin resembles the traditional program offered at many liberal arts colleges utilizing a core of interdisciplinary courses:

The IDEAS Program is based upon a core of six courses taken by all students as the foundation of the College's liberal arts program. This common, shared encounter is intended to help the student formulate and express responses to experience, to the social and political environment, and to the culture that constitutes the varied responses to similar experiences by people at various times and places.

The six core courses . . . are as follows:

Communication/Inquiry: one course
Heritage of Western Culture: three courses
Policy Research: one course, and
Individual Development: one course credit

An individually designed *Exploratory Sequence* provides breadth to the student's education and an introduction to various "modes of thought." In conjunction with the mentor, at least six courses not closely related to the student's field of concentration are chosen to reflect personal needs and interests and express a personal commitment to liberal education.

A concentration consists of a minimum of seven courses to a maximum of eleven courses in the field depending on the stated requirements for the particular discipline.

There is usually considerable room in the student's degree plan for a number of electives [Austin College, 1980, pp. 8-12].

The Special Program at Austin closely resembles the individualized contracting procedure that we will discuss with reference to student-created majors:

The "Special Program" is primarily utilized by students wishing to have a nontraditional or interdisciplinary concentration that needs to be individually designed based on the student's own background and goals. This option requires considerable initiative and effort since the student needs to describe carefully in writing his or her educational background, levels of achievement, goals, objectives, and how these all fit together.

The student and mentor discuss the written analysis and broad plan and work out a detailed plan or learning contract for achieving goals and objectives. Beyond the six-course core sequence that must be completed, there is considerable freedom to plan a total program of courses appropriate to the overall educational plan that is developed.

The "Special Program" is particularly adaptable to the needs of students interested in studying interdisciplinary subject areas or in preparing for unique career fields not spelled out within the standard liberal arts program. A student may be interested in two or more fields, such as psychology and art, history and political science, religion and sociology, or biology and physics; or the student may be interested in a career field, such as banking, biological art, computer programming, forestry, or social work. For any of these fields and for many others, a special program of study can be planned, in some instances involving field study off campus as an integral part of the plan.

The degree plan typically should include in essay form a statement of the design of the concentration and how courses and experiences will be used to achieve an education of breadth and depth. The student also will

outline how the special degree plan will serve to provide for an exploratory
sequence and for good use of electives [Austin College, 1980, p. 14].

The College Honors Program combines many of the features of a traditional honors program with those of an individualized, student-created degree program. Participation in the
College Honors Program is limited to 3 percent of the student
body at Austin, and students are invited to candidacy in the
program. Candidates submit an essay and general plan for their
work in the program. Faculty recommendations and personal
interviews also are often required.

The main features of the College Honors Program are:

1. Careful planning of the junior and senior years with special attention
    to independent research as well as to mutual investigation with other
    students in the program of topics of scholarly concern in both the
    arts and the sciences;
2. Honors courses by faculty whose areas of expertise are broadened for
    the sake of all students in the program regardless of their individual
    academic fields of study;
3. Considerable latitude in scheduling of work beyond the structures of
    regular course offerings or the confines of the regular academic term
    and year;
4. Some opportunity for accelerated progress toward a degree so long as
    that progress is marked by consistent attention to the variety of aca-
    demic disciplines and modes of inquiry which constitute liberal learn-
    ing.

When students are not admitted to the College Honors Program
until near the end of their second year at the College, an optional, entry-
level program in honors education may be offered to a select group of
freshmen and sophomores each year. This features an Honors Colloquium
that is related in part to the core curriculum [Austin College, 1980, p. 14].

Student-Created Degree Program. Although very few collegiate institutions offer three different degree options, as do
Vassar and Austin, many provide students with at least the informal option of designing their own degree program. Levine
and Weingart noted in 1973 that nine of the twenty-eight collegiate institutions they were studying offered student-created
programs: Antioch (Ohio), Bowdoin (Maine), Brown (R.I.),

Haverford (Pa.), Reed (Ore.), Stanford (Calif.), the University of California at Santa Cruz, Trinity (Conn.), and Yale (Conn.). Most of the student-created majors observed in the study either combined two (or occasionally three) disciplines or focused on a particular period, problem, or culture by using materials from several departments. "The structure of student-created concentrations is remarkably similar at each of the schools studied. No school reserves this option for a select group such as honors students. Rather, any student can write a proposal for a concentration—including, in most cases, a description of the courses and independent study he plans to undertake and, where relevant, a proposal for a senior project. The number of courses required for a student-created concentration is usually the same as that required for the average departmental major, and schools that require a senior project or examination . . . easily fit that institution into their student-created major" (Levine and Weingart, 1973, p. 68).

According to Levine and Weingart, the number of students who participated in this self-design option at traditional institutions was small. Students in the early 1980s may be even more hesitant to take the initiative in designing their own program. Student-created degree programs seem to be particularly successful when adult students are involved (for example, in external degree programs such as are found at Empire State College, N.Y., and in the Vermont State College system or in individualized programs for adults) or in colleges that serve traditional-aged students yet require a student-created program and provide sufficient faculty support to enable the planning process to be successful. At Justin Morrill College (Michigan State University), for instance, all juniors are expected to choose a faculty adviser who will help the student design his or her own major area of concentration. The major can be either departmental or interdepartmental and need only meet certain basic credit requirements and have the faculty adviser's approval.

An even more extensive program for facilitating the creation of an academic program by each student is to be found at William Jewell College (Mo.) in its Program of Personal Achievement:

Each student will construct, in his consultation with his Personal Advisory Committee, his individual educational program at William Jewell College. This Program of Personal Achievement will be his distinctive combination of courses and experiences designed to meet his unique background, abilities, and goals.

The student will work out his plans for his college career in a personal booklet, which will remain in his possession. He will be able to visualize his college program as he builds it through successive revisions. At the conclusion of his college years, the booklet will provide a comprehensive review of his educational experiences.

The booklet will include cocurricular and cultural development as well as classes and credits, for the college seeks to make the total environment a part of the student's education.

The first stage in developing the Program of Personal Achievement is for the student to think through his educational goals and state them clearly. These goals will doubtless change during the course of a college career, but the experience of articulating these goals at various stages is seen as crucial to the student's personal growth.

The second stage is to devise a program of courses and cocurricular experiences that will meet these goals. The college has long experience as a liberal arts institution and asks its students to take certain programs as part of a "General Education": exposure to a wide variety of learning matter. Other courses are selected in terms of a student's specific goals: for example, to become certified as a teacher, to enter medical school or graduate school. Many courses are free electives [William Jewell College, 1978, pp. 9-10].

Planning assistance is also comprehensive and systematic in colleges that rely on contracting processes for student degree planning. The New College at the University of Alabama, Birmingham-Southern College (Ala.), and Johnston College at the University of Redlands (Calif.), for instance, require each student to negotiate a contract with the college indicating how he or she wishes to use the resources of the institution (formal courses, seminars, fieldwork, supervised independent study), achieve certain educational outcomes that are related to current or future intellectual interests and/or career plans, and fulfill certain degree requirements that are imposed by the college, institution, or state. The college, in turn, makes a commitment to provide the needed resources in a responsive manner and to help the student assess his or her progress toward the stated educational goals.

Student-designed degree programs typically rely on strong student/adviser relationships and on coherent program designs. They are not designed by students alone, without regard for institutional parameters or requirements of some sort. Although it is most often the older adult student who selects such highly self-directed programs, young, traditional-aged students who are unusually self-directed and clear about their goals have been served as well. In the early 1970s, the University Without Walls program at Loretto Heights College (Colo.) enrolled a number of students between sixteen and twenty years of age. Some were completing their freshman year in college. Other students, often older adults, whose interests were not served by the traditional general education and major field combinations, pursued their own designs, under the guidance and supervision of a faculty adviser. Many times, the degree sequences were "upside down," starting with the area of concentration and ending with liberal learning, reflecting a depth-to-breadth pattern appropriate to meeting the vocational needs and "experience-rich/theory-poor" patterns of a typical working adult's life. At Antioch College (Ohio) and Goddard College (Vt.), a wide age range of students can select from multiple approaches along a continuum of institutionally designed to student designed programs.

A number of public, urban institutions serving many ethnic minority students, such as Chicago State University (Ill.) and Northeastern Illinois University, provide opportunities for extensive student self-design. Minnesota Metropolitan College and the University Without Walls programs of the University of Minnesota and the University of Wisconsin at Green Bay assist adult students to design their degree programs within institutionally framed philosophical parameters, designating particular areas of learning that reflect the special missions of these institutions.

The contracting process that is used at the New College of the University of Alabama illustrates not only the nature and dynamics of the student-centered degree-planning process but also many of the most important features of any curricular planning process (for example, periodic review of plans and use of an advisory group made up of representatives of diverse populations).

After admission, students design their contracts with the assistance of others in regard to educational goals. Aiding the student in the design and fulfillment of the contract, the New College employs a comprehensive system of advising, concentrating on the total development of each individual. The advising committee consists of (1) a student, (2) a New College adviser, (3) typically two other persons—may include faculty, fellow students, or persons from the outside community.

Through the Contract-Advising Committee, the student develops his/her own program and modifies it as interests develop or change. The curriculum includes the following features: a core curriculum of interdisciplinary seminars in the New College, a number of electives, a depth study program, and other experiences agreed upon by the Contract-Advising Committee. Students are strongly encouraged to include in their program an out-of-class learning experience, independent study, and a plan of developing physical as well as mental skills. . . .

Each student develops a demanding and coherent plan for achieving his/her educational goals, based on an analysis of the student's interests, abilities, and previous educational experiences. Then the student, working with his/her Contract-Advising Committee, plans specific academic programs on a semester-by-semester basis. When the student is within one year of graduation, he/she will submit a plan for the final year of course work to the New College faculty and Dean for approval. When the program for the student's final year of study is approved, it becomes the final contract between the university and the student and constitutes the official statement of graduation requirements for that particular student.

The following guidelines provide the context within which the student and his/her Contract-Advising Committee operates in designing a satisfactory program:

Completion of Interdisciplinary General Education Seminars: Includes completion of seminars in the humanities, social sciences, and natural sciences (or substituted academic work) as agreed upon by the Contract-Advising Committee and as approved by the New College faculty and Dean.

Completion of a Depth-Study Program: The usual depth-study program will consist of from ten to twelve courses. Each student is expected to complete satisfactorily the courses designed for his/her particular depth-study program and agreed upon by the Contract-Advising Committee.

Each student in the New College selects a depth-study area on the basis of his/her interest, previous experience, and personal goals. The choice of a depth-study area as well as the specific courses and other requirements of the depth-study program are determined by the student and his/her Contract-Advising Committee.

In the event that there is a question about the student's qualifications for, or of the appropriateness of, one or more educational experiences approved by the Contract-Advising Committee, the Dean of the New College, having taken care to check with faculty members and the department chairman in the student's primary area of interest, will make a recommendation on the matter, informing the student and his/her Contract-Advising Committee of any decisions made. In the event that a student wishes to put together a depth-study program that does not fall within a traditional academic discipline, the Dean of the New College may appoint a student-faculty committee to review the curriculum within one year of graduation and make suggestions for any possible revision to the student, his/her Contract-Advising Committee, and the Dean of the New College for final approval. . . .

Electives: Usually a minimum of twelve elective courses are taken in order to ensure that students will take the opportunity to explore new and broader interests not developed in their depth-study and general education programs. Each student should select with the Contract-Advising Committee several elective courses that are directly relevant to his/her depth-study program and several others—not necessarily related to one another—that are especially interesting. . . .

Off-Campus Learning Experience: It is strongly recommended, but not required, that every student plan a practical or supplementary off-campus learning experience for the equivalent of one semester during the time he/she is enrolled at the university (twelve credit hours maximum unless otherwise approved by the Contract-Advising Committee). The successful completion of this off-campus learning experience will be evaluated by the person(s) chosen to supervise the student's off-campus work and related studies, considering the goals of the experience and what the student has learned from it compared with what he/she set out to learn as established in the guidelines for that particular off-campus learning experience [New College at the University of Alabama, 1975, pp. 217, 220-221].

Like any collegiate institution that is offering a nontraditional, individualized, or multiple-track degree program, the contracting college or university must embrace a departmental structure that is comparable to the student's degree program or is sufficiently malleable to adapt to the specific designs of individual students. A college, for instance, that agrees to accommodate a student who has contracted for a combined program in philosophy and physics must be one in which faculty members in these two disciplines can work together easily, with minimal interdepartmental rivalry or bureaucratic barriers. We shall turn to a more detailed consideration of this aspect of curricular organization after examining another aspect of the curriculum that must also be considered when designing a degree program—the sequencing of degree elements. One must keep in mind that students change and develop during their undergraduate years. The sequencing of general education, concentration, and elective elements in the curriculum may be more important than the overall percentage of time devoted to each element.

Sequencing of Curricular Elements

Required Elements at Entry Level. Colleges and universities differ not only in the way they design the concentration, general education, and elective elements of the curriculum and the relative emphases they give to these elements but also in the way these three elements are sequenced. Typically, collegiate institutions offer their required courses to freshmen and sophomore students. Simon's Rock Early College (Mass.), which serves students younger than the usual college age, offers a required program called "The Transition Year," which includes a semester-long, issues-oriented seminar, a set of introductory-level courses that are specifically designed to facilitate the acquisition of basic skills, and various residential living resources and activities. Similarly, in the late 1960s, Albion College (Mich.) offered an interdisciplinary seminar program ("Basic Ideas") to all freshmen, which "deliberately focuses on some of the value conflicts of greatest urgency to youth today as they struggle to answer such questions as: Who am I? Where am I going and why? What are the values that make life worth living and a society worth fighting for? How can I cope with all the pressures exerted by my parents, my peers, and my environment?" (Padgett, 1969, p. 296).

Similar general education courses were required of all freshmen or freshmen and sophomores at many colleges and universities before the late 1960s. Brown University (R.I.) provided one of the most innovative of these entry-level programs in its "Modes of Thought" courses. As in the Albion "Basic

Ideas" program, students at Brown were exposed to the processes of learning and problem solving through participation in seminars focusing on particular interdisciplinary themes.

A contemporary version of the entry-level core program is offered at Carnegie-Mellon University (Pa.), where freshmen and sophomores in the College of Humanities and Social Sciences are required to take five interdisciplinary clusters of courses, minicourses, and learning modules: fundamental methods and skills; humanities; social values; social, political, and economic systems; and science and technology. This core program tends to reflect the change in emphasis from the personal problems of young people as they enter a new era of their life to the broader societal problems that confront all people.

Although the development-oriented programs at Simon's Rock and Albion may be appropriate for many young students, they clearly are not responsive to the needs of older students or of young students who enter college with a fair amount of sophistication and self-understanding. For these latter groups of learners, one must either eliminate all required entry-level courses or offer entry-level courses that are more responsive to their needs and interests. Carnegie-Mellon has responded by offering a required core program that focuses on the academic response to complex social issues.

Other institutions, such as the School of New Resources at the College of New Rochelle (N.Y.), offer liberal arts programs for adult learners that build on previous life experiences and yet respond to many of the same questions that were asked by the younger Albion College freshmen of the early 1960s:

> The *entry core* offered to beginning students is entitled Experience, Learning, and Identity. Its chief purpose is to introduce students to college-level work; the emphasis lies in overcoming the fears and uncertainties of entering students to enable them to become active participants in the educational process. To this end, the instructor must seek to develop a community of learners and establish a close, reassuring rapport with them. To overcome the apprehensions of the beginning or newly returned student, three components are needed: (1) the leadership and direction of a skilled and informed instructor who is able to arouse interest in ideas and create a climate in which individual goals can be set and measured; (2) a serious academic program through which students can master

critical reading, discussion, reflection, and writing skills by dealing with ten or eleven books selected from the fields of literature, philosophy, and psychology; and (3) a forum in which students form a community of learners and work together to address such questions as: Who am I? What are my values, perceptions, and goals? What is the meaning of education? What is its relation to knowledge and experience? What are the ways of knowing the levels of experience? How can the readings give me a greater understanding of myself and the quality of my life? Students are thus able to break out of the limits of too great a fidelity to specific experiences and extrapolate from them into a more universal realm of discourse [Dowd, 1979, p. 14].

Required Elements at Exit Level. For many adult students, as well as experienced younger students, the first two years of college are not the time when they need an integrative, global perspective. For many of these students, college is a place to prepare for particular careers or solve particular problems; therefore, they want their degree program to be immediately individualized and pragmatic. They want to be able to take specialized courses that meet pressing needs. By the end of the program, however, they may be ready to reflect on what they have accomplished and on the educational and problem-solving processes in which they have participated. In the final year of the program, they can trace out the implications of what they have learned about themselves as learners. A general education program that is required at the end of the degree program may be more appropriate for some students than an introductory-level program. If a college or university is committed to the promotion of lifelong learning, it is particularly appropriate to consider a set of required courses or integrative experiences that prepare students for independent learning after graduation.

At both the University of Florida at Gainesville and the University of Minnesota (School of Cross-Disciplinary Studies), the interdisciplinary, general education element of the curriculum has been placed in the senior year. The University of Florida offers a set of "core courses" in the senior year ("Humanistic Perspectives on the Professions") that encourages students to face fundamental issues related to the professions for which they are preparing, such as abortion, the law as a paradox of constraints and liberation, and the ethics and concerns of the marketplace (Mayville, 1978). An interdisciplinary, integrative sequence of courses and programs has been designed at the University of Minnesota because the faculty members and administrators in the School of Cross-Disciplinary Studies maintain that "gaining special knowledge and experience in diverse areas and the ability to grasp interrelations and to perceive general applications requires that students be comfortable with the pertinent disciplinary concepts and techniques of analysis or expression. All this learning must be accomplished before fruitful, interdisciplinary work can be undertaken" (Mayville, 1978, p. 54).

Evergreen State College (Wash.) and Western Washington State University offer "upside-down" degree programs (Greenberg, O'Donnell, and Bergquist, 1980), wherein a graduate of a two-year community college who has received training primarily in a trade or profession can obtain a more general, liberal education in his or her third and fourth years of study. Thus, while the traditional college education calls for a movement from general education to more specialized training, the upside-down program reverses this order and, together with the other curriculums that place general, interdisciplinary courses at the end of the degree program, calls into question the assumption that learners need a general perspective before approaching more specialized training.

Finally, in many highly individualized programs, especially those intended to serve older adult learners, the undergraduate program concludes with an integrative learning project. This final project, often called a "major work" or "thesis," resembles the capstone thesis in a master's program or the dissertation in a doctoral program—except that its scope may be more limited. There are many variations on this theme: some final projects focus on the major area of concentration. In the performing or visual arts, students may complete a recital or one-person art show. In the social sciences, students may design and carry out new social service programs. Often, degree committees are assembled to observe and evaluate these projects, much as in graduate programs. The common feature of all these designs is the attempt at integration and the effort to avoid fragmentation and mere credit-accumulation degree programs. These integrative components give added coherence and rigor to individualized programs that otherwise might seem a purposeless hodgepodge or an exercise in self-indulgence.

Required Elements Throughout the Program. Several colleges have attempted to combine the advantages of general education courses at entry and exit levels by providing such courses at all levels. Dominican College of San Rafael (Calif.) offers twelve- to fifteen-credit-hour interdisciplinary colloquia, each consisting of three or more closely related courses and a conference/seminar that correlates the content and concepts developed in these courses. These colloquia focus on such diverse topics as "From Intellect to Intuition: Basic Perspectives on Human Knowledge," "The Russian 'Soul,' " and "Great Men in Pursuit of Excellence: Integrated Study of Eight Great Men." In addition to completing a three-course colloquium, Dominican students in their junior and senior years participate in an integrative seminar that involves in-depth study of a major humanities topic, preparation and presentation of a seminar paper, and completion of an independent senior project.

Beloit College (Wisc.) requires both "a freshman Great Books course that deals with the great ideas and issues of man and an upper-division seminar on contemporary issues" (Heiss, 1973, p. 68). Each of these courses lasts one year and is taught in a seminar. Students at Hobart and Smith College (N.Y.) also participate in a lower-division and an upper-division interdisciplinary course. Both courses are "bidisciplinary," bringing together faculty members and students from two areas to work on a problem or theme.

The innovative curriculums at Austin College (Texas), St. Andrews Presbyterian College (N.C.), and Fairhaven College (Western Washington State University) incorporate general education units at all stages of the degree program. Austin requires all students to take an "Encounter with the Arts and Sciences" program and "Heritage of Western Man," as well as "Policy Research," an upper-division course that examines social issues and attempts to develop alternative policies. The St. Andrews Studies program is required of all students at St. Andrews Presbyterian

College and, like the Austin program, ranges across both the lower and upper divisions. Following is an excerpt from a recent bulletin of this college that describes the program in some detail:

St. Andrews Studies is a three-year, general education program in the fine arts, the humanities, and the social and behavioral sciences required of freshmen, sophomores, and seniors. The program moves from the development of skills of critical inquiry and a progressive consideration of disciplinary methods converging in an interdisciplinary understanding of the contemporary world. All three levels engage the student in serious consideration of moral values. Each course offers a variety of options in format and content. These options will vary from year to year. Common learning experiences in small and large groups (festivals, concerts, films, lectures, workshops, etc.) complement the course.

101, 102 Freshman Tutorials: 4 hpw

Develop intellectual, imaginative, and social skills in the context of learning groups of fifteen to eighteen students led by faculty and advanced student advising teams. Tutorials in the fall term concentrate on informal writing, self-understanding, and the nature of liberal learning, while encouraging students to explore academic and career options for the college years and beyond. Spring term tutorials emphasize the development of formal skills in expository writing and one other communications skill.

201, 202 Sophomore Disciplinary Studies: 4 hpw

Introduces the methodologies of the arts, the humanities, and the social and behavioral sciences and fosters an appreciation of the distinctiveness, value, and limitations of the disciplines. The focus for each semester is either a historical epoch or a geographic area of the world. Students approach the study of the epoch or geographical area in separate sections employing the methodology of an academic discipline. Two or more sections will meet together from time to time to share the results of their disciplinary study.

The junior year is designated as the time for intensive work in the major and, therefore, does not contain a St. Andrews Studies component.

401, 402 Senior Interdisciplinary Seminars: 4 hpw

Explores issues and topics requiring resources and information from several academic areas reflecting the students' majors. The emphasis is on the development of skills of interdisciplinary communication as well as refining the skills acquired in the first two years of the program. Seminars in the fall term deal with social issues in contemporary international society; seminars in the spring term focus on the transition from college into career and family life [St. Andrews Presbyterian College, 1977, p. 38].

The faculty at Fairhaven has formulated a three-stage curricular sequence that emphasizes general education at both the first stage ("exploration") and the third ("generalization and application"). A recent Fairhaven *Bulletin* thoughtfully summarizes these three stages and clearly articulates the assumptions made by many colleges and universities that have introduced general education throughout the degree program:

Fairhaven's curriculum recognizes that *how* one learns changes as one progresses through the learning process; it complements, directs, and supports the students at each stage of their progress; its focus is on the learners and their development.

Stage One: The first stage is one of exploration, what Alfred North Whitehead, upon whose theory of learning Fairhaven's curriculum is patterned, called a period of "romance." This is a time to explore what's out there to be learned, a time for introductions to areas and methods of study, ways of knowing, purposes of an education, and a time for study of the self in relation to intellectual and social experiences. Special seminars are offered in which learners new to college in general and Fairhaven in particular are encouraged to explore and develop their interests, are taught ways of learning independently and in cooperative groups, and are instructed in the improvement of their reading, writing, and research skills. A broad range of introductory courses are offered, and to ensure their explorations have breadth, students are encouraged to study with as many resource people as possible.

The exploratory stage of learning usually lasts from three to five quarters and ends—or rather, the learners naturally move to the next stage in the process—when they are ready to concentrate on their chosen subjects for a period of time. With the advice and help of their tutors, students select five topics that have engaged their interest during their initial studies; they also pick two faculty members and one advanced student with whom they feel comfortable and, for a time, talk about these subjects that excite them, answer questions, and receive suggestions about further study of these topics, especially about the topic or topics upon which they plan to concentrate during the second stage of their learning. When the group is assured the student is ready to proceed, and when the student has also demonstrated to two faculty members that she or he can write competently, the transition to stage two is completed.

Stage Two: The satisfactions during the second stage are different from those of stage one and focus on coming to know one subject as deeply as possible, using the breadth of acquaintance gained in the first stage as a base upon which to build. This period of concentration can be pursued in two ways: (1) Some students may find their areas of interest covered in one of the majors offered in another college of Western [Washington State College]. For them, completion of stage two is signaled by completion of the requirements for that major and, additionally, by presentation to the tutor of a statement discussing the rationale, content, and value of that major. (2) Others may find that their area of interest crosses the disciplines of two or more standard majors or even that no standard major treats what they wish to study. In consultation with a concentration adviser, these students may construct for themselves a *Fairhaven Interdisciplinary Concentration* that combines Fairhaven studies with a minimum of fifty non-Fairhaven credit hours. Approval of the plan for the concentration should be secured soon after beginning stage two. Completion of stage two for these students is signaled by approval of the completed concentration.

Stage Three: Study at Fairhaven culminates in at least one quarter of working with faculty and other advanced students to demonstrate an understanding of the implications of the specialized study and attained skills and to search for ways in which one's focused studies relate to other areas of knowledge and to the world. Students in stage three are asked to participate in at least one advanced seminar and to be involved in some activity that shares with the community the fruits of their study through teaching, a performance, a presentation, or social action. The process of education does not simply stop with the completion of college work; it leads somewhere, hopefully to wisdom; and wisdom, Webster tells us, is the "intelligent application of knowledge."

The Fairhaven College Curriculum: Fairhaven curricular structure can be schematized as follows. In addition to completion of all three stages and transition requirements, a minimum of 180 credits must be earned.

Stage 1, Exploration (three to five quarters)

Introduction to areas and methods of study, development and assessment of educational goals.

Transition: (1) Study with several Fairhaven faculty; (2) demonstration of writing competency; (3) discussion (written or oral) on five topics selected by student under advisement, with two faculty and one advanced student.

Stage 2, Concentration (six to eight quarters)

Acquisition of extended knowledge and study in depth.

Transition: (1) Approval of: (a) completed major at WWSC; or (b) Fairhaven interdisciplinary concentration; (2) presentation of a statement discussing content, rationale, and value of major; for those doing a major, this is additional; for those doing a concentration, this is an integral part of the final draft.

Stage 3, Generalization and Application (one quarter)

Practical application of acquired learning and skills; consideration of ramifications of one's studies and relation to other areas of knowledge.

Transition: (1) Community-sharing activity; for example, teaching, a performance, a presentation, social action; (2) participation in at least one advanced seminar [Western Washington State University, 1977, pp. 52-53].

Arrangement of Academic Administrative Units

Disciplinary Units. The way the academic administration of a college or university is organized has a pervasive and often subtle impact on the character of the curriculum. Particularly in the area of interdisciplinary studies, most colleges and universities confront significant problems when the academic administrative units are arranged in a manner that is incompatible with this interdisciplinarity.

Most larger collegiate institutions are organized into academic departments, typically composed of faculty members with training and expertise in a particular discipline. New departments are usually created as a result of formal recognition of an interdisciplinary field that has gained its own identity (for example, biochemistry, sociobiology). This reorganization is less responsive to the needs of students than to the gradually changing nature of the academic world. To the extent that a college or university is preparing students for graduate education or wishes to expose students to the particular analytic and problem-solving approaches and tools of a modern academic discipline, the organization of academic administrative units by disciplines seems appropriate. A college or university that intends to offer a classical liberal arts education (inherently interdisciplinary) or wishes to be directly responsive to particular themes, problems, or values or to prepare students for particular nonacademic careers may wish to explore one of the other types of organization that will now be described.

Multidisciplinary Units. Many small colleges have avoided or moved away from disciplinary departmental units, not because of a lack of support for the disciplines, but because they do not have enough faculty members in most disciplines to constitute a reasonable-size academic unit. Many large public institutions have also moved away from departments, not because of a lack of support for disciplines or an insufficient faculty, but because of a desire or demand to reduce the number of academic administrators. Most of these small colleges and large public institutions have constructed multidisciplinary divisions, schools, or colleges. The term *multidisciplinary* is used rather than *interdisciplinary* because in many (if not most) instances, the faculty members in these divisions continue to teach exclusively within their own disciplines and engage with faculty members from other disciplines in planning the overall curriculum and degree programs but not individual courses. As a rule, the curricular and degree-program planning is itself a matter of making decisions about the distribution of requirements among various disciplines rather than developing fully integrated and interdisciplinary courses or programs.

Even colleges and universities with discipline-based departments often have a higher-level divisional structure or, in larger institutions, a higher-level school or college structure. These higher-level units are usually multidisciplinary, though, in some instances (as we shall soon note), they can be interdisciplinary. The higher-level units generally are not the source of significant curricular or instructional planning but are the source of important academic budgetary control. When budget control and curricular planning are handled at two different levels, there is often ambiguity and conflict in the formulation of academic plans and programs. People in the lower-level unit (department or division) operate without full knowledge of budgetary constraints; hence, their planning and expectations may be unrealistic. Those at the upper level (division or college), however, are often out of touch with students, are not fully knowledgeable about the plans being presented by the faculty, and find themselves in the uncomfortable position of always having to respond with a "yes" or "no" to an innovative curricular idea rather than being in a position to generate new ideas themselves. The most effective multidisciplinary academic units are often those having both substantive academic and budgetary control over the curriculum. One also must acknowledge, however, that when substantive and budgetary controls are held at the lower levels of a collegiate institution, faculty members operating in these units sometimes tend to make decisions that are self-serving, parochial, and unresponsive to broad institutional needs and interests. Alternative organizational structures that encourage faculty members to think and plan in interdisciplinary and institutional terms may be more effective.

Interdisciplinary Units. During the late 1960s and early 1970s, there was a remarkable flourishing of interdisciplinary programs in American higher education and an accompanying proliferation of interdisciplinary academic units. At colleges and universities throughout the United States, departments of eth nic studies, women's studies, community service, ecological studies, and urban studies appeared with considerable fanfare and struggle—but sometimes with little longevity. It is note-worthy, however, that in 1980 there were about 350 women's studies programs on college campuses, and another 600 institutions offered at least twenty-five women's studies courses though not an organized program. About 20,000 women's studies courses exist nationwide (Rubin and Howe, 1980).

At the divisional level, several colleges have organized all their academic units around interdisciplinary themes. The College of the Atlantic (Maine), for instance, has four interdisciplinary divisions: environmental design, environmental sciences, social and cultural studies, and values and consciousness. At many other colleges, such as Davis and Elkins (W. Va.) and St. Andrews Presbyterian (N.C.), one division is specifically designated for interdisciplinary studies.

A number of larger institutions have created entire colleges or schools that are devoted to a particular interdisciplinary theme or problem. In her inventory of academic innovations, Heiss (1973) identified a number of these larger interdisciplinary units—for example, the College of Human Resources and Education (University of West Virginia), School of Community Services and Public Affairs (University of Oregon), College of Environmental Design (University of California), College of Human Development (Pennsylvania State University), and College of Human Ecology (Cornell University, N.Y.).

The interdisciplinary school or college has been even more ambitiously embraced by collegiate institutions that have organized or reorganized around a cluster college model. Until recently, the University of the Pacific (Calif.) housed three autonomous cluster colleges, two of which exemplified a particular interdisciplinary theme: Covell College (Latin American) and Callison College (non-Western world). Similarly, at the University of California campuses at Santa Cruz and San Diego, several cluster colleges emphasize curricular themes. The cluster college movement holds great potential as a vehicle for the promotion of diversity and distinctiveness in American higher education. It is unfortunate that this movement has been short-lived and that so few institutions have been able to initiate and retain cluster colleges (Gaff and Associates, 1970).

The difficulty experienced by many collegiate institutions in organizing academic administrative units around interdisciplinary themes can be attributed to several factors. First, the faculty members who staff these interdisciplinary academic units have themselves inherited a discipline: most are graduates of a disciplinary doctoral program. These faculty members are often unable to break out of their disciplinary molds because of lack of motivation, lack of sufficient knowledge in and about other disciplines, or inability to communicate across the jargon-laden gaps between contemporary academic disciplines.

Second, the power in many colleges and universities resides in the disciplines. Faculty members are selected, promoted, and moved into positions of leadership mainly as a result of publications in disciplinary journals, attendance at disciplinary conferences, effective teaching of "standard" (disciplinary) courses, and chairing of disciplinary departments. The budgets and personnel of interdisciplinary programs are usually taken out of disciplinary departments. The disciplinary departments, therefore, have veto power over the reallocation of these resources and can determine the life or death of these interdisciplinary programs. Finally, interdisciplinary programs are often built around themes or problems that are changing rapidly or are transitory in character. The program, therefore, is either constantly in flux or inherently short-lived. In all, there are few incentives for faculty members to be enthusiastic and motivated to move in an interdisciplinary direction.

Two strategies have been taken to confront these problems associated with interdisciplinarity. One strategy is to make use of matrix organizations; the other is to set up short-term or highly flexible centers or institutes. We turn now to a consideration of these organizational alternatives.

Matrix Units. In recent years, major corporations and

businesses have begun to explore alternatives to the traditional pyramidal organization. Among the most widely used and debated of these alternative organizational structures is the "matrix organization," a structure in which multiple sources of information and control exist at virtually all levels of the organization. In a matrix organization, an employee has two or more bosses. He or she might, for instance, be responsible for both the development and promotion of a particular product and hence might report to both the vice-president for product development and the vice-president for sales.

Typically, matrix organizations are complex and difficult to operate. As Davis and Lawrence (1977, pp. 7-8) have noted, "If you do not really need it [a matrix organization], leave it alone. There are easier ways to manage organizations." Yet, if an institution is simultaneously faced with three conditions, then a matrix structure may be justified: (1) the organization is confronted with two or more central goals, (2) the organization must meet changing and relatively unpredictable demands with diverse and complex services or goods, and (3) the organization must promote the extensive sharing of resources. Many colleges and universities that are faced with conflicting goals, complex and varying student and societal demands, and limited resources may find it beneficial to consider a matrix organization.

Two of the collegiate institutions that now make use of matrix or modified matrix organizations are the University of Wisconsin at Green Bay (UWGB) and Ottawa University (Kans.). At UWGB, faculty members and students are involved simultaneously in two types of academic organization. They are members of a particular interdisciplinary college: community sciences, creative communication, environmental sciences, or human biology. They are also affiliated with a particular program unit that is discipline-based. Thus, a student might be majoring in environmental sciences from a political science perspective. Similarly, a faculty member may be affiliated not only with the College of Community Sciences but also with the "department" of psychology.

At Ottawa University, each faculty member is a member of a department that represents a certain discipline. He or she also belongs to one of four interdisciplinary "academic centers": the Center for Communication, Expression, and Value Clarification; the Center for the Study of Organizational and Cultural Issues; the Center on Issues of Individuality and Personal Value; and the Center for the Study of Human Interaction with the Environment. These four centers, according to a recent Ottawa catalogue (Ottawa University, 1976, p. 20), "sponsor regular courses, independent studies, and seminars, assist in depth-study development, provide support and direction to advising within the area of concern of the center and with regard to career options, sponsor special programs, and provide a focus for ongoing interchange among faculty and students whose educational and career goals fall within the center interest."

A matrix organization can be successful if its two axes (department and division or department and center) are given equal status and control. At UWGB and Ottawa, the interdisciplinary divisions or centers must be just as influential in determining the nature of the curriculum and allocation of resources as the disciplinary departments. The matrix also will be successful only if people are selected for the institution who can readily adjust to and live in the complex organizational climate of the matrix. Professional development should accompany any movement toward a matrix.

Ottawa University has recently abandoned its matrix organization. Dean Shumway (1980) has commented on the reasons for this change:

> [Our] specific matrix format . . . did not function well for us because it replaced the divisional structure more than was useful. While departments were able to retain an identity due to specific curricular offerings, the natural affinity within certain traditional divisional lines was not supported organizationally, and centers provided no "natural" connection other than an arbitrary gathering together of people who might be interested in proposing and supporting a particular course or two. Further, the centers were dependent upon strong leadership with an entrepreneurial flavor that could recurrently gather together and motivate the members of the center to either maintain existing programs or explore new options. For that reason they were of uncertain impact and apart from an occasional success did not function well. In the academic year 1977-78, the

faculty reorganized into a divisional structure that it refers to as "faculties" (the faculty of arts and humanities, the faculty of natural sciences, and the faculty of the social and behavioral sciences). Even so, the interdisciplinary and cross-disciplinary connections that had been established in the earlier center matrix were maintained, and programs still exist that cross over divisional lines. Thus, I would judge that the matrix experiment was one that was worth exploring and had some lasting value but did not have enough power in itself to be maintained as we had designed it.

A matrix organization holds several distinct advantages for collegiate institutions over the traditional pyramidal organization. First, a matrix allows a college or university to retain the stability and respectability of the disciplines while incorporating the flexibility and responsiveness of interdisciplinary structures. A college or university can assign each faculty member to an academic department that is discipline-based. This will serve as a home base for the faculty member throughout his or her tenure at the institution. Courses are taught and major programs of study are offered by each of these departments. In addition, each faculty member selects one or more interdisciplinary divisions or programs in which he or she will also work for several years. A faculty member might be a member of the history department and, for two or three years, also a member of the faculty in the Center for Urban Studies.

Second, matrix organizations allow a college or university to use the existing, discipline-based resources of the faculty as well as more specialized, interdisciplinary expertise in particular theme or problem areas. Whereas the discipline-based departments would be chaired by permanent faculty members, the interdisciplinary division or program would be headed by someone who is brought in with specific expertise in the area of study. A Center for Urban Studies, for instance, might be directed by an urbanologist hired on a nontenure-track basis at an excellent salary for the three years of the program. Members of the regular faculty, from a variety of disciplines, would work with the urbanologist in planning and teaching couses in this interdisciplinary field.

Third, a matrix organization enables a college or university to offer diverse and enriching interdisciplinary experiences for both its students and faculty. The professional developmental potential that is inherent in the matrix organization is impressive. Faculty members can work in a new interdisciplinary field every two to four years without sacrificing their continuing contact with and allegiance to the home discipline. A faculty member will be working with an expert in an interdisciplinary field as well as with faculty colleagues who are also drawn to this field.

Matrix organizations require a strong, yet flexible academic leader (dean or academic vice-president) who can oversee the multiple operations of the matrix and can negotiate conflicts between departments and divisions that may arise. Matrix organizations should also be structured so that programs offered in the temporary, interdisciplinary divisions or centers can become more permanent if the need for the program continues to exist and if the program staff has been particularly successful and remains interested in the project. The program is given permanence by being transferred to the departmental axis of the matrix. Individual faculty members must choose whether to stay with their original disciplinary department. This transfer of a temporary program to permanent status should be rare, however, for the matrix can easily become overbalanced toward the departmental units and will soon take on the appearance of any other traditional, discipline-based collegiate organization.

Temporary Units. Another way to address the difficult problem of introducing interdisciplinary studies into the curriculum is through the establishment of short- or medium-term institutes or centers that supplement the traditional offerings of a college or university. Heiss (1973, p. 85) identifies the unique character and value of this type of academic organization: "A few colleges and universities have introduced the institute concept as an alternative to the course or program concept. These relatively short-lived structures deal with subjects of broad design, emphasize collegiate planning, are taught by a team of three or more professors, and have an exclusive lien on the time of the students who enroll. . . . Freed from the constraints of time or obligations to other duties, the faculty is able to experiment with a wide variety of pedagogical methods and experiences."

Examples of institutes being offered by collegiate institutions include the Educational Studies, International Studies, Religious Studies, Urban and Environmental Studies, and Developmental Skills Institutes being conducted at the Grand Valley State Colleges (Mich.), the Student Administrative Development Training Laboratory at Berea College (Ky.), the Institute on Aging at Santa Clara University (Calif.), and the International Language Institute conducted in conjunction with many colleges in the United States. Typically, institutes last from several weeks to an entire term. They focus on a theme or problem, may be conducted only once, and usually involve residential living/learning.

Whereas the institute tends to be of very limited duration and usually is equated with a specific and single-purpose educational program, the center is a longer-lasting academic enterprise that will offer several types of services during its existence. In the early 1970s, the University of California at Santa Barbara established a Center for Black Studies and a Center for Chicano Studies that not only provided instructional programs but also sponsored research, policy studies, and the development of library resources. Though called an institute, the Sigurd Olson Institute of Environmental Studies associated with Northland College (Wisc.) serves as an excellent model of a center. This institute, founded by Northland in 1972, provides regional conferences and workshops on environmental problems and issues, conducts community education projects, maintains an environmental-information clearinghouse, sponsors a lecture series, and conducts research. Similarly, at Augustana College (S. Dak.), the Center for Western Studies provides educational and research services in the region, serving as a resource for both the college and the community. Other colleges similarly might establish urban studies, rural studies, or regional studies centers that meet local needs, serve as bridges between the college and community, provide students and faculty members with practicum experiences, and enable the college to move into new interdisciplinary areas with partial funding from fees collected by the center for services rendered.

Concluding Comments: Organization and Flexibility. The curriculum can be organized around disciplines, themes, problems, issues, or processes. What is important is that there be a coherent rationale around which these curriculum-organization decisions are made and that this rationale be made explicit to a variety of audiences, the most important of which is the student and potential student. The rationale chosen will reflect a range of assumptions about the world of the future, the nature of the student group served, the mission and commitments of the institution, and the ideal of "an educated person." The organization of a college's curriculum cannot be merely the result of administrative history if it is to be defensible and of quality.

Static departments built around traditional disciplines may be inappropriate in a world that is changing rapidly. Matrix organizations, institutes, and centers enable a college or university to retain the best of two worlds. These organizational alternatives provide flexibility and relevance without sacrificing disciplinary resources and precedence. They allow a collegiate institution to retain its traditions without limiting itself to these traditions. Although future conditions may force colleges and universities to abandon disciplinary units entirely, matrix organizations, institutes, and centers may delay the need for such drastic action. The way a college or university organizes its academic offerings will certainly have much to do with its capacity to survive the unpredictable 1980s and 1990s.

— V —

PROCEDURES

Planning, Implementing, and Evaluating Instructional Units

Cross (1975) has spoken of the three levels to be found in any college curriculum. At one level there is a curriculum that is described in the college catalogue; at another level there is a curriculum that is taught by the faculty; and at a third level there is a curriculum that is learned by students. The fifth and sixth dimensions of the undergraduate college curriculum (procedures and outcomes) cross over all three levels of the curriculum more than the four other dimensions (time, space, resources, and organization) do. It is in the daily application of specific instructional procedures and in the definition and application of specific educational outcomes that a curriculum comes alive and affects the work of both the faculty members and students. In this chapter, we will consider four procedural concerns: procedures for planning a degree program, procedures for granting academic credit, procedures for teaching inside and outside the classroom, and procedures for assessing student performance.

Program Planning

Faculty/Institution-Determined. Typically, the curriculum of a college or university and the content and structure of courses in this curriculum are determined by individual faculty members and faculty committees. Students are faced with catalogue requirements when planning their academic programs. They are given the freedom only to choose among courses that have already been designed and described in the catalogue. Many courses are not available to some students because of prerequisites and because each student must meet certain distribution requirements for graduation. Thus, responsibility for curricular planning is held mainly by faculty members rather than students.

Faculty-planned curriculums are pervasive and respond to the legitimate need of students for clear and detailed information about the courses they will take and the courses of study they will follow for particular careers. Many students do not want to participate in a planning process that is unpredictable or one that will produce an educational program that is not acceptable for employment or graduate or professional school. However, other students who have different educational needs may not be particularly concerned about the career-preparation aspects of a collegiate curriculum. They wish to have greater voice in what they will study, and they may find the traditional faculty-dominated planning process unacceptable. These students are often older and more experienced. Their developmental needs are different from those of young adults, who tend to be more exploratory as they prepare to enter the adult world (Weathersby and Tarule, 1980). These older students represent a large segment of the student population that will be attending college in the near future. Many colleges and universities, therefore, may soon have to consider alternative procedures to involve students more actively in the planning process.

Faculty/Student-Negotiated. In several ways, faculty and students at collegiate institutions have worked together in formulating individual courses and study programs. At one level, joint planning occurs when the student incorporates into his or her program of study both required courses (faculty-determined) and electives (student-determined). Many colleges and universities fit this category of negotiated program planning, though several institutions have given relatively greater emphasis to the student's role. At Worcester Polytechnic Institute (Mass.), a far-sighted and highly innovative technical school, the student is required to take a set of five thematically related courses and a related independent studies project (accounting for a total of one quarter of his or her degree program). One half of each student's degree program is filled with a qualifying project of the student's choice that applies technology to a social or human problem and a major qualifying project that relates to the student's chosen field. The remaining quarter of the degree program is made up of course work.

Like Worcester Polytechnic, William James College (Grand Valley State Colleges, Mich.) prepares students for a particular career within a liberal arts context and blends required courses with extensive freedom of choice for students in planning other elements of their degree program. "There are very few survey courses at William James," a recent catalogue notes (Grand Valley State Colleges, 1977, p. 110). The college emphasizes instead students' participation in independent studies, internships, tutorials, and other activities over which they have significant control. Students and faculty members at William James also jointly negotiate new courses each term.

This second approach to joint planning—negotiated contracts between a faculty member and a group of students—has been used at Johnston College (University of Redlands, Calif.) and Evergreen State College (Wash.). When Johnston was in existence, faculty members posted courses they would like to give and, in turn, students posted courses they would like to take. Courses were selected through faculty/student negotiation, and course content was negotiated during the initial class meeting and renegotiated as expectations and perceptions changed and goals became clear.

The Evergreen planning process combines this second planning model (faculty negotiation with a group of students) with a third model (faculty negotiation with an individual student). Students at Evergreen enroll in a single program each quarter and choose from three negotiation models.

> *Coordinated Study:* A group of faculty (three to five) and students (usually sixty to a hundred) studying a common theme or problem together using ideas and materials from several "major fields" (disciplines). Coordinated Studies are offered at both basic and advanced levels.
> *Group Contract:* A small type of program, usually one or two faculty with, at most, twenty-five to forty-five students, involving in-depth study of a single topic. As a rule, only one or two "major fields" (disciplines) are involved—depending on the educational background of the faculty members. Group contracts involve work at an advanced or intermediate college level.
> *Individual Contract:* A negotiated agreement between a single student and a faculty member for a fixed period of study, normally one quarter. Learning goals and methods of evaluation of the student's work are spelled out explicitly in a written contract worked out in advance. In general, individual contract work is intended to be advanced and specialized [Evergreen State College, 1977, p. 18].

The first two of these options closely approximate the planning procedures used at Johnston College, though because Johnston was smaller, negotiations there could be more flexible and responsive to individual students' needs. Evergreen State College has been able, in part, to provide flexibility through the third option—a contract between an individual faculty member and a student.

Other collegiate institutions that have chosen this third type of negotiated planning process include Goddard College (Vt.), Governors State University (Ill.), Thomas Jefferson College (Grand Valley State Colleges, Mich.), New College (University of South Florida), Empire State College (N.Y.), Mary Baldwin College's Adult Degree Program (Va.), and the more than thirty University Without Walls programs throughout the United States. At Loretto Heights College, UWW students develop individualized degree plans that are approved at four points between admission and graduation: (1) a tentative degree plan proposed in the application for admission, (2) an updated and revised degree plan submitted at the completion of sixty semester credits or with the advanced-standing proposal for prior noncollege learning (whichever comes first), (3) an almost completed degree plan approved at the predegree review session (held at least eight weeks before graduation), and (4) the final completed degree program (presented at the individual degree review session, a celebration held by each student with his or her faculty adviser and team of resource persons). Negotiations and changes are made all along the way. All degree plans require a minimum of 128 semester credits, with one third (or forty-three credits) in "breadth" and a minimum of thirty credits in a "depth" area of concentration. All degree programs are required to contain four "balances": (1) theory and practice, (2) depth and breadth, (3) affective and cognitive learning, and (4) a mix of learning resources (Loretto Heights College, 1971).

At Goddard College, each student's educational program is planned individually on a semester-by-semester basis through a conference between the student and his or her faculty adviser: "Taken into account in the planning are the student's interests, her needs, as much as they can be identified, her educational experience to date, criteria for moving through the program, and the resources the college can offer. Because Goddard is based on a respect for individual freedom, the final decision is the student's; but because freedom is understood as something very different from whim, the decision comes only after considerable examination of the various matters which affect it. Counselors arc faculty members (occasionally members of the nonteaching professional staff) chosen for their ability to help students. A student is expected to meet with his counselor for as long or as short a time as they may find appropriate, at least every three weeks. The topic for these meetings is the student's ongoing education, with that word redefined in its largest sense" (Goddard College, 1978, pp. 23-24).

At Thomas Jefferson College and New College (University of South Florida), students also plan their program on a term-by-term basis, an individually designed learning program being jointly devised by student and faculty adviser (tutor).

Academic planning for the student's entire tenure at Governors State University is initiated when the student first arrives on campus, and planning is reviewed periodically and modified

during the student's stay at the university. The study plan negotiated by the student and his or her adviser indicates the instructional programs to be taken, the approximate time needed to
meet the student's academic objectives at Governors State, and
the relation among the student's objectives, the competencies
expected of graduates from the university, and the methods to
be used in attaining each expected competency (whether regularly scheduled modules, self-instructional materials, cooperative education jobs, independent readings and investigation,
courses transferred from other institutions, or prior nonacademic learning experiences).

Student-Determined. In 1973, Heiss noted that "there
has been widespread growth in the number of institutions that
have expanded their curricular options or have given their students their own study programs. Usually students who select
this option are required to consult with a faculty adviser and to
work within the framework of the institution's educational
aims. In some of these institutions the student is required to fulfill certain course requirements or graduation prerequisites, but
in others he is given wide freedom in designing his study plan"
(p. 82).

As with faculty/student-negotiated plans, some student-
determined plans encompass the entire four years of residence,
whereas in other instances the planning is done at the start or
end of each semester. Heiss (1973) identified special degree programs at the University of Iowa, Cornell College (Iowa), the
University of Minnesota, New York University, Antioch College
(Ohio), Stephens College (Mo.), and Sarah Lawrence College
(N.Y.) as examples of institutions that allow students to design
their own degree programs.

Several experimental colleges, including Raymond College (a cluster college housed in the University of the Pacific,
Calif.) and Hampshire College (Mass.), have initiated student-
controlled curricular planning procedures. Raymond College
students have an almost unlimited choice of courses and are
given considerable freedom in choosing among the available options. Similarly, at Hampshire College, "students are expected
to devise their own program of classes, make up their own tests,

and pace their own degree progress. To implement these expectations, required courses have been eliminated, most classes use the seminar format, and students receive no specific reading or other assignments unless they request them. Performance is evaluated on a pass-fail distinction rating in all courses. During the January interim, the student writes a report of his educational experiences that emphasizes self-evaluation and self-discovery" (Heiss, 1973, p. 3).

In recent years, Schoolcraft College (Mich.) has given students considerable autonomy in planning their curriculum through the college's Independent Human Studies (IHS) program. As described by William Mayville (1978, p. 36), the students at Schoolcraft "design their own projects with minimal guidance from faculty. There are no prescribed courses, and all the students' academic energy is focused on their project. At the beginning of the semester, the student, aided by an IHS facilitator and student member of the group, develops an idea for [his or her] interdisciplinary endeavors. The student then determines what academic departments can offer the most guidance and will assign credit for the work. A contract is devised that lists goals, processes, resources, and schedules to be met. The work is largely independent although the resources of academic departments and the community are drawn upon."

Students can do curricular planning not only alone but also in groups. They benefit from the assistance of other students in initiating their own projects. An independent student planning group has been established at the Davis campus of the University of California to assist with individualized educational projects. The Student Center for Educational Research and Innovation is managed by students and is currently involved in "counseling those undergraduates interested in self-initiated and group research projects and providing assistance and direction for developing new courses. This process includes clarification of the student's objectives regarding the project; help in securing a faculty sponsor with similar interests or research; aid in the completion of a written proposal and application for credit; provision of financial assistance when necessary; oversight and evaluation of current projects; and ongoing communication with faculty to maintain [the Student Center's] files on faculty research projects and interests" (Fund for the Improvement of Postsecondary Education, 1979b, p. 18).

In both the faculty/student-negotiated and student-controlled curricular planning processes, a new role is emerging for the American college and university. Rather than necessarily being primarily a source of knowledge and content expertise, these institutions eventually may be in the business of helping a person who wishes to gain greater clarity concerning his or her learning needs to formulate a plan by which these needs can be met and to gain access to the resources needed to implement the plan. A collegiate institution can provide advisement, problem solving, and resource linkage to a learner, thereby providing him or her with a lifelong service.

A college or university that can provide effective planning assistance need not worry about the loss of traditional college-age students or the reduced need for higher education among adult learners. It can look forward to many years of support from the community it serves. For such a college, the procedure whereby degree and nondegree educational programs are planned may become the most significant feature of its curriculum and may turn it into an educational institution that is responsive to learners of all ages. Educational brokerage functions of this type are being explored currently at a variety of traditional and nontraditional collegiate and noncollegiate institutions, such as the University of Indiana and the American Center for the Quality of Work Life in Washington, D.C. (both recent recipients of grants in this area from the Fund for the Improvement of Post-Secondary Education).

In addition, recent research in developmental psychology, adult development, and intellectual and ethical development suggests that the matter of control over learning flows from developmental sequences (Chickering and Associates, 1981; Levinson, 1978; Loevinger, 1976; Perry, 1968; Weathersby, 1977). The general pattern suggested by these studies is that as people develop from dependence to independence, from dualistic thinking to relationistic thinking, and from other-directedness to self-directedness, they view the roles of teachers, education, and learning differently. Lower stages imply the teacher and the school as the sources of authority. At higher stages, decisions about learning reside more with the learner. These hierarchal developmental patterns are not necessarily related to ages across the life cycle, but are related to development at various stages as people change perspectives about themselves and the world around them.

These theoretical perspectives will be increasingly tested in the years ahead. Some research has already begun (Chickering and Associates, 1981; Goldberger, 1980). The potential power of these ideas to transform the college curriculum seems promising, especially in relation to who makes the decisions about what students will learn and how this process is controlled. Should this developmental-research trend bear fruit, curricular control is likely to shift to the arena of the learner, and the curriculum may be determined more by the diversity of the learner population than by the preferences of the faculty and the institution.

Crediting

Credit by Successful Completion of Instructional Unit. In most instances, a college awards credit on the basis of successful completion of a particular instructional unit (usually a course). Although very few educators are willing to go to the extreme of equating the amount of time spent in a course with the amount of learning that has taken place, most colleges and universities make this equation when granting credit for an educational experience. Even some colleges that have moved toward competency-based education, which emphasizes outcomes rather than inputs (such as time spent in a course), have used course completion as demonstration of competency. It is assumed at these competency-based institutions that the evaluation taking place in the course assesses student competence and that if a student does not exhibit competency, he or she will not pass the course. This assumption is based, in turn, on the assumption that faculty members are evaluating each student with reference to an absolute standard (minimal competence) rather than relative to the performance of other students (grading "on the curve").

Transfer of College Credits. In addition to granting credit for courses completed on campus, virtually all colleges and universities accept credit from other accredited collegiate institutions. This practice not only facilitates the transfer of students between two colleges or universities, it also enables students to remain enrolled at one collegiate institution while taking courses at another. This interinstitutional exchange is particularly successful and valuable for students when negotiated through a formal interinstitutional consortium. Many regional consortia—for example, College Center of the Finger Lakes (N.Y.)—have promoted interinstitutional agreements regarding the cross-registration of students at member institutions. Other consortia—for example, the Semester in Washington program—are set up specifically to facilitate this transfer.

Assessment of Prior Learning. Although most colleges grant a large majority of credit hours for formal courses completed on campus or at another collegiate institution, they may also grant credit on the basis of an assessment of the student's learning prior to coming to the institution. The increased enrollment of adult students who have learned much outside the formal college classroom has increased the need for the effective and equitable assessment of prior learning and the granting of academic credit in recognition of this learning.

Some of the first attempts to assess and credit prior learning were done not with adult students, but rather with gifted entering freshmen under age eighteen. At the University of Chicago and elsewhere, students were able to "place out of" many courses upon entering college by passing one or more entrance examinations. Some colleges and universities still make routine use of examinations to grant college credit, employing a national examination (for example, College-Level Examination Program, Advanced Placement, or American College Testing Program exams), regional or state exams, or exams designed by faculty members at the institution. Thomas Edison College (N.J.) makes extensive use of written exams to generate credits for entering students.

A recent survey indicates that 708 colleges and universities have designed procedures whereby a student may prepare a proposal or portfolio for the assessment of prior noncollege learning (American Council on Education, 1980). Assessment procedures vary but usually include faculty members, mentors, counselors, and/or community professionals who review past experiences to determine the amount and type of learning that is inherent in these experiences. An appropriate amount of academic credit is then granted, ranging from a few credits (perhaps three to six) to possibly all but the final year of the total credits needed to graduate from the institution. Those past experiences that are often considered appropriate to document for academic credit include work in a profession, in-service training, volunteer work, proprietary education, military training, apprenticeships, independent reading, creative arts, personal-growth workshops, proposal writing, and project management.

A comprehensive report on a survey conducted by the Office on Educational Credit and Credentials of the American Council on Education (ACE, 1980) is expected to be available in 1981. Preliminary findings of the survey reveal that 97.5 percent of academic institutions that responded award credit for extrainstitutional learning. Examinations, the most frequently used method, are used by 96 percent. Seventy-five percent use the ACE Military Guide. Portfolio assessment, faculty-committee assessment, personal interviews, the National Guide (ACE), and hands-on demonstration follow in frequency, in that order.

Portfolio assessment ranks second in frequency of use by private institutions and third by public institutions. This volume is remarkable, given that the portfolio assessment process was essentially begun in the early seventies and has developed in sophistication and popularity only over the past decade. The increasing rate of return of older, experienced adult learners to colleges and universities is primarily responsible for this phenomenon. However, efforts to formally assess learning that has taken place outside academic institutions can be documented as early as 1963 at Queens College, City University of New York (Meyer, 1975, p. xvii).

A significant amount of support for the growth of portfolio assessment of prior noncollege learning is attributed to the research and training and developmental activities of the Council for the Advancement of Experiential Learning (CAEL), established in 1974 with grants from the Carnegie Corporation of New York. Under the leadership of Morris Keeton, CAEL has received support from the Lilly Endowment, the Fund for the Improvement of Postsecondary Education, the Babcock Foundation, and the Ford Foundation and has grown to include more than 350 public and private colleges and universities as members (Council for the Advancement of Experiential Learning, 1979-80).

CAEL's early research work in partnership with the Educational Testing Service resulted in a wide array of publications to guide institutions interested in developing quality prior-learning assessment programs. Six steps in assessment form the basis of CAEL's *Principles of Good Practice in Assessing Experiential Learning* (Willingham, 1977), as follows: (1) identify learning, (2) articulate learning, (3) document learning, (4) measure learning, (5) evaluate learning, and (6) transcribe learning. Policies, procedures, guidelines, assessors, costs, and quality-assurance issues are critical in an institution's decision to implement an assessment process. Good assessment programs distinguish carefully between experience per se and learning that results from experience. The latter is the focus of CAEL's interests.

Portfolio assessment programs shorten the time spent in completing a degree, save the student time and money, reduce duplication in learning experiences, and focus attention on learning outcomes as opposed to where, when, and with whom the learning took place. Portfolios are often large and comprehensive documents that take many months for students to prepare. The process is often assisted by special workshops or courses that guide the student in writing and presenting his or her learning. For the student, the process is an introspective and powerful experience, as one's entire adult life is often reviewed and described. Students come to value their skills and knowledge, recognize areas of weakness or omission, and are engaged in creative degree-, career-, and life-planning activities with faculty members and advisers. Although the initial motivation for portfolio preparation is often to gain academic credit, the results are frequently more personal and profound as adult students analyze and synthesize their learnings and their lives.

Procedures and policies for prior-learning assessment are developed by each institution. One critical issue, for example, is whether credit proposals must be equivalencies of courses offered or can be credited on their own integrity. Guidelines range from one-page outlines to extensive handbooks, videotapes, and films ("Transitions . . . ," 1981). Assessments may be done by a single faculty member, a standing assessment committee, a departmental committee, an assessment center staff, or a review committee that may include community professionals along with institutional faculty members and administrators.

Contrary to popular mythology, the portfolio preparation and assessment process is neither easy nor quick. This process may be one of the central elements of a quality lifelong education approach for diverse adult learners. As colleges seek to serve a broader student constituency in the years ahead, it should be expected that consideration of the assessment of prior noncollege learning will become an important agenda item for all postsecondary institutions.

At Marylhurst College (Ore.), adult students participate in a Prior Learning Experience (PLE) program, which includes two activities—a PLE workshop and a PLE portfolio. At the workshop, students are assisted in completing the portfolio. Experiences are described, assessed, and documented with specific focus on the learning that occurred and the knowledge, skills, and values that were gained. On completion of the workshop, the student submits his or her portfolio to a review committee for evaluation. The committee is composed of Marylhurst faculty and staff and members of the local academic and professional community. The committee can approve up to ninety hours of credit toward a baccalaureate degree. The college requires 180 hours for graduation.

Comparable procedures are followed at other collegiate institutions that offer credit for prior experience. Many of these other institutions, however, do not prepare students for assessment so diligently. Clark University (Mass.) is a clear exception, for it provides students with extensive assistance through its Learning Support Project. Participants in this project earn academic credits "for a reflective analysis of a life experience using concepts provided by the disciplines in the university. This work is supported by a two-semester 'Life Experience Seminar.' In this seminar the student learns to produce a 'portfolio' that unites focused life experience with an appropriate theoretical framework. The portfolio is awarded variable academic credit by a 'mentor' who has worked with the student on the project. This person is usually a member of the Clark faculty" (Fund for the Improvement of Postsecondary Education, 1979a, p. 27).

No Credit. For some colleges and universities, credits do not seem an appropriate vehicle for indicating the amount of learning that has occurred or for determining successful completion of a baccalaureate program. Rather than taking courses to generate credits for graduation, a student takes a course to prepare for a set of examinations, global assessment by a board of examiners or review committee, or a competency-assessment procedure. A student graduates when he or she has completed the exam successfully, passed the board or committee, or demonstrated the attainment of certain competencies.

A general examination is used extensively to determine graduation in European universities as well as at most graduate and professional schools and some undergraduate institutions in the United States. Most American colleges and universities using such an exam also require a minimum number of academic credits. Boards of examiners and student review committees are also used extensively in European universities but at only some undergraduate American colleges and universities, such as St. John's (Md.), that are modeled after these European institutions. The American equivalent of the board of examiners is the new movement toward the assessment of competencies as a means of determining eligibility for graduation.

Alverno College (Wisc.) currently offers a "purer" competency-based program than any other college. Although Alverno still counts semester hours for student transfer, funding, and other outside reporting, the primary emphasis is on gaining and assessing four levels of competency in each of eight outcome areas. An assessment team is assigned to each of the competency levels, with overall coordination of the assessment activities in the hands of a campuswide assessment committee.

Sterling College (Kans.), Mars Hill College (N.C.), and MacMurray College (Ill.) combine credit-free assessment of competencies with the traditional credit-generating requirements of course attendance. At all three institutions, competence can be demonstrated, at least in part, through successful completion of certain courses. Furthermore, all three colleges require completion of a certain number of credit hours before graduation. At Sterling College, most of the competencies are demonstrated through successful completion of specified courses or of one course selected by the student from several options.

Mars Hill College, like Alverno, uses assessment teams to determine the acquisition of six basic competencies. These teams are composed of faculty members, community people, students, and administrators. "Students who believe themselves qualified without college courses and able to demonstrate competence in any given area may contact the assessment team responsible for that area and be assessed" (Mars Hill College, 1979, p. 9). All students major in a particular discipline, with requirements for each major specified in terms of measurable competencies. The assessment of these competencies in each department is usually based on completion of certain courses, demonstration of certain skills and knowledge, and completion of certain projects.

MacMurray College (1977, p. 36) offers each student several ways to indicate competence in each of eleven areas, or "elements" (three skill areas and eight awareness areas):

A student may elect to design a project based on his talents or previous experiences. Each of these projects will be presented to an evaluation team composed of faculty and students. A second alternative allows the student to satisfy a competence through an appropriate major. Students may, if they wish, satisfy each of the elements . . . through course work, but they will be urged to choose other alternatives whenever possible. While the graduation requirements continue to be 128 hours, each time a student chooses an alternative other than course work, he increases the flexibility of his schedule and can use those course hours to complete a second area of concentration or to work in teacher preparation or cooperative education. . . . The fourth alternative allows students to satisfy a competence through examination. CLEP exams, proficiency exams, and advanced-placement credit may be used to indicate competence for several of the elements.

The MacMurray program parallels the multiple-track degree-granting procedures at Vassar College (N.Y.) and Austin College (Texas) described earlier. Students can choose a procedure for demonstrating competency that is compatible with their own style of learning and relating to faculty members and fellow students. The multiple-track program at MacMurray also allows for differences in attitudes and skills among faculty members in regard to the assessment of student learning outcomes. Other colleges that are hesitant to embrace a "pure" form of competency, such as that found at Alverno or Mars Hill, might wish to examine MacMurray's "hybrid" model or consider Sterling College's use of course completion as the primary index of competence.

Teaching

Any teaching event involves the interrelation between two entities: (1) the student/learner and (2) a body of content or an experience that the student/learner is, in some sense, to acquire. The faculty member, as teacher, is expected to mediate and assist in the student's acquisition of this content or experience. In this mediating/assisting role, the faculty member will choose to attend either to the content or to the student. A faculty member who attends to the content usually indicates greatest concern for the subject matter being taught. He or she views the teaching enterprise primarily as an opportunity for students to learn something in an effective and efficient manner from someone who knows more about the subject than they. A good content-based teacher will clearly specify the instructional objectives to be achieved, will provide an equitable means of evaluating student achievement of these outcomes, will use teaching methods that maximize student interest in the content of the course, and will individualize the course of study to accommodate students' differing learning styles, life-styles, ages, skills, and backgrounds.

Michael Polanyi (1967), the noted scientist-turned-philosopher, has observed that we not only attend to things, we also attend from other things. We are focally aware of that to which we are attending but are only tacitly (indirectly) aware of that from which we are attending. We are always, for instance, attending from a wide variety of bodily functions (for example, keeping our balance) when we operate in our world, yet we are rarely aware of these functions in the sense of attending to them, for to do so would require that we withdraw our attention from other matters out in the world. The content-based teacher usually attends to the content that is being taught. At the same time, the teacher is attending from a set of assumptions about what students need and want. The content-based teacher can usually provide an articulate statement about reasons for organizing content in a certain way. Furthermore, the teacher tends to be quite knowledgeable about the subject area (or at least is centrally concerned about acquiring this knowledge). Of these issues, the content-based teacher is focally aware. However, this teacher is usually much less articulate about, or even aware of, his or her assumptions concerning why students should learn or how they can best learn this content.

Assumptions about student needs, motives, concerns, learning styles, and so forth definitely influence the content-based teacher's performance in the classroom, for the teacher is inevitably attending from these assumptions to the content. Much as Kuhn (1970) speaks of the implicit paradigms that inform the operations of science, so are we speaking of the tacit assumptions about students that inform the teaching of content-based faculty members in a way and to an extent that most of these teachers seldom acknowledge.

Other faculty members are inclined to attend to, and be focally aware of, students and, in doing so, attend from, and are only tacitly aware of, the content being taught. These teachers address themselves mainly to the needs of students. They view themselves as being primarily in the business of helping students learn what they want to learn and what they need to learn (given the students' personally defined career and life goals). A good student-centered teacher will help a student identify current needs and resources and desired learning outcomes for a particular course of study or experience. This teacher also will help the student to identify and obtain institutional or community resources needed to achieve these outcomes, to evaluate the extent to which these outcomes have been achieved, and to learn something about the processes of learning itself—in the words of Donald Michael (1973), "learning to plan and planning to learn."

Given the enormous demand on student-centered teachers for exclusive attention to students' needs and concerns, it is not surprising to find that these teachers will attend from a set of tacit assumptions about the content of the teaching enterprise. The student-centered teacher's own biases, values, and concerns are not unimportant; rather, they significantly influence ways in which this teacher interacts with students—ways of which the student-centered teacher is often unaware and may not acknowledge.

A classic example of the influence that tacitly held values have had on student-centered teachers is to be found in the humanistic psychology movement of the late 1960s and early 1970s. Faculty members who espoused humanistic psychology principles often have done meaningful work with students and are to be commended for the extraordinary attention they gave to many confused young men and women of this era. Yet their ultimate failure, in many instances, may be attributable to a lack of focal awareness concerning the white middle-class values that underlay much of their work and, as a result, the extent to which their consciousness-raising activities ("the greening of America") ignored important social, economic, and political realities.

In many ways, content-based and student-centered teachers operate in the same manner. Both are concerned with clear specification of desired learning outcomes. For the content-based teacher, these outcomes are to be specified by the teacher as one who knows more about the content, presumably, than the students do. The student-centered teacher is an advocate for specification of desired outcomes by the student (who supposedly knows more about his or her own personal learning needs than the teacher does). Thus, the main difference between the content- and student-centered teacher is a matter of control: Who specifies outcomes? The great debates over traditional versus nontraditional and behavioristic versus humanistic education have centered on this issue of control.

A third type of teacher disagrees with the content-based *and* the student-centered teacher concerning the specification of desired learning outcomes by either the teacher or the student and believes that learning takes place primarily through interaction between teacher and student, student and student, teacher and teacher, or student and experience (vicarious, simulated, or real). The learning to be derived from these interactions can never be fully specified ahead of time because two or more independent entities (students, teachers, experiences) are meeting to interact from two or more different perspectives. Even if desired learning outcomes could be specified by the student and/or faculty member ahead of time, these outcomes would begin to interplay and modify one another once the faculty member, student, and/or experience began to interact.

An interaction-based faculty member is primarily interested in creating instructional settings in which a maximum amount of fruitful interaction will take place. This teacher is also concerned with the analysis and synthesis of learnings that have emerged from the interaction. A good interaction-based teacher could be viewed as a creative educational architect, designing educational programs that are exciting, diverse, and challenging for himself or herself as well as the students. There will be support for students as they confront the ambiguity of this type of education, and attempts will be made to provide clarity where clarity is possible. This teacher will both prepare students for and "debrief" students from the rich learning experiences they will have.

The interaction-based teacher is attending to the interaction between the student and the content, attending from his or her own role as teacher. For both the content-based and student-based faculty member, their teaching role is relatively clear to themselves and others. The content-based teacher is the primary conveyer of content to the students, actively and visibly involved in helping students learn a basic body of information. Similarly, the student-centered teacher is actively and visibly involved in helping students obtain their self-defined learning goals. Once the issue of control is worked out, the content- and student-centered teachers can settle into rather easily defined roles.

The interaction-based teacher does not readily find this comfort. This role is rarely defined with clarity, for work is often done behind the scenes, the teacher being more the director than the actor, more the architect than the builder. The interaction-based teacher attends from a whole set of assumptions about his or her own role as a teacher, and because these assumptions are rarely made explicit and rarely tested, they are often in conflict.

An interaction-based teacher, for instance, often operates from the assumption that he or she must be quite active initially and even charismatic in order to spark interaction among students. The interactive instructor might even make a false statement in order to provoke discussion. This strategy may be appropriate and can be successful as long as the teacher is not tacitly assuming that instruction should always be active and entertaining.

This tripartite distinction among content, student, and interaction-based teaching has direct implications for the methods of instruction a faculty member uses. Certain instructional methods are particularly appropriate for content-based teaching, for they can be used to transmit information effectively and efficiently from the teacher (or other information source) to the student in a sensitive and exciting manner. Other instructional methods are not appropriate to content-based teaching because they do not provide the faculty member with sufficient control and predictability or because the method relies on student judgment and choice. Similarly, some methods are appropriate and others inappropriate for use with student-based and interaction-based teaching. Some of the most serious problems confronted by faculty members are associated with a mismatch between the instructional method being used and the mode of teaching that the faculty member desires.

Figure 4 lists twenty teaching methods that are used at least occasionally in undergraduate instruction. Of these twenty

Figure 4. Appropriate Instructional Methods for Each of Three Modes of Teaching.

Content-Based Teaching

Lecturing
Question and answer/recitation
Reading
Programmed instruction/computer-assisted instruction
Audiovisual instruction
Audiotutorial instruction
Personalized system of instruction
Fantasy/suggestopedia

Interaction-Based Teaching

Seminar/discussion
Laboratory/studio
Symposium/debate
Team teaching
Case study/Socratic method
In-class discussion (buzz groups/learning cells)
Simulations
Role playing

Student-Based Teaching

Tutorials/independent study
Learning contracts
Field placements
Student-generated courses

methods, eight are most often appropriate when used for content-based teaching. Eight others are most often appropriate when used for instruction that is interaction-based. The final four methods are most often associated with, and are appropriate for, student-based teaching. Following are descriptions and discussions of each of these twenty methods of teaching.

Content-Based

Lecturing. Lecturing is appropriate in a variety of instances when a body of content is to be conveyed to students.

First, when information is not contained in a book, set of slides, movie, videotape, or other resource, then it may have to be communicated by lecture. Second, a faculty member can convey not only a body of content but also enthusiasm or unique perspectives concerning this content during the lecture. Third, the lecture enables a student to see "a mind working." An effective lecturer often will move over into an interactive mode when exploring, analyzing, or synthesizing new ideas. The lecturer is demonstrating the processes of exploration, analysis, and synthesis while speaking. Students can learn something about learning as well as about a body of knowledge.

On the negative side, lecturing is not a particularly efficient mode of knowledge transfer. Other methods (particularly reading) are more efficient. Second, a lecture is often a one-way communication process. There is usually very little feedback to the lecturer on his or her performance. Students rarely receive immediate feedback, either, on their own acquisition of the lecture content. Other content-based methods (for example, a personalized system of instruction) provide better feedback mechanisms.

Both these problems are partly overcome by instructors who make use of "minilectures" of five to fifteen minutes to introduce a concept or to convey enthusiasm or a unique perspective on a concept. The instructor then uses some other content-based method (for example, audiovisual) or an interactive method (such as a seminar or buzz group) to test for or increase student comprehension.

A third problem is the primarily oral nature of lectures. As a number of educational researchers and practitioners (for example, Hill and Nunnery, 1973) have recently noted, some students seem to learn primarily through visual or kinesthetic rather than auditory modes. An effective lecturer must be redundant in his or her presentation—not in the sense of verbally repeating the same idea a second or third time, but rather by presenting the idea visually on a blackboard or flip chart or by acting out the idea by means of physical models, gestures, action-oriented metaphors, and so forth.

Question and Answer/Recitation. Most college teachers

try to overcome the one-way communication problems of lectures by interspersing lecturing with question-and-answer or recitation sessions. Typically, a faculty member will encourage students to ask questions at any time during a lecture when they are unclear or wish to add something to the discussion. Alternatively, a faculty member may pause periodically to entertain questions or to ask questions. The questions that a faculty member asks can be either open-ended or closed-ended. Closed-ended questions are those with a specific right answer ("Who was the first president of the United States?"), whereas open-ended questions have no definitive answers ("What might have happened if George Washington had chosen to be king rather than president?"). Open-ended questions tend to move a faculty member over to an interactive mode of teaching, whereas closed-ended questions lead into recitation.

Recitation is a rather antiquated word that evokes images of willow-stick discipline and an emphasis on the three Rs. Yet, recitation is used frequently in the contemporary college classroom (especially in foreign language courses) and may be used with even greater frequency as many experts in the field of literacy advocate more oral recitation and reading in the college classroom to improve reading and writing (for example, Schultz, 1977). Recitation usually involves a request by the faculty member for certain information from the students or for demonstration of a particular skill. The faculty member often will call on students to ensure that they have done their homework or to gather systematic information about current levels of student performance. When carefully prepared and equitably conducted, recitation can be an effective and even enjoyable teaching device. A trusting and supportive environment may be essential for recitation to be constructive for students. Usually, this implies that recitation is used to encourage learning and to ensure that all students have been given adequate attention but not as a means of student evaluation (which can better take place in other settings, using other devices).

Reading. Along with lecturing and question-and-answer sessions, assigned reading is the most common method of instruction. It is surprising, in fact, that reading has not become even more dominant. With the invention of the printing press, lecturing might have been more thoroughly superseded by reading than it has been. Many contemporary faculty members, in fact, complain about their students' inability to read. As a result, they tend to lecture even more than in the past and assign less reading.

Reading holds several distinct advantages over virtually any other instructional method. It is highly efficient as a vehicle for transmitting information and involves minimum faculty involvement in the form of precourse planning and one-on-one interaction with the student. Reading is the most portable of instructional methods. It can take place at any time and in many settings. It is a very inexpensive method of instruction, at least for the institution, since students usually purchase their own books (though when the cost of library books and facilities is added in, institutional costs significantly increase).

Finally, reading enables a student to receive highly diverse, up-to-date, expert information from more than one source. No faculty member, in isolation, can hope to compete with several carefully selected books in providing insightful and provocative information. Certainly, one of the most important roles played by faculty members is the review and selection of books to assign.

Several disadvantages should also be noted. First, a book does not provide students with direct human contact. Second, the book can rarely offer students very useful feedback on their own level of comprehension or performance. Third, students are rarely motivated to read unless they are stimulated by some other source of ideas (teacher, fellow students, experience, or something else).

The more recent innovations regarding college textbooks include the opportunity for faculty members to compose their own book of readings (which is printed and bound by a publisher) and the availability of some textbooks not only in a single-bound edition but also in separately bound sections for teachers who would like their students to read only a portion of the book. There have been major breakthroughs in the use of graphics to supplement the printed word. Graphics contribute esthetically to the book. They also prove valuable to the non-verbally oriented student. With tighter student and institutional budgets, however, one wonders how long these new graphics will be provided in textbooks.

Programmed Instruction/Computer-Assisted Instruction. Programmed instruction is the first of the so-called nontraditional methods that we will discuss. Like many of the other "nontraditional" methods described, programmed instruction was offered by some of its early, ardent advocates as a panacea for many of the instructional ills of the academic world. Like these other methods, programmed instruction was not enthusiastically embraced by many faculty members. It took its place alongside these other nontraditional methods as one of a variety of instructional tools available to serve a diversity of learning needs.

Initially, programmed instruction was proposed as a means of overcoming feedback problems associated with both lecturing and assigned reading. A basic tenet of behavioristic learning theory is the value of providing immediate reinforcement for successful performance of a specific task. Programmed instruction provides immediate reinforcement as well as ensuring that a student masters one set of instructional materials before proceeding to the next and that a student periodically reviews past sets of materials before moving on to new materials.

In the past, programmed instruction was primarily mediated through the printed word. Students were given a programmed instructional text that first introduced students to some information (for example, "William Shakespeare was a major playwright during the Elizabethan era in English history"). Then, on a second page (usually interspersed with new information), the student was asked a closed-ended question about this information—for example, "During what era in English history did William Shakespeare write plays?" The question often not only tested for retention of some part of the initial informational statement ("During what era . . . ?") but also repeated (reinforced) other parts of the statement (" . . . William Shakespeare write plays?"). Later in the programmed text, a different question might be asked that tested for retention of (and reinforced) other parts of the statement—for example, "For what type of artistic endeavor was William Shakespeare noted during the Elizabethan era in English history?"

Typically, the question was answered by selecting one or more responses from a multiple-choice format. The student answered the question and then determined the correct response (usually by turning to the next page of the programmed text). If the student's response matched the correct response, then the student proceeded to the next material. If the student's response did not match the correct answer, then he or she was asked to note the correct answer; or, if the correct answer required some explanation, the student was referred back to the initial statement.

The student proceeded through the programmed text in this manner, being intermittently exposed to new information, tested for retention of old information, and referred to previous information if unable to give the correct response. When observing a group of students working through a programmed text, one is usually impressed with the sound of rustling pages as students turn back to previous statements, check out answers on succeeding pages, or turn to information on new pages.

Programmed instruction has never been very popular outside courses taught by ardent behavioral psychologists and some biological scientists. The major criticisms that have been voiced are that (1) a programmed text interrupts the flow of information, so that it is hard to build a concept step by step; (2) a programmed text is often frustrating and not very exciting for students (at least after their initial interest in the "gaming" quality of the text has waned); (3) very few programmed texts are available outside the behavioral sciences; (4) composing one's own text is time-consuming; and (5) programmed texts cannot easily test for appreciation, synthesis, or other higher-order learning.

Programmed instruction is useful and appropriate in several settings and for several purposes. First, in learning and retaining a set of definitions, numbers, locations, or other such "facts," a short programmed text can be quite helpful. It can be intriguing and gamelike for students who are not used to this type of instruction. This type of text also increases the probability that students really will know the "facts" once they have completed the text. Second, programmed instruction is appropriate when an instructor is not available. Programmed ("self-instructional") texts have been used successfully to serve students in remote locations, hospitals, prisons, and so on. If feedback and encouragement from an instructor are not available, then programmed instruction is a practical alternative.

Third, programmed instruction can be used successfully when conveyed and monitored by a computer rather than printed textbooks. Computer-assisted instruction (CAI) has kept programmed instruction alive during the past five to ten years and holds the promise of becoming a widely used instructional tool by 1990. In making use of CAI, a student sits at a computer keyboard and interacts with the computer much as a student would interact with the programmed textbook—with several important differences.

Generally, while signing in, the student is asked his or her name by the computer as well as information about the material he or she wishes to cover during the session. The computer begins by providing the student with some printed information. For example:

> *Computer:* Hi, Jean. Today you've said you wanted to work on some ideas about William Shakespeare, a famous English playwright. First of all, do you know what a playwright is? Which of the following definitions of a playwright seems most accurate:
> 1.   Someone who writes short stories about sports,
> 2.   Someone who writes dramatic presentations for the theater, or
> 3.   Someone who writes novels.

Joan: (Types in "2.")

> *Computer:* Good, Jean, you're right. Okay. Let's talk a bit about where and when William Shakespeare wrote plays. . . .

The interaction between Jean and the computer would continue with the computer providing new information, testing Jean's retention of this information, and re-presenting information when Jean made the wrong response (for example, "Sorry, Jean, you gave the wrong answer. Let's go back and review some things we talked about earlier"). This branching and recycling program is not difficult to write, though much more complex and sophisticated routines have been written. The most widely known and used CAI program is PLATO, developed at the University of Illinois. The literature on the use of computer-assisted instruction in the college classroom is growing at a rapid rate. Several recent articles reflect the diverse use of CAI in a variety of disciplines: geography (Collins and others, 1980), medicine (Votaw and Farquhar, 1978), logic (Larson and others, 1978), music (Hofstetter, 1978), economics (Henry and Ramsett, 1978), and sociology (Lavin, 1980).

Computer-assisted instruction holds several major advantages over programmed instruction textbooks and many other instructional methods as well. One advantage concerns logistics. A CAI student does not have to fumble back and forth through pages of a book. The computer rapidly returns to a previous statement, asks a question, provides an answer, and so forth. Second, whereas programmed instruction textbooks often seem remedial and are offensive to students who prefer to read "straight" books, the computer is a new and widely respected (or at least feared) tool. As a result, students in remedial programs are usually not ashamed to inform peers that they are "going over to work on the computer for a while." Although the impressive quality of computers will soon diminish, CAI now is blessed with the aura and mystery of high technology. Furthermore, in working with computers, the CAI student is becoming acquainted with a tool that may be of significant value in future vocational activities.

Another advantage of the computer as an instructional tool is its capacity to forget. Although computers are usually touted for their memory, the ability of the computer to forget past failures is extremely important. One student in a Boston-area college recently commented that she liked CAI because she could return to the computer after doing miserably and the computer would treat her like a student who had never made an error. Very few faculty members are so willing to forget past failures. The computer is infinitely patient. It will keep working with a student until the student wishes to stop, and it never conveys any signs of boredom or contempt (unless programmed to do so!).

Audiovisual Instruction. As with programmed instruction, some prophets and advocates in the higher education community were convinced during the 1950s and early 1960s that various audiovisual technologies were going to reform teaching and learning in collegiate institutions. During the golden years of the sixties, when there were significantly more dollars for collegiate instruction, a large amount of money was spent on movie projectors, television monitors, and 35-mm slide projectors as well as for A-V facilities and staff to maintain and monitor this equipment. Much of this money was wasted, unfortunately, for very few dollars were spent teaching faculty members how to use audiovisual technologies in their classrooms or even in trying to convince them that A-V is not a dirty word.

Audiovisual technologies have not revolutionized higher education. However, they are clearly here to stay, and in an attempt to assess the nontraditional learner more successfully, many educators are now turning to educational television, motion pictures, and other media. An important lesson that is just now being learned by most faculty members who use A-V, however, is that they cannot compete with the mass media for the student's attention. Faculty members who produce their own videotapes often end up with "talking heads" that pale in comparison with the programs produced by educational and commercial television. Faculty members must use television and movies in ways that are not yet possible for the mass media. A faculty member, for example, can use a videotape as a basis for classroom discussion, interrupting the tape frequently for reaction and clarification. Students will usually feel freer to criticize and argue with a speaker on videotape than a speaker in person.

Faculty members have found audiovisual technologies to be of value in several respects. First, A-V provides stimulus variation. Students who grow tired of listening to the instructor's voice and viewpoints may pay closer attention to another person or to information that is presented visually. Second, A-V technologies provide yet another means whereby a faculty member can teach to students who prefer different instructional modalities (visual or kinesthetic). Third, professionally prepared A-V presentations often are more interesting and transmit more information in a shorter time than a lecture can. An A-V presentation usually avoids the redundancies inevitable in a lecture.

A fourth value is often ignored by the conscientious faculty member. A teacher usually does not have to be present for the movie, slide show, or videotape replay. The instructor can use the time to work more extensively on other aspects of the course (for example, advising or design). Furthermore, A-V materials can be made available to students on an individualized basis (equivalent to delivering an individual lecture to each student). We turn now to an instructional method that makes full use of this individualization capacity of audiovisual technology.

Audiotutorial Instruction. If a faculty member does not have to be present during an A-V presentation, then it also is apparent that the students need not all be assembled at the same place and at the same time to receive instruction. One can set up A-V equipment at a particular location and ask students to come there at a time of their own choosing (within limits) to view, listen to, or work with A-V materials. This allows for maximum individualization of time and duration of instruction and gives students immediate access to A-V equipment and other instructional materials that are not available in the usual classroom.

As described by Schiller and Markle (1978, p. 157), the audiotutorial method or system "typically uses a multimedia approach often with study guides provided by audiotape rather than by written text. It uses a central study-laboratory where students can view films, inspect demonstration experiments, conduct simple experiments themselves, and work through other instructional materials at their own pace. Self-pacing and control over repetition are present; however, in early versions of the system, examinations were scheduled at common times, and mastery was not enforced, with grades being given in the conventional manner. Later versions have instituted the mastery requirement and differ from PSI [Personalized System of Instruction, to be discussed later] primarily in the heavy investment in media which Keller [the founder of PSI] did not rule out, but which he perceived as luxuries."

The audiotutorial method has at least two sources of inspiration. One is the language laboratory, used for the teaching of foreign languages for many years. The second, more direct source is Samuel N. Postlethwait, a biologist at Purdue University, who first made use of tape-recorded study guides, related texts, and films placed at study areas in a laboratory setting.

Typically, an audiotutorial room is set aside for at least part of a term. Usually this is more easily accomplished in natural science, behavioral science, or professional school courses (where laboratories have been set aside for specific courses) than in a humanities course, for which a specific room is rarely assigned. If a classroom cannot be found, an audiotutorial lab can be set up in a reserve-book room, at a series of carrels in the library, in a dormitory, or even in a student union.

An audiotutorial lab usually contains booths in which are placed books, slide projectors, video recorders, audio recorders, television monitors, record players, pictures, artifacts, research equipment, models, and/or tape-loop projectors. Each booth holds instructional materials on a single topic. Typically, a student will move from booth to booth over a period of several weeks or an entire term. Work at each booth usually takes about one hour.

A lounge area is sometimes provided in the audiotutorial lab where students can converse informally with one another or with the instructor or a teaching assistant. Coffee and soft drinks are often provided. The instructor or teaching assistant is available not only to monitor student progress and the A-V equipment but also to become acquainted with the students, answer questions that might arise from materials presented in the lab, and engage in discussions about particularly interesting ideas that have emerged from the instructional materials. Many faculty members who use the audiotutorial method speak of having more time to talk with students than when making extensive use of lecturing or other nonlaboratory methods. A faculty member may also place a log book in the laboratory or in each booth. Students make comments and ask questions in this book. The instructor periodically checks the book, offering ob servations and answering questions.

A wide variety of topics have been taught in audiotutorial labs, mostly in the sciences. The lab is probably being used most extensively in biology, though recent articles have described its use in chemistry (Youmans, 1976) and physiology (Kalmbach, 1980). One course, "A Survey of Western Religions," has effectively incorporated the audiotutorial method by assigning a booth to each religion being studied. Information about and images of each religion were conveyed through books, slides, recorders, audiotaped discussions, and pictures posted on the walls of the booth. An ecology course has been designed in an even more ambitious manner. Each booth is enclosed, and the environment inside the booth (dry, moist, hot, cold) duplicates the ecological conditions described by materials located in that booth.

An audiotutorial laboratory can be quite limited in scope or quite extensive. At one extreme, the laboratory might be set up for one week near the start of a course. Four or five short modules would be offered that introduce several of the major themes of the course as well as some terminology. At the other extreme, an entire course can be structured around the audio-tutorial laboratory, with ten to fifteen modules of one to two hours' duration offered to students.

Like any instructional method, the audiotutorial laboratory can be overused. When first using an audiotutorial lab, a faculty member should limit its scope. The lab is usually most successful when used to create an impression or image of a particular time or place in order to convey something about the context within which a particular event has occurred, a work of art has been produced, or a decision has been made. This broad image or context can be conveyed through pictures, posters, music, or speeches, while the focal event, work of art, or decision is conveyed through the written word, slides, and the like. The audiotutorial lab is often used to spice up dull material (terms, definitions, taxonomies) that must be learned.

Some faculty members shy away from audiotutorial labs because of the work involved in setting them up. This problem can be overcome by assigning the task of designing each module to students in an advanced course or to students taking the course one term before the use of the audiotutorial lab. Students in an upper-division course on Shakespeare, for instance, might be given the task of selecting printed works, dramatic recordings, and period music and then constructing a booth in which these materials can be placed. This booth then becomes one module in an introductory-level "Survey of World Literature" course. Students in the Shakespeare course will find this task interesting and challenging. They will learn about Shakespeare and probably construct a better instructional module for their fellow students than the instructor could working alone.

Similarly, students in a "Survey of World Literature" course could learn about several famous authors by creating audiotutorial modules for one another. Each student in the course would be a member of a small task group that is assigned a particular author. This group would be responsible for constructing this author's module. Members of the group would also review, critique, and help to improve the other modules. A completed audiotutorial lab would be available the next time this survey course was taught. Students in the subsequent course might be given the task of further improving the existing modules or of creating new modules that focus on other major authors. The audiotutorial lab can be an engaging learning device in both its construction and its use.

Personalized System of Instruction. Just as the audiotutorial laboratory is a logical extension beyond the use of audiovisual equipment in the classroom, so is the so-called Personalized System of Instruction (PSI) a logical extension beyond programmed instruction. PSI was developed by Fred Keller, a Skinnerian psychologist, who was given the challenging task of designing a psychology program from scratch for a new Brazilian university. Two major concepts underlie PSI and its various derivations: mastery and self-paced learning.

Initially, Keller (1968) identified five distinctive features of a "pure" PSI course design:

1. The go-at-your-own-pace feature, which permits a student
    to move through the course at a speed commensurate with
    the student's ability and other demands on his or her time.
2. The unit-perfection requirement for advance, which lets the
    student go ahead to new material only after demonstrating
    mastery of that which preceded.
3. The use of lectures and demonstrations as vehicles of moti-
    vation rather than sources of critical information.
4. The related stress on the written word in teacher/student
    communication.
5. The use of proctors, which permits repeated testing, imme-
    diate scoring, almost unavoidable tutoring, and marked en-
    hancement of the personal/social aspect of the educational
    process.

We emphasize the first two of these features because the remaining three are no longer common to all PSI courses or seem
to be secondary in importance to the first two.

Mastery learning begins with the assumption that if certain
instructional units of a course are prerequisite to other units,
then a student should have mastered this prerequisite material
before moving on to the next unit. In an introductory psychology course, for instance, the instructor may believe that students should learn about perception, learning, and motivation
before tackling personality theory or social psychology. Advocates of mastery learning argue that if perception, learning, and
motivation are prerequisites, then a student who exhibits inadequate knowledge of this material (for example, a score of 60
percent on a multiple-choice test) should not move on to personality theory or social psychology until acceptable levels are
attained and exhibited (for example, a 90 percent score on the
test). Mastery is typically set at a rather high level (90-95 percent correct), and students are given ample time and assistance,
ideally, when studying for the tests. Mastery learning requires
that multiple versions of a test be available so that a student can
be retested if unable to reach mastery during the first testing
period.

An alternative to Keller's PSI method exemplifies the use

of mastery without self-pacing: the Mastery Learning system, developed by Benjamin Bloom (Schiller and Markle, 1978), includes mastery (unit perfection) but in many instances does not allow for self-pacing because students may work together with a teacher until their performance on a mastery test shows that some need remedial work.

The second concept, self-pacing, builds on the assumption that people learn in different ways and at different rates. An advocate of self-pacing would propose that it is unfair to test all students in the same room at the same time. Some students learn best when covering a rather large body of material in a relatively short time (blocked learning), while other students learn best when new material is acquired in small chunks over a relatively long time (spaced learning). Students who prefer blocked learning will want to take tests on the acquired material at different times and at different intervals than students who prefer spaced learning. These two kinds of learners will acquire the same amount of material in the same amount of time. Standards need not differ for them. Only the ways new materials are presented and the ways tests are given on these materials need be diversified.

Those disagreeing with this argument note that students must learn how to learn in a variety of ways: block learners must learn how to learn when information is provided in small chunks; conversely, spaced learners must learn how to "cram" when there is a short period of time in which to learn a great deal of material.

When mastery learning and self-pacing are brought together in PSI, students are confronted, typically, with a series of instructional units (modules). If PSI is the only mode of instruction being used, there are usually seven to fifteen modules per course, each of which an average student will complete in about one or two weeks. If PSI is used for only part of a course or in conjunction with other instructional methods, then the modules will be fewer and/or of shorter duration.

Each module usually begins with a pretest to determine the student's current level of knowledge and/or proficiency in this area of instruction. If the student already exhibits mastery-level ability, he or she can move on to the next module. Usually mastery is not yet exhibited, and the student participates in some instructional program through which the material of this module is presented. A variety of instructional methods can be used in this segment of the PSI procedure. Often, reading and programmed instruction are used. The audiotutorial laboratory is compatible with PSI, each booth providing the instructional program for one PSI module.

When the student has completed the instructional materials in a module, he or she takes a posttest on this material. If mastery is exhibited on this posttest, the student proceeds to the next module. If the student has not attained mastery, exposure to the instructional materials associated with this module is repeated. A different instructional method might be used or new instructional materials presented to ensure that the student has been given every opportunity to learn this material. A second posttest is then given, as are third and fourth posttests if necessary. If the student does not pass the second or third posttest, the instructor will usually offer a different type of test or will sit down with the student to find out what he or she knows and what the problem might be with the instructional materials or tests. A tutor might be assigned to students who are encountering problems with a particular module.

The PSI method of instruction offers several advantages over other methods as well as being burdened with several disadvantages. One advantage is a shift in the role of the instructor, who can operate more directly in behalf of the student. PSI enables the instructor to establish certain standards against which the student's performance is judged (called "criterion-referenced" instruction). When a student has met these standards (after having completed a particular instructional unit designed or selected by the instructor), then the student is likely to reflect positively on both himself or herself and the instructor—assuming that the standards are acceptable to the instructor's colleagues.

By contrast, when "grading on the curve" (norm-referenced instruction) is in effect, the faculty member is not judged positively by peers if all students receive high grades, for in this way, the faculty member may be seen as contributing to the deterioration of academic standards and to grade inflation. If a faculty member who uses PSI is able to solicit agreement from colleagues that the tests being given are satisfactory, if the standards of mastery that have been set are acceptable, and if the students all attain mastery, the instructor should be commended for excellence in teaching rather than condemned for lowering the standards. Placed in this position, the PSI instructor is usually more amenable to helping students prepare for tests and overcome learning blocks and test anxiety. The faculty member is then not caught in the ambiguous position of having to "find" the lowest student quartile (D's and F's) in order to preserve a well-formed grading curve.

A second advantage concerns flexibility and individualization for students. Within limits, each student can work at his or her own pace and take tests at a convenient time. Optimally, students may choose among several instructional methods and several modes of testing, at least if they encounter problems the first time through the module. With the use of pretests, a student can avoid sitting through lectures or reading books that cover material already acquired. If students come into a course with widely divergent backgrounds and skills—as is increasingly the case—then the pretests are particularly valuable. A student should be given the opportunity to test out of certain modules if a course is required or prerequisite to other popular courses.

A third advantage is the opportunity for a PSI instructor to focus attention on students who find the course difficult. Often, students who are overwhelmed with a course will be quiet during classroom discussions or will cease attending class. They are often reticent to ask for the instructor's assistance. PSI provides a monitoring device whereby these students can be identified and served. If a student is not progressing at a normal rate through the modules or is encountering difficulties with a particular module, the instructor will know immediately and can set up special appointments and/or tutoring for this student.

Faculty members who use other content-based methods can monitor student progress through the frequent use of short quizzes. Unfortunately, quiz results may reveal more about the poor timing of the test for a student than about any inherent problems the student is experiencing with the subject matter. Even if such faculty members identify students in trouble, other course obligations (lecturing, discussion groups, and so on) may preclude extensive attention to these problem students. The PSI instructor is usually freed from many of these distracting obligations and hence can devote adequate time and attention to the problem student.

As Schiller and Markle (1978) have noted, "A benefit that is an outgrowth of the gradual improvement of the course is the reduction in instructor preparation time that is required for successive offerings. Although the initial offering will require at least as much time as any well-prepared conventional course, and probably more, each successive offering typically requires less and less instructor effort until little is required beyond setting up the mechanics. . . . assuming, of course, that the course content is not something that changes drastically in short periods" (pp. 168-169).

One major disadvantage of PSI is its incompatibility with the registration, crediting, and scheduling procedures of most collegiate institutions. Rarely is a student allowed to take an unlimited amount of time to complete a course. Usually, if a student has not completed a course by the end of the term, he or she is assigned a low grade or given an Incomplete, which will be changed to an F if the course is not finished shortly. At most collegiate institutions, therefore, a "pure" form of self-paced PSI is not feasible. A student must keep in mind that all the modules must be completed by the end of the term (or some other deadline set by the instructor).

A second, related issue concerns the assignment of grades in a PSI course. If a student has "mastered" all the modules in a course, shouldn't a grade of A be assigned for the course? If all students in a course have completed the modules, then shouldn't they all receive A's? At some colleges and universities, this is called "grade inflation." At others, it is not. PSI has been modified in several ways to accommodate this problem. Sometimes a separate set of quizzes or a final examination is given for grading purposes. The pre- and posttests associated with each module are used not for grading purposes, but rather to help a student monitor progress and prepare for the graded quizzes or exams. Alternatively, time is used as a grading criterion. Students who finish the PSI modules first receive A's. Those who finish the modules at a slower pace receive B's, and so forth. Both these grading procedures (especially the latter one) seem to defeat the purpose and spirit of PSI.

A somewhat more satisfactory grading procedure builds on the need for tutorial assistance in a PSI course. To get an A, a student must not only complete the PSI modules but also provide a certain number of hours of tutorial assistance for other students. For a B, a lesser number of tutorial hours is required. The student is not being rewarded for working faster per se. Rather, the reward is for teaching other people, having rapidly completed the modules. A justifiable assumption is made that the student will learn more about the content of the module if he or she must teach it to someone else. Through use of this grading option, the instructor receives valuable tutorial assistance.

The grading problem can also be solved by including PSI as only one element in a course. A faculty member, for instance, might use several PSI modules near the start of a course to introduce the basic terminology, definitions, and concepts of the course. Students are told that they must complete the PSI modules by the fourth week of the course if they are to comprehend and use the concepts to be presented during the rest of the term. Or the instructor might be a bit more persuasive by stating that these modules must be completed by the fourth week of the term if the student is to receive an A or B for the course. Another approach might be that these modules must be completed by the fourth week if the student is to remain in the course.

PSI modules can be used alongside other instructional methods. An instructor might give lectures, hold discussion sessions, and provide periodic simulations or case-study sessions along with the PSI modules. A final grade would be determined on the basis of performance in all segments of the course. Thus, all students completing the PSI modules could receive grades of

A for this segment of the course, yet not necessarily receive an A for the entire course.

The problem of tutorial assistance in a PSI course can be confronted in several ways other than making use of students taking the class. The problem is actually much broader than just tutorial assistance. A PSI instructor is faced with a number of clerical demands, including test administration and recordkeeping as well as the higher-level demands for the construction of tests and the production or selection of instructional materials. Some instructors in larger institutions who are using PSI in introductory courses are able to hire teaching assistants to administer the tests and keep records. In smaller institutions, the instructor may have to obtain work-study assistance or ask students enrolled in advanced courses to provide these services. The latter solution to the clerical problem is not very satisfactory, however, for student assistance with clerical tasks can rarely be justified as an educational experience, whereas tutorial assistance can be. Thus, clerical demands are a serious disadvantage for PSI, particularly in small institutions.

Problems associated with test construction and preparation of instructional materials are more easily solved—at least for introductory-level courses—if the instructor is willing to use tests and materials prepared by other people. The Center for Personalized Instruction at Georgetown University (Washington, D.C.) has information about existing PSI courses in many fields. Instructors can also borrow sample test items from the numerous textbooks that they receive each year. Small-college instructors should consider setting up a consortial arrangement, cooperatively preparing or selecting instructional materials and constructing test items, with faculty members from nearby colleges who teach in the same discipline and wish to use PSI for similar introductory courses.

Students in advanced-level courses can help prepare instructional materials and construct test items. Like designing and building audiotutorial booths, this assistance can be justified as an educational activity. In preparing materials and test items, advanced students will often be more creative and sensitive to the needs and learning styles of introductory-level students than the instructor might be.

A final disadvantage of PSI is student reaction against this method. Although some students appreciate the clarity of course structure and requirements in PSI, others react against the seemingly "inhuman" or "mechanistic" quality of the design. Many students cannot find sufficient self-discipline to manage a self-paced course. This disadvantage is most apparent when a course is designed exclusively around PSI.

Despite these major disadvantages, PSI is being used widely, and a growing body of literature concerning the use of PSI in a variety of fields is now available. Some of the fields in which articles have recently been written include chemistry (Hughes and others, 1978), human physiology (Giese and Lawler, 1978), mathematics (Hassett and Thompson, 1978), and geology (Andrews, 1977). This method is probably being most extensively used in psychology, in keeping with its origins. Professional schools (particularly nursing) are just beginning to make use of PSI.

Fantasy/Suggestopedia. Among the ingredients of a particularly effective lecture is often the speaker's ability to convey or elicit vivid visual images. One widely respected lecturer on twentieth-century Irish literature, for instance, is able to bring the students into the Irish Rebellion through the use of carefully chosen stories, images, and illustrations and through tone of voice, pauses, and gestures. The student's own fantasy work is central to this lecturer's goal of conveying something about the context within which Irish writers create works of art.

Fantasy can be conceived of as slowed-down lecturing. Rather than speaking at 150 to 200 words per minute, an instructor might provide only 30 to 60 words per minute, relying on the student to produce a rich fantasy based on these words. This "directed" or "guided" fantasy technique has been used in a variety of disciplines. In an ecology course, an instructor may ask students to imagine that they are about to wake up in the year 2020. The instructor then asks them to imagine living through a typical day in the year 2020 and, in doing so, presents several statements about what the world might be like then. Having fantasized either in their heads or on paper, the students are encouraged to describe and talk about their images and the implications of these images for current and future pub-

lic policy. Discussions about future conditions are often richer
and more insightful when based on students' fantasies about the
future than when based solely on verbal discussions about the
future.

Fantasy can be used profitably in the sciences and mathematics. Three-dimensional models can often be conveyed more
effectively through fantasy than by being drawn as two-dimen-
sional figures on a blackboard. Students can image walking
around to the back side of a cube that is floating in space. They
can image a hypothetical animal that could exist if adapting to a
specific and unusual set of environmental conditions. Fantasy can
be broadly and creatively used, not only to help a student become immersed in a particular story, painting, or musical composition but also (as in the case of the Irish literature lecturer)
to become immersed in the context within which the artist is
working.

To successfully employ fantasy in the classroom, it is essential for the instructor to establish a restful and reflective atmosphere. If possible, a comfortable room should be selected.
The lights should not be bright, and outside noises and visual dis-
tractions should be kept to a minimum. If the instructor feels
comfortable in doing so, he or she should have students lean
back in their chairs or even lie on the floor, close their eyes, and
spend a few moments divorcing themselves from outside concerns and activities. This latter process of disengagement can be
facilitated by asking the students to spend a few moments concentrating on their breathing. If the instructor is familiar with
progressive relaxation techniques, these also can be used in preparing students for a fantasy. Faculty members who are not sat-
isfied with the outcomes of a fantasy conducted in the classroom often have not given sufficient attention to these prelimi-
naries.

In foreign language fields—and increasingly in other fields
as well—fantasy has been used in a somewhat different manner.
A technique called "suggestopedia," first used in Bulgaria and
more recently used by American educators in teaching German,
French, and Spanish, relies heavily on fantasy. Suggestopedia is
probably the most controversial of the content-based instruc-

tional methods we have considered. It also may be of greater potential benefit to students than any of the previously described methods.

Suggestopedia is a subtle and complex process for which instructors must be trained. Several of its intriguing goals and features are (1) conveying a positive attitude about the ease with which seemingly difficult material (for example, German grammar) can be learned; (2) providing a warm environment that is conducive to receptive and relaxed learning; (3) aiding the memorization of terms or rules through the use of music and rhythm; and (4) aiding the acquisition of concepts through use of fantasy (for example, encouraging students to imagine that they are a particular verb that changes form and location as a function of its relationship with a particular noun).

Faculty members who have used suggestopedia report impressive success in teaching the rudiments of a foreign language in a short time to students (and even faculty members) who previously experienced considerable difficulty in learning a second language. The techniques of suggestopedia are now being modified for broader use and have even been popularized under the banner of "superlearning." Several recent articles on suggestopedia provide an overview of the use of this method in foreign language instruction (Mignault, 1978; Milivojevic, 1979; Racle, 1979).

Interaction-Based

Seminar-Discussion. Along with lecturing and tutorials, seminars form the historical base for contemporary college teaching. Most of the other interaction-based instructional methods derive from the seminar format, at least for instruction in the humanities. Laboratories and studios provide comparable bases in the sciences and arts. An effective seminar provides an environment in which a faculty member and students can openly interact to discuss issues, problems, and perspectives that do not lend themselves to easy resolution or solution. A seminar is often ineffective because the faculty member wishes to use it as a forum for the dissemination of specific information or for the promotion of particular perspectives or solutions to particular problems. The content-based methods described above (for example, lectures, audiotutorial lab, PSI) are more appropriate for these goals.

At other times, faculty members are unsuccessful in conducting a seminar or discussion group because they use this setting as a vehicle for encouraging student control of the instructional process. The seminar or discussion group becomes the place in which students "have their say." Although students in interaction with the faculty member might help define the direction a discussion will take, they should not dominate design issues, for there will inevitably be a diverse set of student learning goals and interests that must be mediated and integrated by the faculty member with the students' assistance. Student control is more successfully incorporated in individualized methods that are student-based (see descriptions below concerning independent study, learning contracts, field placements, and student-generated courses).

In the role of designer and facilitator, as well as resource person, a faculty member can contribute greatly to the interactive processes of a seminar or discussion group. As the designer of a seminar or discussion group, a faculty member can encourage a discussion process that is both thoughtful and interesting, is both creative and systematic, and enhances each participant's sense of his or her own worth as a contributor to this process. Of the several designs found successful in meeting these objectives, one called "synectics" (Gordon, 1961; Prince, 1970) is particularly valuable, for it enhances the quality as well as equity of seminar discussions. Under synectics guidelines, a seminar participant is encouraged (or even required) to paraphrase the central idea conveyed by the immediately preceding speaker and to indicate at least three positive features of this idea before stating his or her own idea or criticizing the previous speaker's. Synectics guidelines encourage active listening, constructive reactions to ideas, and intellectual interaction. Since seminar participants who are verbally active often do not listen to or build on the ideas of other participants, synectics discourages overactive participation. Whereas synectics encourages convergent thinking, with each participant building on the ideas of others, several other group techniques—in particular, brainstorming (Clark, 1958) and divergent delphi (Bergquist and Phillips, 1977)—enhance the quality and equity of discussion by encouraging divergent, creative thinking.

Classroom discussion can also be facilitated by starting each session with some common experience to which all seminar members can respond and which will elicit reactions from virtually everyone—perhaps a short movie, an oral recitation, or a questionnaire. Other interactive methods might be similarly used: short simulations, case studies, role plays, or debates. Barnes-McConnell (1978, pp. 71-72) has recently noted, in this regard, that in a discussion group "all students should have at least one, and preferably multiple, common experiences or frames of reference from which to begin. Examples include a written common experience such as a case history, a story, a report, a news article, a book, and so on, the reading of which is required of all students. It might be a class handout or homework assignment. A common verbal experience might be a lecture, a speech, a guest presentation, or a panel. Movies, slide shows, television programs, or media interviews are common audiovisual experiences. A common simulated experience might be a role-playing session or a simulation game; and a common real-life experience might be participation in a community research survey, individually assigned visits to community agencies, group field trips, or observation of some community activity."

Alternatively, the instructor or a student might begin the seminar by posing a problem with which participants must grapple or an open-ended question that will be the topic of discussion throughout the seminar. The noted anthropologist and systems theorist Gregory Bateson (1979) describes a class that he began by placing a crab shell on the table. The participants were to determine how they would know this had once been a living thing if they had come from another planet.

Laboratory/Studio. As is true of most interaction-based methods of instruction, there is always a lingering temptation for the scientist to make use of the laboratory and, to a lesser extent, for the artist to make use of the studio as a place in which to teach specific subject matter. When the laboratory or studio becomes a tool for content-based instruction, it loses its vitality and purpose. Even though the outcomes of almost any contemporary laboratory experiment are known to the instructor, and the student is being asked to learn particular laboratory skills, there is still room for ingenuity and individual diversity in the way the student conducts the investigation, analyzes the resulting data, and writes up a report. If the student is merely walking step by step through a laboratory "cookbook," then the value of the laboratory should be questioned. There are much more time-efficient ways to learn about specific steps that have been taken in the past to solve certain problems or scientific puzzles. Science instructors can overcome the problem of "dry labs" by making the laboratory experiments interesting and open-ended.

A laboratory experience should be opened up in yet another way. Biological, physical, and behavioral scientists should not lay exclusive claim to the laboratory. This mode of instruction should be available to all faculty members in all disciplines. "Traditional" faculty members in physics, biology, or psychology who have had years of experience in designing and running laboratory-based courses can assist their colleagues in the arts and humanities in the innovative use of laboratory procedures in other disciplines. This linkage not only aids the course-design process but also helps to break down long-term barriers between the sciences and humanities and encourages the science faculty member to change his or her self-definition as a "traditional" instructor, thereby opening up to consideration other methodologies in the classroom.

What might a laboratory look like in the humanities or arts? Several areas lend themselves readily to the laboratory. Logic can be taught in a laboratory setting, as can historiography. An English literature course on the contemporary novel might include a laboratory in which students are given excerpts from certain novels and asked to critique them from a particular perspective (for example, that of a certain school of literary criticism). A painting laboratory might require a student to examine systematically the visual and esthetic effect of different types of brushstrokes or the predominant use of dark colors at the top or bottom of a still life or landscape.

The traditional barriers between the arts and other academic disciplines can be similarly dismantled by asking faculty members outside the arts to consider the use of studio instruction in one or more of their courses. What does the art or music professor do in the studio that can be done with comparable impact in other disciplines? How, for instance, does the art professor know when to encourage the student to work on technical skills and when to push toward greater creativity? Isn't sensitivity to the appropriate balance between a student's technical competence and his or her creativity vital for all teachers?

Symposium/Debate. There is a long-standing tradition of deliberation and debate in the history of American higher education. This tradition is evident in the debating societies that played a central role in the intellectual and social lives of many students during the nineteenth and early twentieth centuries. It is also evident, more subtly, in the contemporary emphasis in American higher education on the development of analytic and critical skills. American higher education has less of a symposium tradition, though this mode of instruction has deep, classic roots and is accepted as a valid and even laudable instructional method by most faculty members in American collegiate institutions.

Typically, a symposium involves three or more panelists and an audience. The essence of an exciting and provocative symposium is usually not the opening comment, but rather the discussion that takes place among panelists or between panelists and members of the audience. Symposia that emphasize the panelists' opening comments often seem to neglect the chief characteristic of the symposium—namely, the gathering of several experts or articulate spokespersons for a particular perspective. If the panelists are not given ample time to interact, one wonders why they were brought together in the first place, given the logistic problems and significant costs often associated with this union.

Colleges frequently conduct symposia outside the formal academic course schedule. Many colleges and universities, for

example, offer one or more special thematic conferences each
year during which several symposia are conducted. The University of Idaho offers the "Borah Symposium" each year on the
issue of war and peace. A special trust fund has been established
to partly defray costs associated with bringing together interna-
tionally known scholars, statesmen, and politicians.

An assumption is often made in planning for and funding
such a symposium: that it offers extraordinary educational opportunities for students, faculty members, and other members
of the academic community (as well as bringing some visibility
and even increased credibility to the college or university). One
can challenge this assumption. Students (and faculty members)
are rarely provided with any background information to prepare
for the symposium. Ideally, a series of "in-house" educational
activities should precede an institutionwide symposium in order
for participants to benefit fully from the viewpoints being presented. Furthermore, several educational events should be
scheduled after the symposium so that its rich offerings can be
fully discussed and digested. Videotapes of symposium presentations and discussions, for instance, might be viewed and discussed by groups of students and faculty members after the
event. If the symposium is of a general nature (such as war and
peace), it might even be discussed in many of the courses taught
during the term when the symposium is offered.

The symposium mode of instruction should not be restricted to institutionwide events, but should instead be brought
into individual courses. A faculty member can invite several colleagues, knowledgeable members of the local community, or
knowledgeable students to sit as members of a symposium panel.
Team teaching need not be restricted to the formal assignment
of two or more faculty members to one course. A faculty member who is formally assigned to teach a course can ask colleagues
to join together for one or more symposia. Although most faculty members are aware of this option, it is rarely used. Reasons
for the neglect of colleague resources are obvious and numerous: lack of time, scheduling difficulties, uneasiness about in-
vading another faculty member's turf, disruption in course continuity, and so forth. Most of these problems can be overcome

through planning, exchange agreements, or a basic shift in attitudes about academic freedom and autonomy.

As in the case of PSI, faculty members may wish to explore interinstitutional consortial arrangements with colleagues
from nearby colleges and universities, who are often excellent
symposium panelists. They provide not only expertise in the
field of discussion but also an alternative perspective—especially
if they come from an institution with a different background
and tradition. A symposium on war and peace, for instance,
might involve participants from both civilian and military educational institutions, or from a liberal arts college, school of
business, and school of law.

Another way symposia can be used concerns the courses
that students take to meet a distribution requirement for graduation. If a cluster of courses all can fulfill distribution requirements in one area (such as foreign language proficiency, critical
thinking, or math "literacy"), then a "cross-course" symposium
might be held each term, which would involve students enrolled
in each of these courses. Such a symposium would involve faculty members from each course, other faculty members at the
institution, and/or outside experts and could be addressed to a
theme that integrates disparate courses. A symposium on the
nature of language and culture, for instance, might involve all
students who are taking a foreign language course (or computer
science course) to meet a distribution requirement. Or a symposium on "alienation and modern life" or some similar theme
(which may be changed each term) may be required of all students taking humanities courses to meet a distribution requirement in Western civilization.

This type of integrating symposium can be of value not
only as a compromise between a standard required core curriculum and distribution requirements but also as an annual or semi-
annual faculty development activity. It encourages interdisciplinary and integrative thinking, discussions, and research among
faculty members who must prepare for the symposium. With
minimal additional time or money, most colleges and universities with distribution requirements in their general education
program can improve the overall quality of this program (and

faculty teaching in the program) through use of cross-course symposia.

In recent years, debates, like symposia, have been conducted outside the confines of individual courses. Many colleges and universities support intercolleigate debate teams or host intramural debates on contemporary issues. Debates should be used more frequently in the classroom. They can be effectively integrated with several other interactive methods that we will describe (team teaching, case studies, Socratic dialogue, learning cells, buzz groups, and role playing).

The ultimate "neutrality" of debate in the classroom must be preserved. An effective debater should be able to argue on either side of an issue, to identify the strengths and weaknesses of any position, and to recognize the validity of multiple perspectives on an issue or problem. Two students in a course, for example, might be given the assignment of researching both sides of a particular issue. When beginning the debate, each student is arbitrarily assigned to argue one side or the other. In this way, students grow to appreciate the complexity of contemporary issues and the inherent danger of simplistic thinking.

A debate could have one or more judges who assess the relative worth of each debater's argument. Often the role of judge can be as educative as the role of debater. A panel of students can be assigned the task of weighing both sets of arguments presented by the debaters. The judges' critical faculties must be brought to bear in making a decision. Just as students who are working on a case study must ultimately make a difficult decision when faced with a wealth of conflicting data, so must debate judges make a difficult decision while faced with complexity. After making a decision, judges are faced also with the task of communicating their reasons for the decision and of providing each debater with constructive feedback about his or her performance.

A classroom debate can often be enriched and enlivened by setting the debate in a historical context. A debate on fishing rights in the Atlantic Ocean, for instance, can be enhanced by asking students to imagine that this is an international hearing at the United Nations. Students might be asked to read recent

United Nations reports. The topic of debate might be extracted directly from an actual hearing. Similarly, a theological debate might be set, hypothetically, in a Dayton, Tennessee, courtroom, the papal chambers, or a Buddhist monastery. A debate need not be conducted as a sterile, intellectual exercise, for it will (or at least should) involve issues of historical or contemporary importance.

Team Teaching. One might argue that team teaching is not an instructional method, but rather a description of the instructional resources available in a course. *Team teaching* implies that two or more faculty members are formally assigned to teach a course. Yet, team teaching is more than this—or at least should be. Simply to put two or more faculty members in a classroom together is not to ensure that the learning of students (or the faculty members) will be in any way enhanced. Most team teaching, in fact, operates on a rotational basis. One faculty member teaches for a while (perhaps one class period or one week), and then the other. Alternatively, the two faculty members teach together, usually in a seminar format, and dominate discussion. While the intellectual exchange may be exciting for the faculty members and even amusing or intriguing for the students, very little real communication may take place between the faculty members and students.

Effective team teaching always involves a complex and often tenuous balance among three parties: faculty member A, faculty member B, and the students. The relationship between each faculty member and the students is just as important as the relationship between the faculty members. The three parties in a team-teaching situation can interrelate in a variety of ways. One faculty member can preside, with the second serving as a monitor, mediator, or discussion facilitator. The presiding faculty member may be the content expert, allowing the second faculty member to attend extensively to the process of the classroom. Who isn't being heard? How do we encourage the quiet students? What can be done to elevate the level of trust and increase risk-taking behavior in this classroom? Ideally, these roles will be frequently reversed so that each faculty member can attend primarily at times to the content and at other times to the process. Alternatively, one of the faculty members can serve as the "teacher" for one or more segments of the course, while the second serves as a "master learner" (see Chapter Four).

A third possible relationship between team-teaching faculty members and students leads us into role playing and back to debate. Each faculty member assumes a particular role, as some historical figure or as the spokesperson for some school of thought. Each role might be consistently played by one faculty member throughout a term, or faculty members may shift roles. In a team-taught course on "Psychology and Society," one professor represents a Skinnerian perspective on society throughout the course, while a second professor represents a perspective that Carl Rogers would take on society. Since both the faculty members and students might weary of each professor's consistently playing one role, the two could switch roles periodically. The students also might assume certain roles that complement those being played by the faculty members.

From week to week, members of the faculty team might assume new roles appropriate to the different topics being addressed. In a philosophy course, for instance, two faculty members might initially assume the roles and philosophical positions of Socrates and Aristotle. Later they might assume other complementary roles as famous philosophers or theologians (for example, Augustine and Aquinas or Russell and Wittgenstein) or representatives of major schools (for example, positivist and existential).

As we shall note more fully later, the roles need not be played in a theatrical manner. A faculty member need only attempt to represent the intellectual perspective and spirit of the person or school being represented. Team teaching that incorporates role playing, the master-learning concept, or the mediator/facilitator function can yield rich learning experiences for students who usually are inaccessible to the faculty member who teaches alone.

Case Study/Socratic Method. An unfortunate consequence of the typical isolation of professional schools from undergraduate education is the failure of most liberal arts faculty members to understand and appreciate the potential use of the instructional methods used in professional schools. The case-study method, which is used extensively in business schools and in law schools, and the "Socratic" method, used in many forms in most law schools, are appropriate for instruction in any discipline. The two methods are quite similar, the case-study method usually involving more preclass preparation by the student than the Socratic method.

The case-study method is most closely associated with the Harvard University School of Business, though it is used in most graduate schools of business and management in the United States. Charles Fisher (1978, p. 262) describes the method: "A case study may be defined as the factual account of human experience centered in a problem or issue faced by a person, a group of persons, or an organization. It describes real situations in real settings that require or suggest the need for discretionary action. The case-study method, then, is the process of using this written case to effect learning by involving the participant in at least three interdependent stages of activity: reading and contemplating the case by oneself; analyzing and discussing the case with others in a group session or sessions; and subsequent reflection upon the case, the discussion, and his or her own attitudes and behavior." The Harvard "case method" has been modified in a number of ways for use with a variety of students and in a variety of content areas. R. C. Bauer (quoted in Fisher, 1978, p. 260) has identified several types of case methods of instruction: "the *case problem,* which briefly presents the facts and the problem itself; the *case report,* which provides the basic elements with little supporting information and gives the decision(s) and results; the *case study* (or *history*), which is a longer, more complete account, not necessarily with a readily identifiable problem, but containing the results and sometimes the implications and analysis of actions; and the *research case,* which is the most comprehensive, including more on observable events, factors, and a complete diagnosis."

Several features stand out as critical to use of the case-study method in all its variations. First, the case itself must be carefully prepared. Some say that effective case writing is an

art. It certainly involves highly sophisticated narration. Fisher
(1978, pp. 268-269) offers a description of the typical written
case study: "Typically, the beginning of a case study presents a
brief overview of the problem or situation, thus involving the
reader. The setting and other descriptive information follow.
The facts are presented, either chronologically or else in a manner relating to salient aspects of the problem, so as to lead up to
major decisions that must be made or to significant circumstances that require analysis and discretionary evaluation. Therefore, the ends are often left untied, with the outcome not
known, the actions unjudged, and the motives not presumed.
The participants are required to make their own analysis and
judgments, assessing for themselves the consequences or implications of various decisions or actions." A case usually contains
a brief description of a real problem that has confronted someone or some group at one time. Action must be taken. The
alternative courses of action are sometimes spelled out. At other
times, the reader is expected to identify the alternatives. The
case contains a brief description of the background behind the
problem being confronted. Documents (statistical tables, correspondence, verbatim transcripts, and so on) that support or
expand on the background description are often included as
well.

In some instances, a case is broken into two or more
parts. The reader is given the first part of the case and is asked
how he or she would solve the problem. Later the reader is
given a second part of the case, which describes the decision
that was actually made in response to this problem. The reader
can in this way compare his or her own proposed action with
that actually taken. Often the reader is then presented with a
new or modified problem emerging from the actual action that
was taken, is asked once again to respond to this problem, and
is given information later about the action that actually was
taken. This routine may be repeated three or four times if the
case is rich and detailed or if it involves actions that were taken
over a long period.

A case should usually be presented in no more than twenty to thirty pages (including documents). Longer cases tend to

offer too much detail. Furthermore, they are inclined to be didactic rather than provocative. An effective case will encourage reflection, deliberation, and discussion. It will not provide answers or offer analysis. If carefully selected, the case will defy simple solutions or unidimensional analyses. The reader of a case should be confronted with a problem that can be approached from a number of perspectives, each of which is valid and useful.

Most cases close with a set of questions formulated by the case writer (or others who have used the case). These questions serve as catalysts for deliberation and discussion rather than definitive statements about how the case should be approached. These questions are often just as important as the case itself.

When the case-study method is applied outside schools of business, law, and public policy, the cases may take on a somewhat different form. In a literature course, for instance, the "case" may be the first half of a short story or play. Readers are asked at this point how they think the story or play will or should proceed. Comparisons can then be drawn between the readers' predicted or suggested scenarios and the scenario that was actually developed by the author.

In other fields, such as police science, psychotherapy, or nursing, the "case" may be a videotape. A particular scene is enacted up to a certain point. The tape is then halted, and the viewer is asked what action he or she would take at that point. The viewer may then be shown a second videotaped "playlet" and asked to make a second set of decisions, and so forth. In the natural or behavioral sciences, a case may consist of the first two thirds of a research report, including the introduction, methods, and results sections. The reader is asked how the discussion and conclusion sections would be organized.

A second central feature of the case method concerns student preparation for the class discussion of a case. Students are asked not just to read a case but also to prepare their decisions about actions to be taken, on the basis of an analysis of the central features of the case. A student must be able to justify his or her decisions and actions. Because a case should not have one "right" answer, the analysis and justification are more important than the student's particular choice.

In most instances, students prepare for the case not only in isolation but also as members of a case-study group or team. Each student meets with a small number of colleagues to discuss the case and arrive at a consensus about the action to be taken. Some case instructors ask one or more of these case-study groups to make a classroom presentation or to lead a classroom discussion of the case. In other instances, the instructor is interested mainly in the responses of individual students and uses the case-study groups primarily to refine students' ideas before they enter class.

Some case instructors prefer to let case-study groups work on their own, while others assign a tutor or teaching assistant to the group. This assistant is usually an advanced student with previous experience in this particular area of study and the case-study method. Occasionally, group leaders are selected from among current students in the class. Some instructors first lead a case-study group themselves, composed of their teaching assistants or tutors. This special case group deals with each case before the regular groups do and serves as a forum not only for deliberations on the case but also for discussions about how the teaching assistants or tutors should facilitate the students' deliberation.

A third central feature of the case-study method is the way classroom discussions of the case are managed. At this point the interactive quality of the case-study method is particularly apparent. Instructors who come from a content-based perspective are likely to run into trouble. A case study should not be used if the instructor wishes to make a particular point. A short lecture, with illustrative examples, is more appropriate. A case instructor should encourage discussion and debate among students. By verbal and nonverbal probes and reactions, the instructor can encourage risk-taking behavior and divergent thinking. If students feel that the instructor has a particular solution in mind for the case, they may expend energy trying to figure out the instructor's preference (to agree with it or to take issue) rather than their own preference.

Several strategies are often used to elicit substantial and vigorous case discussions. First, an instructor might ask one student or case-study group to present one or more of the central "facts" of the case and then ask the rest of the class to discuss the validity of these facts and their bearing on the decision to be made in this case. The instructor then asks another student or group to present some of the facts. This is followed by more critique and discussion. The instructor then turns to students' or groups' decisions on the problem confronted in the case, as well as other students' comments and critiques concerning these decisions, in order to help students clarify their own perspectives and opinions.

A case-study instructor may instead encourage an open and freewheeling discussion of the case, subtly structuring the students' deliberations through the use of questioning strategies and blackboard (or flip-chart) space. Before the class begins, the instructor determines the major categories within which the students' comments about the case are likely to fall. Assessment of the various tracks that students are likely to take in successfully confronting the case is made, and those tracks that are filled with pitfalls and dead ends are identified. The instructor sets aside areas of the blackboard for different categories and develops questioning strategies that are likely to encourage student movement along successful lines of thought.

The instructor opens discussion with some general question, such as "What seems to be going on in this case?" Some students' responses to this question are placed at a particular location on the blackboard. The responses of other students are placed in other locations. Students may not even be aware of the instructor's classification scheme. They will be aware, however, of the relations among various ideas that are being presented by their colleagues. Some ideas will cluster together. Other ideas will be located at opposite ends of the blackboard. Students will learn something about the analysis of a problem as well as the synthesis of wide-ranging and seemingly disparate information by observing their instructor in action.

A fourth central feature of the case method is not as readily apparent as the first three, yet is of equal importance.

This feature concerns the attitude of the instructor toward the case materials he or she is using. Whereas faculty members using most methods feel some exclusive right to the materials they have developed (for example, a lecture or set of seminar questions) and have some reticence about using materials developed by other faculty members (with the exception of textbooks), case instructors typically use case studies that others have developed and feel honored if their case is being used by others. In many disciplines and fields of study (particularly business, law, and public administration), extensive collections of case studies are available. In some disciplines and at some collegiate institutions, publication of a case is considered just as prestigious as publication of a research report or scholarly journal article.

A fifth central feature of case methodology is also somewhat elusive. An effective case study destroys the traditional dichotomy between head and heart. It is truly an interactive method in that a student cannot sit back and speculate with detachment about alternative courses of action in a complex setting. Choices must be made; values, conceptual skills, and even intuition are put on the line. Many traditional-age students (eighteen to twenty-two years old) are uneasy when first confronting this aspect of case methodology. They are used to viewing the classroom as a world of ideas rather than as a world of decisions and actions. Case studies may be particularly appropriate in courses offered to undergraduates at the end of their academic careers. Case studies enable students to experience the "real world" of decision making and problem solving while the resources (and protective shield) of the academic institution are still available.

The Socratic method, like the case method, forces a student into making difficult decisions. In doing so, the student examines his or her own values, learns new conceptual skills, and gains experience in the acquisition and distillation of complex and often contradictory information. Although the Socratic method has been used primarily in legal education, it is potentially of value in virtually any discipline. The Socratic method, as it is used in most contemporary legal (and even philosophical) education, only vaguely resembles the educational methods used by Socrates. Whereas Socrates was the primary speaker (his educational method might be described as an interrupted monologue), the contemporary "Socratic" instructor primarily makes use of open-ended or leading questions to provoke discussion among students.

Typically, the instructor poses a particular problem at the start of a class session to which students are to respond. How would you solve this problem? Why would you solve it in this manner? The instructor then will either comment on or ask other students to comment on the strengths or flaws of this solution, will add something to the problem, or will change its character slightly so that students must reexamine the appropriateness of the principles they are applying in attempting to solve this problem.

A law instructor might begin by describing a particular auto accident in which one driver is clearly at fault. The case involves financial claims made by one of the parties. Students are to assume the role of judge or lawyer. They are asked to make a decision about fault and/or financial responsibility or to be the attorney for one or the other party. Specific principles of law can be applied to this case. The instructor may then add a complication to the case—for example, noting that the driver who was not at fault had been drinking before the accident. Students must now grapple with this somewhat more complex problem, to which simple and straightforward principles may not apply. Typically, the instructor continues in this way, adding various "complicating" conditions to the case and challenging the students to become problem analyzers and solvers rather than just the transmitters or enforcers of "black letter" law.

In a philosophy course, an instructor might similarly challenge students by asking them to examine their own simplistic solutions to particular philosophical problems. Philosophy professors often use the Socratic method in challenging a student's definition of *fact* or *truth*. They begin with a simple hypothetical situation in which a student is asked to determine whether something is "true" (for example, "Is it true that Columbus discovered America?"). The instructor may then challenge the students' response to this situation (for example, "What about the

Indians who met Columbus? Didn't they 'discover' America? There was no 'America' when Columbus landed on San Salvador Island. What, then, did Columbus discover? Columbus's name was actually Cristoforo Colombo. What does this imply about 'truth'?"). A student is asked to grapple with these complex conditions and, in doing so, to confront and perhaps modify his or her own conceptions of "truth."

The Socratic method is also appropriate in less obvious disciplines. A political science or economics professor might wish to use this method in helping a student develop critical appreciation of, or healthy skepticism toward, current public policy. A nursing instructor might use a Socratic dialogue to expand students' awareness of alternative approaches to patient care or the effect of certain public or hospital policies on patient care.

In-Class Discussion. A large class or one structured primarily around lectures and question-and-answer sessions need not exclude interaction-based methods. Two in-class discussion methods are particularly appropriate for use in conjunction with lectures and large classes—the "buzz group" and the "learning cell."

The buzz group (named for the sound generated by many people talking at once) enables members of a class to converse with one another and be heard and understood by at least a small number of student colleagues. Usually when a faculty member tries to elicit discussion in a large class or in a class that is accustomed to lecturing, most of the students are reticent to speak. No one wants to make a fool of himself in front of a large number of people. Hence, students may either remain quiet or risk a statement only when quite confident of its validity. Thus, discussions tend to be either nonexistent or mundane. Those remarks that are made tend to be directed primarily to the instructor (especially if he or she just finished lecturing). A few students may be quite active in classroom discussion, but their contributions are not always helpful, nor does their often indiscriminate participation tend to encourage the participation of other students.

If the class is periodically broken up into groups of six to

ten students, then discussion will take place. Students are more
likely to be verbally active in a small-group setting among their
peers. Furthermore, unorthodox ideas can be expressed in the
safe confines of the buzz group. These ideas will also be more
readily expressed before the whole class by a student representing the group, for this person is conveying the ideas of anony-
mous members of the group rather than necessarily his or her
own ideas. In a buzz group, each student has sufficient "air
time" to present his or her own opinions. If these ideas win the
day, this student will usually also have an opportunity to share
them with the whole class. The overall quality of classroom discussion is improved through the use of buzz groups. Usually
only the best or most interesting ideas are expressed when the
groups are asked to share their discussion outcomes. Mundane
or ill-formed ideas are generally ignored in brief reporting sessions.

Some faculty members find that buzz groups—or "cau-
cus" groups, to use a more respectable sounding term—are not
successful in eliciting discussion. This lack of success is often
due to one of several errors. First, the instructor might not have
made clear what is to be discussed in the buzz group. Students
should be given a particular question to answer, problem to
solve, or issue to discuss. One or more groups should be expected to report on the outcome of their discussion once the
total class has been reconvened. If a group knows it might be
chosen, the discussion is likely to remain focused and directly
related to the topic at hand.

Second, the buzz group might have been convened for
too long. In most instances, buzz groups should meet for no
more than ten or fifteen minutes. If a narrow topic is being addressed and the group is small, that should be sufficient time. If
the topic is particularly complex, the total class might convene
after fifteen minutes, with one or more buzz groups reporting
on the outcomes of their discussion up to that point. With the
best ideas from several groups in mind, the buzz groups would
then reconvene for another ten to fifteen minutes of discussion.
In any one-hour class period, buzz groups might meet for two
fifteen-minute periods, each period being followed by a ten-

minute report from several groups and a five-minute summary or new statement of the question, problem, or issue by the instructor.

Third, some faculty members run into logistic problems and related time problems. Buzz groups are assigned to adjacent classrooms or to other areas of the building. Hence, a great deal of time is lost in moving from place to place. Continuity is disrupted and confusion prevails. These difficulties can be eliminated by having all the buzz groups meet in the same classroom. The room may be noisy, and students may initially have a hard time hearing one another; however, they soon learn how to attend. The noise level often adds excitement to the discussion. Students overhear other discussions and fragments of discussions, which leads to broader perspectives and adds continuity. The one prerequisite to using buzz groups in a single classroom is the portability of chairs. Students must be able to draw into small circles, yet also be able to face the front of the classroom for general discussion. Buzz groups are hard to conduct when chairs are bolted to the floor or must not be moved because of administrative policy.

Fourth, a faculty member may not have tried the buzz group a sufficient number of times before abandoning it. Students are not accustomed to this mode of instruction and hence are often uncomfortable in talking with fellow students in small groups. Furthermore, students (and the faculty member) may have to try buzz groups several times before these groups work smoothly. After three or four buzz-group sessions, new buzz groups can usually be formed and underway in less than two minutes. The efficiency of buzz groups can be further increased by keeping membership in each buzz group constant. Each group of students always sits together (highly efficient but a bit regimented) or has its own place in the room. In the latter case, members of a group move to chairs in their designated place whenever buzz groups are convened.

Several variations on the buzz group have been successfully employed. Each buzz group can be assigned a particular school of thought or person in history. Whenever the class breaks into buzz groups, each group must tackle the question, problem, or issue being posed by the instructor from the perspective of this particular school of thought or person. This technique is particularly effective when used in conjunction with faculty role playing (discussed later).

Another variation on the buzz group is the "fishbowl," in which one buzz group works on a question, problem, or issue while another observes without making comments. After a short period (ten to fifteen minutes), the observing group members are asked to make comments on the observed group's discussion. These comments might focus on the content of the discussion or the way the group approached the question, problem, or issue. Sometimes feedback is given to the total buzz group being observed. In other instances, the feedback is given by individual members of the group that is observing to individual members of the group being observed. Usually, the two groups will switch places during a second buzz-group session.

A third alternative use of the buzz group involves the selection of different, though interrelated, topics of discussion for each buzz group and the structuring of relationships between buzz groups. This alternative moves classroom discussion toward the simulation mode. The total class is given the task of generating solutions to a particular problem described by the instructor. One set of buzz groups (approximately two thirds of the groups) works on the outer ring of the classroom, generating alternative solutions to the problem. At the same time, one buzz group situated in the middle of the room defines a set of criteria for evaluating solutions. A third set of buzz groups is given the task of determining strategies whereby they can select the best solution generated by the outer groups and sell this idea to the inner group. This third set of buzz groups is located between the inner and outer groups.

Each buzz group first meets for fifteen minutes. Then members of the outer group present their ideas to one or more of the middle groups for fifteen minutes. The approach to be taken is determined by members of the outer and middle groups. While this is going on, the inner group decides how it will conduct the review of proposals. At the start of a third fifteen-minute period, each middle group presents to the inner group the best of the solutions it has received from the outer groups, some combination of solutions recommended by several of the outer groups, or its own solution. The inner group then judges the worth of each solution, using the criteria it has established. A general classroom discussion follows, focusing systematically on each stage of the problem-solving process. A similar buzz-group variant is offered by Charles Wales and Robert Stager in their "Guided Design" method (Barnes-McConnell, 1978, pp. 84-87). In small groups, students work their way through an organized set of decision-making steps that are arranged hierarchically and lead the students to the resolution of a real-life problem.

A learning cell, like the buzz group, relies heavily on peer learning. It differs from a buzz group in that the method is used to facilitate not small-group discussions but rather the sharing of information among two persons or two or more groups of people. The usual learning cell consists of two persons, each of whom has been given responsibility for learning a different set of information. During class (or during a special session), the two students meet together as a learning cell to share information and, at times, to test each other on acquisition of this information. This sharing of information among students, based on selective reading by each student, is often done informally outside the classroom when students form their own study groups, each member of the group taking primary responsibility for one section of the course material to be covered. The learning cell legitimizes this sharing of ideas and brings it into the classroom.

A learning cell can be justified on several grounds. First, many faculty members confront students with the ambitious goal of gaining some knowledge in a large number of areas and extensive knowledge in one or two areas. A learning cell fits nicely with this model. A student will become quite knowledgeable in one or more areas. By teaching another student about what he or she has learned, this student will gain even greater mastery of this area. In other areas, the student will acquire more limited knowledge. Information acquired from a student colleague will be screened through this second student's own value system, experiences, and so on. Given the probable compatibility between these two students' values and experiences, this screening process is usually appropriate, and the material being presented is relevant to the learner student's own interests.

Learning cells can also be justified as vehicles for interaction and exchange of ideas. Each student has a chance to discuss and clarify ideas with a colleague. In this way, the learning cell serves a comparable function to the buzz group.

Third, the learning cell allows for alternative modes of testing. The "teacher" in a learning cell can be asked to draft a set of questions that will be given to the "learner." The teacher will be graded on the basis of the questions he or she asks and the learner's success in answering these questions. This form of grading reinforces cooperation rather than competition and constantly focuses on the learning of both students.

Several variations on the regular learning cell can be noted. First, a learning cell can be constituted of more than two persons. For instance, it may have the same number of members as the major textbook for a course has chapters. The learning cell thus becomes a "human textbook." Each student reads the entire textbook but concentrates on one chapter, doing additional reading, meeting with members of other learning cells who have been assigned the same chapter, and meeting with the instructor for formal help sessions. When any member of the learning cell has problems with a particular chapter, he or she obtains assistance from the cell's "expert" on this chapter. At the end of the term, when students are reviewing for the final exam, each learning-cell member assumes responsibility for leading his or her colleagues through a review of his or her particular chapter. The final grade for each student might be based in part on the performance of other members of the learning cell on items related to his or her chapter.

Another learning-cell model is similar to one noted above with reference to buzz groups. Each member of the cell is assigned a different school of thought or historical person. Whenever the learning cell meets to study a particular topic, each member of the cell has the task of determining how his or her assigned school of thought or person would relate to this topic.

A third alternative blends the learning-cell and case-study

methods. Each member of a learning cell is assigned the task of
acquiring knowledge in a particular area related to the topic of
the course or of representing a particular discipline in addressing
the interdisciplinary topic of the course. The learning cell meets
as a case study group each week to discuss and analyze one case.
Each member of the learning cell contributes not only in a general way to the group discussion but also specifically with reference to his or her area of expertise or perspective.

Both the buzz group and learning cell encourage extensive interaction in the classroom. Although neither method demands the subtle skills of a case study or Socratic dialogue, they
both can be deceptive in terms of design and execution—in other
words, they may require more work and have more pitfalls than
one might expect. Faculty members may wish to work with colleagues when first making use of these methods. A joint sharing
of problems and observations of each other's classroom can be
of significant value when buzz groups and learning cells are used.

Simulations. Although this instructional method is classi-
cally rooted in the ancient games of Greece and medieval Eur-
ope (see Huizinga, 1955) as well as, more recently, the war
games of nineteenth-century Prussia, its use in undergraduate
education is contemporary and growing. In the past decade, the
number of simulations and instructional games available for collegiate use in a variety of disciplines has at least doubled, as evidenced by the increase in collegiate listings of instructional
simulations between the second (Zuckerman and Horn, 1973)
and third (Horn, 1977) editions of *The Guide to Simulations.*
Possibly as a result of the press by students for more social relevance or more practicality, collegiate faculty members are beginning to make more extensive use of simulations and instructional games as a means of more effectively integrating action
and thought: "Jean Piaget has said, 'Knowledge is not a copy of
reality. To know an object is to act on it. To know is to modify,
to transform the object, and to understand the process of this
transformation, and as a consequence to understand the way
the object is constructed. An operation is thus the essence of
knowledge, it is an internalized action that modifies the object
of knowledge.' He adds, 'Intelligence is born of action' and

'Anything is only understood to the extent that it is reinvented.' People in daily life constantly invent and reinvent situations in order to learn from them. Yet too often people fail to recognize that reinventing a situation in which one has been an actor and perhaps reliving or revising decisions made is, in effect, to play a game" (Abt, 1970, p. 12).

The term *simulation* is elusive and has been used in a variety of ways, particularly in an instructional context. Most theorists and practitioners of instructional simulations would probably agree that a simulation is a representation of some real-world event or setting in a reduced or modified form. This form (the simulation design) highlights certain features of this event or setting in a manner that is economical, reproducible, and/or safe, yet also dynamic and involving (Raser, 1969; Rockler, 1978). A simulation is always at least one step removed from the real world. This distance enables students to risk new behavior and learn from their successes and mistakes in a supportive environment. A simulation also enables students to observe certain phenomena in an environment that is simpler than that found in the real world and has been designed specifically to illuminate or reveal these phenomena.

Simulations may or may not be based on competition and may or may not involve gaming (Shirts, 1972). Most instructionally oriented simulations (as opposed to those used primarily for research purposes) require some form of competition and gaming as a means of involving students more fully in the exercise. Although the designers of simulations have begun to emphasize noncompetitive learning and cooperative instructional games, the terms *simulation, game,* and *contest* can usually be used interchangeably in instructional settings.

An important distinction, however, can be drawn between simulations and role playing. In a simulation, the setting is artificial, but the people who are participating in the simulation are being themselves. Most instructional simulations teach people about what it is like to operate within a certain social structure or physical environment. People are asked to be themselves and do the best job possible, often under difficult circumstances, in relating to other people, making decisions, or performing certain skills. By contrast, in a role play, the setting is real, but people are not being themselves. The role player is expected to relate to other people, make decisions, or perform skilled tasks in a way that is prescribed or at least suggested by the role rather than by his or her own predilections. When both the setting and people are artificial, then "drama" exists, whereas, by definition, if both the setting and participants are real, then the "real world" exists.

A simulation, therefore, involves the design of an artificial situation in which "real people" are placed to act in a realistic manner. This artificial setting may be a simulated classroom, corporate boardroom, or sixteenth-century courtroom. Often a simulation is designed in such a way that one or two of the participants are placed at the center of action, with other participants playing supporting roles. The central players usually work at the "eye of the hurricane" with very little guidance. The central figure may be a school principal, chairman of a corporate board, church leader, or parent in a simulated family. Such simulations often resemble drama or role playing. In other simulations, each participant is given the same amount of information, the same goals, and the same opportunity to achieve these goals. This type of simulation tends to be more "gaming" than the first type. The real world rarely provides as equitable a chance for all people to succeed as does this type of simulation. The first type is often more realistic and hence more frustrating and instructive.

A major decision regarding simulations for many faculty members is whether to use existing designs and/or materials or to produce new ones (or both). In many fields, simulations exist in abundance. They are extensively documented in several publications (Horn, 1977; Stadsklev, 1975; Twelker, 1969; Zuckerman and Horn, 1973). Many of these simulations should be pilot-tested with colleagues or student volunteers before use in the classroom, for they vary widely in quality.

Currently, three kinds of simulations are used for instructional purposes: (1) in-basket, (2) hands-on, and (3) computer-mediated. The in-basket simulation is widely used in undergraduate and graduate business education but is potentially of great value in other areas of study as well. During an in-basket simulation, a student (or group of students) is presented with a problem to solve or decision to make (from the "in-basket"). Once the problem is solved or the decision is made (and placed in the "out-basket"), another problem or decision is posed for individual or group consideration, followed by yet another problem or decision, and so forth. Often, as in a Socratic dialogue, the problems or decisions are initially elementary and easily addressed, through the straightforward application of existing principles, policies, or laws.

Time is often an important factor in an in-basket simulation. Students are given a limited amount of time to consider a certain number of in-basket problems or requests for decisions. Like the case-study method, an in-basket simulation forces an individual or group to make a decision, take action, or select among several alternative solutions under realistic conditions. An in-basket simulation is the easiest type of simulation to design and conduct and requires the least amount of hardware.

"Hands-on" simulations have been so named by computer-simulation practitioners because these simulations require the manipulation of objects without computer mediation. Most board-game simulations and simulations that require a significant amount of interaction between players in a game format are of this type. Typically, the players are placed in some simulated environment in which they are to survive and to achieve some prescribed outcomes. There is not the level of detachment that is usually found in an in-basket simulation. The player does not merely solve a problem: he or she is living with or in the problem or is part of the problem. Decisions are not placed in an out-basket; they are lived out in a "hands-on" simulation: the player must live with the consequences of the decisions being made. Most commercially available simulations are of the hands-on variety. Typically, this type of simulation requires more preparation than the in-basket type and yields (for good or ill) more affectively charged learning than either in-basket or computer-mediated simulations.

Computerized simulations are only now beginning to come into prominence in undergraduate educational settings, having previously been used primarily in research settings. A student (or group of students) is presented, by means of the computer, with a problem to be solved or decision to be made (as in the in-basket simulation). Various factors regarding the problem or decision are also presented to the student or are at least programmed into the computer. Once the decision has been made or the problem solved, the student's response is recorded in the computer. At this point, the full instructional power of the computer becomes evident. The consequences of the student's actions are traced out by the computer and fed back to the student. The student may then change the decision or solution or move on to another problem. Frequently the computer will be programmed to show the student in a graphic manner how this decision or solution affects a variety of other parts of the environment or system being simulated. Interactive terminals and computer graphics have made computer simulations even more instructive and engaging.

Computer simulations are widely available for use in the biological and physical sciences and engineering. The computer is being used to teach principles of ecology, Newtonian physics, and the design of water-treatment systems. The computer could also be used more extensively to simulate complex social environments and even human thought. Many faculty members are beginning to make use of the computer for recordkeeping, test scoring, and programmed instruction (see discussion earlier in this chapter), but its use as a simulator may ultimately be of greatest importance.

If a faculty member decides to design his or her own simulation, then a fair amount of time needs to be set aside for this design process. Horn (1973) suggests a nine-step procedure: (1) define the problem area to be simulated, (2) define the objective and scope of the simulation, (3) define the people and organizations involved, (4) define the motives and purposes of the players, (5) define the resources available to the players, (6) determine the transactions to be simulated and the decision rules to be followed, (7) formulate the evaluation method (how "success" in the simulation is to be defined), (8) develop a simulation/game prototype, and (9) try out and modify the prototype. Although these steps provide valuable guidelines for the novice designer, they tend to be too linear and oriented toward social science simulations. Many simulation designers "play" with the design for a while and let the objectives emerge in a more spontaneous manner. Other designers emphasize the structures of the simulated setting and let the motivations of the players emanate from this structure.

Most simulation designers, however, would seem to agree on two issues: (1) one can best learn about design from actually playing a variety of games and participating in a variety of simulations, and (2) all new simulations should be tested when still an idea and in operation with colleagues, "friendly" students, relatives, and so forth before being used in the classroom. *Jabberwockey* (Washburn, 1971), a simulation on the design of simulations, can be particularly effective in helping a group of faculty members enter into the design process.

In making use of simulations, some instructors focus on the design and implementation of the game without giving adequate consideration to the discussion and reaction session that should follow the game. At least a third as much time is usually devoted to the "debriefing" of a simulation as went into the playing of it. Thus, a three-hour simulation would be followed by at least a one-hour discussion. This session enables the faculty member to defuse the feelings that are generated by the simulation as well as clarify student learnings from the event and consider the application of these learnings in other settings. Because a simulation often focuses on the impact of systems and settings on behavior, the emotions generated by a simulation become important grist for the mill. A simulation participant who experiences profound anger at the behavior of another participant should examine structures of the simulation that precipitated this behavior, the existence of similar structures in "real" settings, and how such anger can best be confronted in these real settings. This type of learning can be significant and far-reaching.

Role Playing. Like simulations, role playing involves artificiality—though, as noted above, the actor rather than the setting is in some sense artificial. Whether a student or faculty

member, the role player assumes a new persona, representing
ideas, perspectives, or interests of a particular person in history.
The role player tries in some way to get into the heart and head
of the person being represented. Whereas one need only understand a particular point of view in order to be able to effectively
represent it in a debate, the role player must be able to empa-
thize with, as well as understand, the point of view of the person being represented.

In some instances, a faculty member may wish to play a
role in order to convey more vividly and accurately something
about a particular person or point of view being studied by his
or her students. A faculty member need not become overly dramatic in this endeavor. Costumes are not needed. The faculty
member need not emulate the mannerisms of the person being
represented or the speaker's accent, favorite phrases, or typical
mode of instruction. Only the spirit and perspective of this person need be captured.

Typically, a faculty member will begin by briefly describing a particular school of thought or historical context and
will then describe the person to be role-played and explain the
reason for selecting this person. The faculty member indicates
that he or she will temporarily "become" this person and answer students' questions as the person probably would respond.
Students should be reminded on occasion that this is a role play
and told that sufficient time will be set aside at the end of the
role play to discuss the merits of the case being made by the
person being role-played. The primary objective of any role play
should not be to determine whether the person being role-
played is "right" or "wrong," but rather to acquire a deeper
appreciation and understanding of this person's point of
view.

The simple act of shifting from a lecture about a person
or idea to a role play in which this person or idea is being represented firsthand can greatly enhance a presentation and enliven
the interaction between students and faculty. As a rule, students are more likely to interact actively and creatively with a
faculty member and to take risks if the faculty member is in
role. As in faculty-centered debates and team teaching, students

also can observe and model the faculty member in his or her efforts to fully appreciate a particular point of view before attempting to critically analyze it.

As noted above, role playing can serve as an effective adjunct to team teaching. Two or more faculty members can each
adopt a different role and then engage in a debate or symposium. This approach is particularly valuable if faculty members
take several minutes after the debate or symposium to reflect
on and discuss their individual roles and relationships with the
other role players. This follow-up discussion is often of greater
value than the actual role play. Students should be actively involved in this discussion, describing what they observed about
the interaction between faculty role players. How did the position espoused by each faculty role player change as a function
of specific interactions with other role players? What docs this
indicate about the point of view being represented by each role
player?

Students also benefit from assuming roles and playing
them out in the classroom. In a seminar on psychobiography,
for instance, each student is asked to present a psychologically
based history of a famous person (for example, Woodrow Wilson or Mahatma Gandhi) from a first-person perspective. The
presenter becomes Wilson or Gandhi, conveying something
about this man's personal history and the impact of this history
on the real-life decisions made and actions taken. The student
role player answers questions from other students and faculty
members from the perspective of the person being played.

During part of the discussion period each week, all students in the course take on the roles of the persons they are
studying and interact with one another in these roles. Thus, if a
particular seminar session focuses on Gandhi, the student playing Wilson might comment on Gandhi's life and contributions as
Wilson might have done. Another student who is studying Martin Luther might similarly comment on Gandhi's life from Luther's perspective. Time should be set aside at the end of the
seminar for general discussion of the seminar and Gandhi's life
and actions. Students should drop their roles during this final
session. This debriefing session is even more critical than in fac-

ulty role playing. The debriefing time is needed to gain perspective on what occurred during the seminar and to defuse any feelings that might have been aroused.

This approach to role playing can be used in a variety of disciplines. An English literature course might be conducted with students playing various roles in a particular novel or representing different schools of literary analysis or different authors. What, for instance, might Shakespeare have to say about the work of James Joyce?

Role playing by either faculty or students holds several advantages over other instructional methods. First, role plays are inherently interesting. One has only to witness the success of Steve Allen's *Meeting of the Minds* on the Public Broadcasting System. This program would probably be rather dull for most listeners if it were no more than a discussion of various topics from the viewpoint of several historical persons. By "embodying" people who represent different ideas, Steve Allen's colleagues infuse the program with unpredictability and insight. This involves more than "good theater" (though the Allen players do wear costumes and use some props). The players must know the ideas and perspectives of the persons they are roleplaying—which brings us to the second advantage of role playing.

Role playing is a highly motivating, educational enterprise for students. When given the assignment of "getting inside" a particular historical figure, students often are inspired and enthusiastic. They are likely to do more background research if asked to play the role of a particular person than if asked only to report on this person's ideas. Furthermore, because the student may have to confront situations that were never posed for the person being role-played or respond to questions to which the role-played person's answers were never recorded, the student must study not only the content of the role-played person's pronouncements but also the person's general perspectives and attitudes, a valuable exercise for any of us living in a complex and changing world.

Role playing holds yet another advantage. It encourages interaction between students. Many students feel safer in the formal exchange of ideas in a classroom when playing a role than when being themselves. The shy or reticent student can often be encouraged to participate in a classroom discussion when given the role of a person who has a perspective that is rather uncomplicated yet relevant to many topics being addressed in the classroom.

When performed by the faculty member, a role play provides variation in the usual classroom presentation and enables the faculty member to explore and speculate on the ideas of the person being role-played without always having to qualify the statements being made ("Freud might have said this, given these circumstances . . ."). Furthermore, the role-playing instructor holds the opportunity of eliciting the full-blown imagination of his students. With minimal costume or scenery, the instructor can turn the classroom into a sixteenth-century studio or a nineteenth-century chemistry laboratory. In this setting, an instructor can explore many dimensions of another person's life and works in interaction with his or her students. This is possible with very few other instructional methods.

Student-Based

Tutorials/Independent Study. Most colleges and universities offer some form of individualized instruction that is responsive to the diverse needs, interests, and competencies of students. In both tutorials and independent study programs, the student is periodically given the full attention of a faculty member (or graduate assistant, instructor, or tutor). The faculty member tailors his or her role, expectations, and resources to this individual student.

Both the tutorial and independent study methods start with a "contracting" phase, during which the faculty member assesses and critiques the student's interests or needs, and written and/or oral plans for the tutorial or independent study program are formulated. Although this initial "contracting" phase may be quite short, it differentiates these two methods from either content-based or interaction-based methods. A faculty member cannot enter into either a tutorial or an independent study program with a totally planned agenda or design. The student must be actively involved in the decision-making processes if the tutorial or independent study program is to be successful.

Tutorials typically differ from independent study programs in four important ways. First, tutorials focus on acquisition of a body of knowledge or skills, whereas independent study programs usually focus on production of a written or oral report, term paper, essay, journal, or research project, which grows out of a variety of learning experiences, readings, and/or field experiences. An independent study frequently increases the learner's freedom, while a tutorial is most often controlled by the instructor.

Second, tutorials usually involve close and regular monitoring of student progress, whereas independent study programs generally are supervised less intensively and may even be sporadic in regard to supervision.

Third, tutorials generally require that the faculty member or tutor serve as the primary resource person to the student. This method is student-based in that the tutor will tailor the approach and presentation to the student's immediate and personal needs. However, in the actual processes of the tutorial, the faculty member or tutor may resemble a content-based instructor—lecturing, questioning, answering questions, and testing for the acquisition of specific content. By contrast, the independent study method more closely resembles interaction-based instruction. The faculty member helps the student grapple with a particular problem and, in doing so, serves as a facilitator of the student's exploration. The instructor may even join the student in this exploration of a new domain of knowledge, creating a mutual, peerlike learning environment.

A fourth difference between tutorials and independent study programs concerns their common uses. Whereas tutorials have been used in recent years primarily to assist students who are having problems in completing their academic work, independent studies are more frequently offered to students with excellent academic records who have exhibited self-discipline and motivation. Faculty members often use independent study designations to individualize the curriculum and to accommodate a diversity of learner needs, interests, abilities, and schedules. The one-to-one relationship established through independent study often enhances the quality of the undergraduate experience, providing for personal time and attention to be given to the student. Further, self-directed learning skills are reinforced through independent study.

Regardless of their differences, the tutorial and independent study methods are often considered to be the same among faculty members. They are the primary means by which the individual differences of undergraduate students have been addressed by American colleges and universities over the past two centuries.

Learning Contracts. Although the independent study and tutorial methods are responsive to students' interests and immediate needs, they may not be of maximum educational benefit to students over the long run, for they often fail to take into account a student's current status and educational goals. Independent study programs usually focus on the student's production of a particular report rather than the student's learning in producing the report. The tutorial does focus on student learning, but it tends to focus on short-term learning goals without reference to how these goals relate to longer-term educational needs. A learning contract enables a faculty member and student to jointly explore the student's past learning, his or her long-term educational goals, the extent to which the gap between current levels of learning or competencies and desired levels can and should be reduced or eliminated, the resources available to the student for achieving the desired levels, and the means by which the student can progress toward the desired levels.

A wide variety of learning-contract procedures are being used in American undergraduate education. Most, however, share certain common properties. Clark (1978a, p. 213), for instance, provides a summary description of the learning-contract procedure that applies to most colleges and universities using this method:

The contract process is one in which two individuals, a faculty member and a student, negotiate about teaching and learning. The process begins with a discussion of who the student is, what the student's goals and objectives are, why the student wants to study particular content and skill areas, how the learning will be accomplished, what resources will be employed, how the learning will be evaluated, and how much credit will be awarded. Similarly, the faculty member indicates what expertness he or she possesses, the alternative ways in which the learning can be accomplished, alternative resources that may be employed, and what level of student performance is expected. The process assumes that there are two active participants, not an active teacher and a passive student. This transaction between student and faculty member is the essential component of contracting.

The outcome of this process is a written agreement, usually called the learning contract. Although institutional practices vary somewhat, most learning contracts have four parts; these are descriptions of (1) the student's long-range purposes, goals, or objectives; (2) the student's specific objectives for the period of time in which the particular contract is in effect; (3) the learning activities in which the student will engage, including a description of the content and/or skills to be mastered and the mode of study to be employed, a designation of what learning resources will be used, and the amount of credit the institution will award upon satisfactory completion of the learning activities; and (4) the methods and criteria or standards that will be used to evaluate the student's performance.

Learning-contract procedures incorporate several basic steps. They begin with some assessment of the student's past learning. Typically, a set of learning categories is identified. These categories may encompass a set of skills, several areas of knowledge, or a set of roles or job functions. In each of these categories the student's current level is assessed. For example, if the categories are skill-based, the student's past experiences in learning how to write, perform mathematical computations, and apply critical thinking might be assessed. What has the student been exposed to inside and outside formal educational institutions that has aided in the acquisition of writing, mathematical, and critical-thinking skills?

Some learning contracts focus on assessment of current levels of competency rather than past experiences. How competent is the student in the areas of writing, mathematical computation, and critical thinking? These competencies might be assessed by means of performance tests, demonstrations, documentation, or self-appraisals.

The student and faculty member next turn to an identification of learning goals. Using the same categories as in the assessment of current status, they identify and clarify the student's learning goals. The student asks: What must I learn in each of these areas to be successful in my chosen field? Given my life or career plans, which categories are most important to me and which are least important? When I confront the problems and challenges that will face me at particular points in my future, what skills, knowledge, or attitudes are going to be most important? Given my unique strengths and weaknesses, which categories are in need of greatest learning and development?

The stage is now set for formulation of a learning contract between the faculty member and student, based on jointly identified gaps between current and desired states. The faculty member and student identify realistic goals for narrowing or eliminating the gap between current and desired learning levels. No one learning contract (or course) will address, let alone eliminate, all gaps. An effective learning contract will reduce or eliminate some of the learning gaps; the immediate interests and resources of both the student and teacher will determine which ones. Other learning contracts will help fill other gaps.

Among traditional students a learning contract is often offered at the end of their academic career. The learning contract is used, in this instance, to ensure that any deficiencies in the student's educational experiences at the college or university are addressed and (ideally) corrected. When used as a terminal educational resource for students, a learning contract should be responsive to all or most of the "learning gaps," for the student will have no other opportunity in this educational institution to respond to these gaps. Alternatively, the student will be given direct assistance with one or more of the gaps and additional assistance in planning for ways in which the other gaps might be narrowed or eliminated after graduation. This latter approach acknowledges that the student is (or should be) a "lifelong learner" who need not meet all desired competency levels while a student.

Having identified realistic goals for a learning contract, the student and faculty member turn to the identification of resources that are available to the student for achieving these goals. Educational resources that are identified may reside primarily in the head of the faculty member, in which case the learning contract will resemble a carefully conceived tutorial. The resources might instead reside primarily in the student and be engaged primarily through the student's active involvement in a particular project. The learning contract may then closely resemble a carefully conceived independent study program.

Often the resources will reside elsewhere in the academic community (other faculty members, other students, books, ongoing campus activities, formal classroom events) or off campus. The faculty member not only helps the student identify relevant resources but also links the student with these resources (telephone calls, letters of reference, institutional funds to support services rendered by the resource, and so on). The faculty member will assist a student in sequencing the use of resources and in preparing the student for the most effective and efficient use of these resources and also help the student determine whether the resources are being properly used.

A faculty member who employs a learning contract usually assists in the evaluation of the educational resources being used and of the student's overall educational experiences under this learning contract. The faculty member will help the student assess levels of competency or learning levels at the end of the project and/or at several points during the learning-contract period to determine the extent to which the learning gaps have been filled. A faculty member often will help the student assess what has been learned about the learning processes and perhaps reassess learning goals or current levels of learning.

With the completion of the learning contract, the student should have successfully reduced or eliminated gaps between current and desired levels in certain of the learning categories. The contract represents an agreement between the faculty member and student that both are accountable for progress toward the student's identified educational goals. Neither party to this contract is solely responsible for the achievement of these goals, and both parties must be held partly responsible for failure to achieve them. A learning contract requires mature interpersonal relationships and educational commitments by both the student and faculty member. Many students (and faculty members) are not prepared to enter into this type of relationship and commitment; hence the learning contract must be used selectively.

A learning contract can be responsive to a variety of student needs and interests. An individualized learning contract will take on one of many forms and structures and encompass a variety of instructional modes (including lectures and seminars), on the basis of the student's and faculty member's assessment of the most appropriate educational resources for the student's achievement of desired educational goals.

Field Placements. Learning contracts provide undergraduate students with linkages to resources throughout the educational community and off campus. Although the learning contract will usually provide diverse experiences that relate directly to a varied set of needs, undergraduate students will sometimes benefit more from a single, intensive field experience that provides continuity and gives the student a sense of accomplishment, much as a successfully completed independent study project does.

Some field experiences are "sheltered"—that is, they give students a taste of the "real world" and yet restrict the number and type of problems confronted by the student in the field experience. A sheltered field experience might take place through an on-campus internship. A business major, for instance, might serve as administrative assistant to an academic department chairperson, or an education major might serve in a staff capacity to a collegewide curriculum committee. A sheltered field experience might instead be set up off campus with an employer/supervisor who is committed to (and perhaps even paid for) the learning of the student. Nursing students are typically placed in this type of sheltered environment when first working in a hospital or clinic.

A "nonsheltered" real-world field placement may be helpful at the end of a student's academic career. It provides an opportunity for the student to pull together a variety of skills, areas of knowledge, and attitudes. The "real world" placement might instead be offered at the start of the student's undergraduate experience, serving as a wilderness experience in which the student is challenged to use existing knowledge and skills and to gain self-reliance and self-confidence. If a student is plunged into a real-life field placement as an orienting experience, then extensive debriefing should follow this placement, and the student should receive adequate peer and supervisory support while in the real-life setting.

In aiding a student through field placement, a faculty member will often have to learn new skills in order to work with the student in a domain that is not of the faculty member's own making. The instructor must be able to anticipate and tolerate unpredictable events and must be able to assist students in extracting new learnings from even the most complex and difficult situation. Just as the interaction-based instructor will use the case method to show students how to solve complex problems, so will the field-placement instructor help students confront complex situations by using problem-solving and interpersonal skills. Faculty development is often required not only to promote this facilitation of student learning in complex settings but also to enhance the faculty member's knowledge of the problems confronted by his or her students in the field placement.

Student-Generated Courses. The tutorial, independent study, learning-contract, and field-placement methods are usually employed outside the formal classroom; a fourth student-based method, the student-generated course, often makes extensive use of the classroom. This classroom, however, is more responsive to the individual and immediate needs of students than it usually is. Student-generated courses may be of three types: initiated by students but led by a faculty member, initiated by a faculty member but led by students, and initiated and led by students.

During the late 1960s and early 1970s, many colleges and universities provided opportunities for students to suggest and even provide design ideas for courses that were to be taught by faculty members. The students often helped select teachers for these courses, though faculty members had the right to refuse this offer. At the University of Oregon, a program entitled "SEARCH" was inaugurated during the late 1960s. It enabled students to propose specific courses and recruit faculty members to teach them. SEARCH courses could be taken for academic credit, though few of these courses were offered during any one term.

Even if students in the early 1980s may be less inclined to control the curriculum of their colleges and universities, there may be room for courses that directly and sensitively respond to their changing needs and concerns. If students are given the opportunity to select the themes for new courses, this curricular responsiveness may be increased. Student-initiated courses give faculty members an excellent opportunity to teach in new areas that directly reflect student interest.

Courses that are initiated by faculty members but taught by students have been offered by undergraduate institutions for many years. They provide exceptional students with an opportunity to meet a challenging teaching assignment, thereby increasing their interest in the knowledge they acquire from the college or university. The faculty-initiated/student-taught course also provides students taking the course with untapped resources (their peers) and helps a college or university expand its range of curricular offerings.

Typically, advanced or honors students are given the opportunity to teach part of a course (perhaps two or three lectures) or to work with one section of a large, introductory course. In other cases, a student might coteach with a faculty member. St. Andrews Presbyterian College (N.C.), for instance, offers highly qualified sophomore students an opportunity to coteach with a faculty member in its freshman core program. Because, as sophomores, these coteachers have themselves just finished the freshman program, they can be a valuable resource to the faculty member in fine-tuning the freshman program to meet the needs of entering St. Andrews students and can be empathetic and knowledgeable resources to freshmen as they confront the new collegiate environment.

Students may be given sole responsibility for teaching a course initiated by faculty members. Foreign students, for instance, are sometimes asked to teach language courses or courses in the history or culture of their homeland. Students returning from an extensive field placement (for example, in a foreign country, on an Indian reservation, or in a corporation) are asked to teach a course based on their experience. A special honors program might be established that identifies exceptional students each year who are given an opportunity to teach a course (for example, in the freshman core) related to an area of personal interest and competence.

The third type of student-generated course harks back to the late 1960s, when a number of courses and even entire academic programs were initiated and conducted by students. These "free universities" were an extreme and culminating outcome of the movement toward increased student autonomy and curricular control. Throughout the United States, free universities sprang up with or without formal institutional affiliation or sanction. Students (and other community people) established curriculums and conducted courses on a variety of topics. Some free universities were free only in terms of the spirit of the program. Students had to pay tuition, just as in a private college. Concerns about finances, facilities, and faculty soon forced many of these free universities into a state of premature respectability, which, along with increased or renewed student concern for credit hours and credentials, led to their demise.

Although the free-university movement often yielded bizarre and counterproductive results, it is a shame that significant learning from this movement was lost in the countermovement back to more traditional educational models. The free-university movement, for instance, provided its "faculty members" with invaluable experiences in curricular planning, management, marketing, and teaching. Few colleges provide students with this type of practical (yet sheltered) experience.

Rather than let the valuable lessons of the late 1960s pass us by, we should instead seek to identify those attributes of the free-university movement that are appropriate to our current educational institutions and those types of learning that are particularly responsive to the unique educational needs of college students today. Any method of instruction might benefit from such an examination.

Assessment

The assessment of student performance provides a bridge between the procedural and outcome dimensions of the undergraduate curriculum, for both the modes of teaching and crediting, on the one hand, and desired outcomes of the instructional process, on the other hand, help to define the appropriate use of assessment procedures. Currently, at least seven types of assessment are used in American undergraduate educational institutions, the first three being by far the most prevalent: (1) closed-ended written tests, (2) open-ended written tests, (3) presentation of academic products, (4) behavioral performance tests, (5) observation of or reflection on performance in the field, (6) systematic documentation of achievement, and (7) global assessment.

Closed-Ended Written Tests. Probably the most commonly used method for assessing student acquisition of specific information is the multiple-choice test, other common methods being true/false, item-matching, and fill-in. Considerable attention has recently been given to improving the design and use of these closed-ended methods (closed-ended in the sense that there are correct and incorrect answers to each question on the test). Faculty members have been encouraged to write test questions that are free of ambiguity or contradictions, to select alternative test-item responses that are not obviously false, and to identify test items that assess student performance at higher levels of Bloom and others' (1956) taxonomy (analysis, synthesis, and evaluation).

Multiple-choice items have often been improved by providing students with a brief case statement (one or two paragraphs) followed by four or five alternative responses to the problem posed in the case. Rather than selecting one "correct" response to the case, students might be asked to evaluate the relative "correctness" of each response (on a five- or seven-point scale or on a ranking basis) and to write a brief argument for their decisions. Payne (1968) makes a number of other valuable suggestions for the improvement of multiple-choice tests as well as other closed-ended tests. Levine (1978, pp. 82-83) summarizes these suggestions and notes several of the advantages and disadvantages of multiple-choice tests:

The advantages of multiple-choice tests are that (1) they are fast and easy to administer; (2) the odds of success at guessing answers are lower than true/false tests; (3) they are easy to grade; (4) they can be returned quickly in large classes, and (5) they are useful in testing facts, dates, and definitions. The disadvantages of multiple-choice tests are that (1) they are poor at testing conceptual learning, integration of knowledge, and complex skills; (2) they reward clever guessing; (3) they are time-consuming to construct and the product is often poor; (4) finding four or more plausible answers for each question is frequently difficult; (5) they can be confusing or misleading owing to extraneous information or cues in the questions; and (6) they are inefficient in contrast to other short-answer tests because they require much reading, which serves to limit the number of questions that can be asked in a fixed period of time.

A frequent variation on the true/false test is a request for the student to correct any "false" statement so that it becomes a "true" or to indicate why the statement is false. Similarly, in item-matching tests, some items may not match with any other item, the student being asked to fill in the correct match or to change one of the existing but unused items so that it will become a match. Fill-in tests might similarly be modified so that for some items there is no appropriate word to place in a blank space, requiring the student to modify the test item or show why it needs to be modified.

Levine offers several advantages and disadvantages for these latter forms of closed-ended written tests. Levine (1978, p. 84) first considers true/false tests:

The advantages . . . are: (1) They are efficient because an examination may include a large number of questions that cover a wide range of subjects; (2) they are easy to administer and grade; (3) they can be returned promptly; and (4) they are useful in testing factual knowledge. The disadvantages . . . are: (1) They reward guessing because the test taker has a 50 percent chance of choosing the correct answer to any question without knowledge of the subject; (2) they may encourage false learning because students assimilate the incorrect statements; (3) they encourage response sets or answers to test items based on the form of a question rather than the content; (4) they are very hard to construct because minor word flaws or ambiguous wording can easily change a true statement into a false statement; (5) the need for an absolute true/false judgment makes this testing technique tenuous for new frontiers of knowledge; and (6) they cannot be used to examine integration of knowledge, conceptual learning, or advanced skills.

Levine (1978, p. 85) next considers the advantages of the fill-in test: "(1) It does not rely upon a limited list of answers that aids students in guessing; (2) it can be easily constructed, administered, and graded; (3) it can be returned quickly; (4) it is efficient; and (5) it is a good means of testing factual knowledge." Disadvantages are that "(1) it is not objective—correct but unanticipated answers are common; (2) items are frequently ambiguous; (3) items are often memory-based; (4) a course cannot usually be fully covered with a fill-in test; and (5) it is suited only for examining student command of facts" (p. 85).

Several advantages and disadvantages of item matching can also be identified. The advantages of this form of testing are that (1) a student cannot easily guess the correct answer, because there are many options; (2) guessing is discouraged, for a wrong match will throw off two answers rather than just one (unless there are more items on one side of the list than the other); (3) the tests can be easily scored and rapidly returned to students; and (4) they are useful in testing for factual knowledge and relations between concepts. Disadvantages include these: (1) such tests are suited primarily for examining student command of facts; (2) it is difficult to select items that do not relate in some way to other items on the list unless the matches are rather mundane (for example, matching authors with literary works); and (3) the last items to be matched by a student can usually be correctly selected by a process of elimination rather than by knowledge of the subject matter.

Just as psychometricians have persuasively argued for the use of multiple measurement techniques in the assessment of personality (Campbell and Fiske, 1959), so might one argue for the use of multiple measures in the assessment of student performance in the classroom. At the very least, a faculty member should consider mixing multiple-choice test items with matching, fill-in, or true/false items so that a student is being tested for knowledge of the subject matter rather than mastery of a particular testing procedure.

One should also recognize that some testing procedures are appropriate for certain modes of thought but not for others. Multiple-choice tests, for instance, generally test for item recognition but not for item recall. A student need not be able to solve a chemistry equation or even be able to recall a formula in order to select the correct solution to the equation or the correct formula on a multiple-choice test. We should not assume that students can recall or work with information just because they can recognize it on a test. The effective use of closed-ended tests requires a rather sophisticated appreciation of test-construction theory and research as well as some knowledge of human-performance theory and research.

Open-Ended Written Tests. Open-ended written tests (essays) require less sophistication and knowledge of the faculty member, because the student's acquisition of information is being tested in a more straightforward manner: the student is asked to recall information or to use information in solving a problem or answering a question. Levine (1978, p. 86) suggests several advantages of this method: "(1) The essay examination is easy to construct; (2) it is optimal for testing depth of knowledge (unlike short-answer [closed-ended] tests, which are optimal for testing breadth of knowledge); (3) it permits students to be creative; (4) it tests higher-order skills, such as writing and the ability to analyze, synthesize, apply, and organize knowledge, in addition to knowledge acquisition, which is examined on short-answer tests; and (5) it is less amenable to in-class cheating than short-answer tests.

The open-ended test holds several obvious disadvantages that lead many faculty members to make exclusive use of closed-ended tests. First, the criteria for evaluating answers on open-ended tests are less clear (at least at first inspection) than the criteria for closed-ended tests. Because there are no right or wrong answers on an essay exam, a faculty member must employ subjective standards in evaluating students' responses and is often influenced more by writing style and literary competencies than by the substance of the answer. We have all heard the story of a student who graduated from college with straight A's because of ability to write a decent English sentence. With the purported decline in literacy among college students, this writing ability may be of even greater benefit in the near future.

Proponents of open-ended written tests usually note that multiple-choice test items also build on the instructor's subjectivity, which is embedded in the construction of test items, se lection of "correct" responses, and assignment of particular grades for choosing a certain number of these "correct" responses. Proponents also note that students must communicate through the written word when they graduate from college and hence should provide written answers to test items while in college. As we move into a "postliterate" society, some people believe, this latter argument loses its force. Others believe that there is even more reason to enforce writing skills in our liberal arts colleges if this "postliterate" era is to be effectively counteracted.

A second disadvantage of the open-ended written test concerns time needed to grade responses. Whereas most closedended tests can now be computer-scored, faculty members must still spend Saturday afternoons reading bluebooks when using open-ended tests. Some make use of teaching assistants to read essay exams. Most, however, either do not have access to TAs or feel it is inappropriate to delegate this major responsibility. A variety of other reading, reviewing, and grading procedures have been used. Written exams, for instance, are sometimes read and graded by other students in the class (as well as by the professor) or by students in an advanced class (as part of their class assignment). Frequently, faculty members ask students to make up their own essay questions. These students are graded on the basis of both their questions and their answers. In other instances, faculty members review (and grade) essay-exam questions that are submitted by all the students in a course. Questions are selected for inclusion on an open-ended written test administered to all students in the course. The students who formulated the selected items are asked to assist in grading them.

Several variations on the traditional essay exam have often been used. Students might be given a brief case study or problem description rather than a question; they are to solve this case or problem. Alternatively, students are given the answer to a question and asked to rework this answer so that it will be more acceptable, persuasive, or accurate. A student might be asked instead to assume a particular role (as a famous person or a representative of a certain school of thought) and respond to a question or solve a problem as this person would. Third, many faculty members set up a hypothetical situation and ask the student to write an essay that describes its probable outcome.

Finally, the student can be asked to make an oral rather than written response to the question. He or she may be given the question ahead of time. An oral exam eliminates some of the problems associated with dependence on literary skills but introduces the problem of oral competence, the pressures of extemporaneous speech, and the prospect of "stage fright." Oral exams seem to be most successful when conducted in an informal setting. A faculty member should serve as an interviewer rather than an interrogator, and the oral exam should be offered as an option or supplement to the written one.

Levine (1978, pp. 88-89) offers several other observations on the advantages and disadvantages of oral exams:

> The advantages of the oral examination are that (1) it increases student-faculty interaction; (2) it drastically reduces the likelihood of students' misunderstanding test questions; (3) it permits follow-up questions; (4) it can be used to test breadth, depth, and whatever skills the teacher is concerned about; and (5) it provides immediate feedback to students. The disadvantages of this testing procedure are that (1) it may favor more verbal and confident students; (2) it is time-consuming; (3) it may be the most anxiety-provoking type of examination; (4) it is hard to keep test questions secret because all students do not take the examinations at the same time; (5) it is a difficult examination for students to prepare for; (6) it is impossible to compare student performance reliably unless the examinations are tape-recorded; (7) it relies upon subjective evaluation; and (8) it often results in varying test conditions and test questions for different students.

Academic Products. The third common method of assessment is the review of a term paper, research report, artwork, or musical composition that is presented by the student. Whereas closed-ended and open-ended written tests are often reported to be educational in their own right, an academic product is clearly educational. In preparing a term paper, report, or other product, a student is obviously learning something about the processes of writing and organizing materials as well as about the topic addressed. Even more than open-ended written tests, however, the academic product holds the disadvantage of being difficult to evaluate and is often biased toward students with writing skills.

Furthermore, one must question the extensive amount of time that usually goes into preparing a term paper. Given that only one person (the instructor) usually reads and critiques a term paper or other academic product, it is not always obvious that students get adequate feedback or an adequate audience to justify their efforts. Furthermore, the skills learned in preparing a term paper or research report may not transfer to many other settings. Many graduates of liberal arts colleges must unlearn term-paper-writing techniques when moving into the corporate world of memos, letters, and succinct reports. Some faculty members have responded to these concerns by exposing the student's academic product to a larger audience (other students, outside readers, student-run journals, and performances) or by requiring products that are more career-related (such as a case study, series of brief reports, or staff research report).

Behavioral Performance Tests. Open-ended written tests give students the opportunity to show what they have learned using words. There are occasions when a professor wants students to show what they have learned through action, particularly when assessing a complex skill (such as teaching children) or subtle attitude (such as empathy for a patient). Typically, a behavioral performance test begins with the presentation of a setting in which the student is to play a particular role or with a problem that the student is to solve through making a decision and taking action. A student might, for instance, be given the task of caring for an elderly client who does not speak English. The client might be played by another student, a TA, or a faculty member. The student's work with this patient is observed by the instructor, live or on videotape. Typically, the instructor rates the student on a set of criteria that are known to the student before the role play.

Alternatively, the instructor might prepare a videotape (or written scenario) of a particular situation. For example, in a police science program, an arrest might be enacted on videotape. The videotape is interrupted at a certain point, and the student is asked how he would respond at that moment. Preferably, the student is given an opportunity to demonstrate actively what he would do. He may, however, be given an opportunity to choose from several alternative courses of action (as in a multiple-choice test) and to indicate why he would take this action. In a large class this latter written mode of examination may be more feasible than an active demonstration.

Behavioral performance tests are used mainly in academic programs that prepare students for particular careers. They could, however, be used just as effectively in many liberal arts programs. A student's knowledge of a foreign culture, for example, could be assessed by asking the student to serve as a member of a community council and to deal with a series of problems as representatives of this culture would. Students in a literature course could be given the first half of a short story by a certain author and asked to sketch out the rest. Although this is a written test, it is classified as a behavioral performance test because the student is not just writing about the author but is instead trying to actively role-play this author by completing his or her story line. This example illustrates the use of a case study for both instructional and assessment purposes. (Earlier in this chapter we offered the example of completing a short story to illustrate the use of case studies in the humanities. Simulations and role plays can similarly be used for either instruction or behavioral performance assessment.)

A behavioral performance test holds an advantage over open-ended written tests in that literacy is not usually required. It is also a more realistic and sensitive test than either closed-ended or open-ended tests in that the student is asked to actually perform rather than just write about a hypothetical situation. The performance test is often impractical, however, for it requires the instructor's observation of an extended performance rather than rapid reading of test responses or a written essay. The criteria for evaluating a performance test are often problematic as well. The desired behavior or performance outcomes are often hard to define precisely or to assess quantitatively. Although performance tests are more realistic than written tests, they still occur in a simulated environment and hence do not necessarily predict accurately the student's competencies in the "real world," where the outcomes of one's performance have actual consequences. We must turn to a fourth type of assessment procedure to capture the advantages of "real world" assessment.

Observation of or Reflection on Performance in the Field. Experienced-based learning holds the advantage of not only providing students with "real world" learning but also providing faculty members with an opportunity to assess this learning as it is exhibited through the student's work in a field setting. A student who has been in a field placement in the engineering department of a local firm, for instance, can be observed in this setting by the field supervisor and faculty member to determine the extent to which skills have been learned or knowledge exhibited.

The one disadvantage of this mode of evaluation is lack of control over the assessment setting. In a simulated setting, tests can be administered that assess a student's performance independent of such confounding variables as the performance of other people, time constraints, competing expectations, or work-related goals. In a real-world placement, a student's performance must be assessed in its complex social and task setting. The faculty member and supervisor must know quite a bit about the work setting before making any judgment about the student's performance. This takes time that often is not available to either the faculty member or the field supervisor—although both these persons should be somewhat knowledgeable about the setting if they are to be effective educational resources for the student while on the field placement.

Another source of assessment in the field setting is the student's own reports on educational accomplishments there. Students can be encouraged or required to prepare journals or learning logs during the field experience. Faculty members can, in turn, periodically review these journals or logs and thereby assess the student's learning. The journal or log becomes not only a valuable educational resource for the student but also an important assessment tool for the faculty member, who cannot be with the student throughout the entire field placement (Bergquist and Phillips, 1975; Chickering and others, 1977).

   Systematic Documentation of Achievement. In recent years the portfolio has gained acceptance in colleges and universities as a tool not only to assess prior learning (see Chapter Six) but also to document learning that has occurred while the student is attending the institution. The portfolio enables an undergraduate institution to assess a student's work in a highly individualized manner. Portfolio evaluation allows a student to retain major control over the means by which achievement of educational goals is documented while sharing control with the instructor (and peers) regarding the nature of these goals and the criteria by which achievement of them is determined.

   Some colleges and universities have interpreted portfolio evaluation as primarily the accumulation of documents by students to show that work for a course has been done. This mode of informal documentation is rarely satisfactory because the student is given little guidance in determining what type of documentation to collect or what skills, attitudes, or knowledge the instructor deems important. As a result, the student may collect documents that are dismissed as unimportant by the instructor; or the instructor will look for documents or evidence of accomplishment in certain areas that are not available in the portfolio. In the two national experimental colleges ("College 1") of the Council for the Advancement of Small Colleges (CASC), an eight-step portfolio procedure that was found to be feasible, educational, and equitable for both students and faculty was used (Bergquist, Lounibos, and Langfitt, 1980). The eight steps are (1) forming a portfolio committee, (2) identifying categories for the assessment of educational achievement, (3) determining the relative importance of each category, (4) planning for accumulation of documents to demonstrate achievement in each category, (5) approval of plans by the portfolio committee, (6) accumulation of documents, (7) presentation of accumulated documents by the students to the portfolio committee, and (8) assessment of students by the portfolio committee on the basis of a review of the documents.

   These eight steps closely follow those outlined in chap. 3

of vol. 2 in CASC's *Handbook for Faculty Development* (Bergquist and Phillips, 1977), although vol. 2 describes a procedure
for evaluating faculty rather than student performance. A college or university could use portfolio evaluation procedures for
both students and faculty members as well as administrators,
academic departments and programs, and even an entire institution. An institutionwide self-study can readily be designed following these same steps and yield an institutional portfolio. A
portfolio evaluation procedure is also directly compatible with
the learning-contract procedure described earlier in this chapter.
A portfolio provides the information needed to accomplish the
first steps in a learning-contract process. Learning-contract and
portfolio committees can be composed of the same people or
constituted as a single group, serving a particular student
throughout assessment (portfolio) and development (learning
contract) phases.

The first step in a portfolio evaluation is formation of a
committee. This committee may be composed of the student
being evaluated, the instructor, and a student peer (chosen by
the student being evaluated). A second faculty member (or a
staff member) with previous portfolio experience may join the
committee, at least periodically, as a facilitator or consultant on
the portfolio process. An external resource person (for example,
a member of the profession for which the student is preparing)
might also be included.

The committee's first task is to identify evaluative categories. In many instances, these categories will already have
been established by the instructor for all students in the course.
These categories must be related to skills (for example, "communication," "writing"), knowledge (for example, "the French
Revolution," "Impressionistic art," or "single-celled organisms"),
or functions (for example, "filing," "analyzing problems," or
"preparing a laboratory report").

Once categories are identified, the relative importance of
each category for this student is established by the committee.
For one student, the category "capacity to analyze problems"
might be particularly important, whereas the category "capacity
to persuade others that this is an important problem" might be

relatively unimportant. For another student, the second category might be more important than the first. The relative importance of each category is established by asking the student to talk about his or her goals for this course or program, about future educational and career plans, and so forth.

Each category might be rated as unimportant, moderately important, or very important. A rating is assigned to each category so that the student being evaluated can determine where he or she must devote little, moderate, or considerable attention when accumulating documents. Categories that are rated low need be given only brief attention. Standard assessment instruments (such as multiple-choice tests) can be used to determine achievement in these categories. Categories with high ratings are subject to extensive attention by the student and committee. Documents should be specifically oriented to this student's unique interests, talents, and educational plans.

These first two steps (establishing categories and category priorities) are usually accomplished at an initial one- to two-hour meeting of the portfolio committee. The student now develops plans for the accumulation of documents to demonstrate accomplishment in each category. The student is encouraged to look at previously completed portfolios or is given a list of alternative evaluation tools. Using the committee's ratings as a guideline, the student formulates an evaluation plan and presents this plan to the committee at a second meeting.

If the committee has done an effective job of clarifying categories and ratings during the first meeting, the second meeting will be brief. The committee briefly reviews, modifies (if necessary), and approves the student's documentation plans. Sometimes the rating for one or more category will be modified or the categories themselves will be changed. With the committee's input and approval, the student begins to accumulate documents for the portfolio. These documents might be test scores, term papers, productions (paintings, essays, poems, research reports), letters of recommendation, audio- or videotape recordings, attendance records, checklists, journal entries, or laboratory logs. The more extensively a faculty member makes use of a portfolio evaluation procedure, the more extensive will be the collection of alternative tools and techniques from which a student can draw in preparing the portfolio.

Having accumulated the appropriate documents for the portfolio, a student meets a third time with the committee, presents the documents, and discusses the implications of these documents and educational achievements for future educational and career plans. If a grade must be assigned, then the committee (including the student being evaluated) makes the determination. Ideally, the committee will have determined specific criteria for the assignment of a grade during its initial meeting. The committee might, for example, determine what an "A-level" performance would be in each category, requiring extensive and persuasive documentation in the categories of greatest importance.

Even if the committee does not assign a grade, it should make a summary or concluding statement about the documentation that the student has accumulated. This statement, together with the documentation (or an abridged version of the documentation), constitutes the student's portfolio. The portfolio is submitted as a formal record of the student's accomplishment in this course or program.

One advantage of the portfolio is its flexibility. It can be designed as a traditional or nontraditional assessment procedure. In a traditional setting, a student might be required to attend class and pass several quizzes to meet minimal criteria in each category, to pass more extensive exams in categories rated as moderately or highly important, and to prepare an acceptable term paper or demonstration project that is relevant to the highest-rated categories. As a nontraditional procedure, the portfolio might be used to encourage highly innovative documentation even in the lowest-rated category.

Another advantage is the attention given to evaluation criteria. On several occasions a portfolio committee must address issues concerning evaluative criteria: (1) How do we know that the student has been successful in each category? (2) Which categories are most important for this student? (3) In what ways do these documents indicate success in these categories? (4) Overall, how do we assess the student's achievements in this course or program? Many students and faculty participants in College 1 reported that they had never given so much attention to evaluative criteria or gained greater clarity about course goals as when using the portfolio. Although some faculty members view portfolios and related evaluation procedures as being "soft" and "nonspecific," these procedures can actually promote exceptional clarity of objectives and expected outcomes if properly designed.

The main disadvantage of the portfolio procedure is time. When first used, a portfolio evaluation requires that a faculty member spend considerable time meeting with students and assisting students in identifying and collecting documents (including preparing and administering tests). The time needed to implement a portfolio evaluation, however, will drop off significantly with experience. Not only will the instructor become familiar with the procedure, he or she will begin to accumulate a set of exemplary portfolios, tests, and nontraditional evaluation procedures from previous students.

A faculty member is advised to consider the use of portfolios in courses or programs that have elusive goals or outcomes. If the faculty member is unable to identify a satisfactory method of evaluation for a particular course or program, a portfolio procedure can tap the energy and imagination of students who are identifying and using documentation to assess these goals and outcomes. The instructor can then choose either to continue using portfolios or to select those modes of documentation that most successfully assess specific goals or outcomes and use these modes in the assessment of all students in future offerings of the course.

Global Assessment. The term *global assessment* implies a comprehensive evaluation process. There are five essential variables in global assessment procedures: (1) *When* does the assessment take place? (2) *Who* is involved? (3) *What* is being assessed? (4) What *methods* are used? (5) By what *criteria* is the assessment done?

On the question of *when* global assessment might take place: The alternatives are to provide for periodic, ongoing assessments throughout the course or program and to assess progress at the end of the particular learning experience. Frequent testing, submission of multiple papers or reports, and/or ongoing discussion between the instructor and the student provide for frequent feedback. The student gains a clear sense of whether he or she is on the right track. Alterations in the learning activity can be made as the student progresses. Additional readings can be provided if necessary. Motivation can be monitored and problems can be identified, making it possible to solve them. A high degree of individualization is possible.

The more informal the ongoing assessment is, the more potential there is for a collaborative relationship to develop between the learner and the instructor. More formal ongoing assessments, such as quizzes and exams, tend to be seen as punitive and hold less potential for constructive growth and learning.

Some students may view ongoing assessment as disruptive and premature, as in an art or research project. Students may not appreciate sharing their work as it is in progress but prefer to struggle through on their own and submit only the final product for evaluation and scrutiny by others. The student's wish for privacy in the creative process should be respected.

In field experiences, ongoing, informal assessment can be especially useful. The student, the instructor, and the field supervisors can track the appropriateness of the field placement, can identify problems early and solve them during the placement, and can work together to clarify roles and expectations.

To some students doing advanced-level independent study, ongoing assessment may seem intrusive or paternalistic; to others, it may be helpful and imply a partnership with the faculty member.

Global assessments that occur only at the end of a course, study, or program can loom as immense hurdles for some students, especially those who are prone to test anxiety. However, this single assessment may also provide the student with a challenge to review and synthesize a comprehensive amount of material in a particular area of study.

Comprehensive examinations in the major are of this type, as are honors papers and theses. More frequently used at the graduate level, these final procedures can also provide undergraduates with opportunities for a comprehensive review of the field, tying together previously disconnected courses. Single, final assessments also provide opportunities for the student to synthesize theory and practice when both course work and field experiences are included in the program. Connections between concepts can be made, and generalization and "meaning making" can take place. End products are often useful and appealing to older adult students and to mature young adults. If introduced in a positive context, such end-of-course global assessments can be very valuable and growth-enhancing for both the learner and the faculty member.

Who is involved in global assessment is the second variable. Most often, such evaluation is done only by the individual faculty member who is the instructor in a course or a student's major adviser. Because one human being with power is judging another without power, the authoritative role of the teacher is potentially exaggerated. Pleasing the powerful "other" may replace learning as the student's motivation.

When the learner also has a self-evaluative role in the global assessment process, much can be gained. Not only is the student encouraged to be self-evaluating, a worthy habit, but development may be enhanced as the learner assumes increasing responsibility for the outcomes of learning activity.

Students can either recommend grades for themselves, thereby gaining a sense of the difficulties inherent in the grading process, or write or present orally a more subjective judgment of their work. They can express their views of their own learning gains and can also gain experience in comparative judgments by comparing their work against that of others or against established national standards.

Involving the student in global assessment of field experiences will enhance critical analysis skills and reinforce mature adult practices. The ultimate responsibility for learning lies with the learner, and educational institutions can support this notion by involving the student in self-evaluation. Moreover, the student can make comparisons between anticipated outcomes and actual outcomes, pointing up the serendipitous nature of most learning activities.

Committee-based global assessments are more typical of European universities than of American colleges and universities. In the United States, group assessments are usually found at the graduate level. But with the increase in undergraduate programs for older adults, committee-based global assessment procedures have increased in this country.

Committees often include several faculty members, field supervisors or community resource persons, peer students or graduates, the student, and perhaps an external evaluator in the same field. Where programs for older adults provide mentors or advisers, these generalists play a key role in committee-based assessment.

Committees may be gathered together to assess portfolios for prior noncollege learning, to assess a field experience or an independent study, or to review an entire degree program near or at its conclusion. Committee assessment provides for a high degree of individualization. It also holds the potential for representation of multiple points of view, especially if the committee includes both theoreticians and practitioners in a particular field. It is collaborative in spirit. And a committee-based global assessment procedure often becomes a planning opportunity for further education and career decision making by the student.

A powerful potential for improving the nature of assessment lies in this committee-based process. In addition, when community persons are included along with faculty members, relationships between "town and gown" can be strengthened. Often, new joint projects, field-placement possibilities, and curricular improvements are catalyzed. Job opportunities can be discovered, and collaborative college/community efforts enhance public relations and mutual confidence-building objectives.

In committee-based global assessment, the student is usually asked to give each member of the committee, before the committee meets, a copy of the final paper or report on the learning experience. If an artistic product or field performance is the basis of evaluation, the committee is invited to view the show or to observe the student working in the field. Coordination of the committee event is usually the student's responsibil-

ity. This task is time-consuming, as schedules and locations
must be arranged.

The student may or may not be present for the assessment and/or the committee's final deliberation on grading. The
more adult the relationship with the student, the more the student is likely to participate. If a context of collaboration and
partnership between equals is established throughout the course
or program, exclusion of the learner at the crucial point of evaluation would be inappropriate.

Although time-consuming, committee-based global assessment has the potential for high-quality individualization. And if
scheduled at critical points throughout a degree program (for
example, beginning, midpoint, and end), committee-based
global assessment procedures are feasible and can reduce the
amount of time needed for one-to-one advisement.

The third variable in global assessment is *what* is being assessed. The method of assessment should be appropriate to the
content of the assessment. For example, if a student's ability to
work with young children is being evaluated, then performance
demonstration in the act of working with children is most appropriate. If knowledge of child growth and development is
being assessed, then a written report on readings and observations or an examination designed to test lecture information
and reading comprehension is appropriate.

If attitudes are being assessed, written essays and/or oral
reports and discussion can best reveal the student's perspectives,
values, and attitudes.

Laboratory experiments and reports reveal the student's
knowledge of research procedures as well as comprehension of
the principles involved in an experiment, while theater performances and art studio activities can best be used to evaluate creative abilities in these areas.

The faculty must be clear about the content of the assessment. A pencil-and-paper examination is not likely to reveal
clinical skills, nor is observation of a student in a field setting
likely to net an accurate assessment of the learner's knowledge
of the literature in a given field.

The *methods* used in global assessment are the fourth variable. A number of these methods have previously been detailed: comprehensive examinations, portfolios, journals, quizzes, reports, research projects, performances, demonstrations of competence, and committee-based oral and written processes.

The methods are sometimes selected by the faculty member but at other times are agreed to by the student with the faculty member. A range of assessment options within a given course or program is possible and accommodates different learning styles, enhancing individualization.

Considerations of method usually involve concerns for time, schedule, and appropriateness. It is important for students to experience a variety of assessment methods throughout their undergraduate experience. The most commonly used methods, written examinations and final papers, are not the only ones that can be used.

There are times when nationally standardized tests can give the faculty important information on the comparative achievement levels of its students. In other cases, such comparisons are of little real value and simply reinforce homogenization and standardization of the curriculum—while a field is changing more rapidly than the curriculum, and the students are changing more rapidly than either.

Reading and grading lengthy papers, although time-consuming for the faculty, are necessary and valuable activities in many instances, especially when the instructor takes time to correct grammar and make substantive written comments on the paper. Merely assigning a grade of C does not help the student learn anything about his or her deficiencies and strengths. Because writing skills are a central concern of most college faculty members, it is helpful for instructors in all fields to comment on the spelling, style, and grammar in papers as well as the content.

In many courses and programs, learning contracts or agreements developed at the beginning of the course specify the methods of assessment to be used. When options are available and agreements are reached between the instructor and the student, a collaborative partnership is enhanced. This partnership reduces the punitive and authoritarian nature of assessment and increases individualization, while maintaining adequate standards without creating unnecessary barriers often associated with assessment.

Finally, the *criteria* for global assessment are critical to the success of the procedure. For example, there is a difference between measuring an individual student's learning gains and comparing the student's learning with that of others in the class or with national norms. This issue is largely a question of instructor and institutional philosophy. But clarity and consistency are important to establish.

A student who starts out knowing nothing about a field of study and reaches a point of elementary knowledge may deserve an A on the basis of his or her own learning increase. However, in the same class, there may be an older adult student who has been working in a particular field for many years. That student might be expected to rise to an advanced level of understanding while the first student functions at a more basic level.

If nationally standardized or institutional tests are used, minimum competence levels for all students might be established. Intermediate and advanced levels of competence can also be recognized according to these norms.

This issue is especially important in competency-based programs and in programs dealing with diverse adult learners. Because adults with a wide variety of levels of competency in various areas of study enroll in colleges, assessment criteria need to be clear and communicable. Where opportunities for assessment of prior learning are available, either by portfolio assessment or by standardized tests, the issue of the criteria for assessment becomes critical. Arbitrary judgments are not sufficient if a college is to gain a reputation for quality and fairness. Criteria designed for inexperienced young adult students are often inappropriate in judging more sophisticated older adults' knowledge and skills.

Criteria for global assessment need to distinguish among theoretical knowledge, performance skills, and attitudes. Few faculty members have made these distinctions in their courses. This effort requires a focus on outcomes, not on inputs. That is, to improve the quality of assessment, intended outcomes become the focus of the evaluation process, not the length or volume of course requirements. This shift from course designs to course intentions implies more complex curriculum management than many instructors are accustomed to. However, many colleges have moved in this direction—for example, Alverno College (Wisc.)—and by so doing have improved the quality of the undergraduate curriculum, which can appropriately serve an increasingly diverse learner population.

Global assessment holds several advantages over previously discussed procedures. First, its informality allows for more flexibility and individualization. Second, it involves the student directly in the assessment process, encouraging development and learner responsibility for learning. Third, it involves multiple perspectives and allows for variations in learning styles while ensuring high standards and rigorous expected outcomes. Fourth, it encourages collaboration while ensuring independence and self-directed learning habits that are the objectives of most undergraduate institutions. And, fifth, global assessment can accommodate a wide diversity of learner background so important to the student populations now using our colleges and universities.

On the negative side, global assessment is often based on ill-defined criteria and relies heavily on the goodwill and subjective judgments of those conducting the assessments. Combining some level of ongoing, continuous feedback with the final comprehensive global assessment best ensures that the integrity of the process will be preserved. This may offer an ideal combination of assessment procedures.

The current trend toward using only final examinations of a standardized nature has the potential to decrease individualization and increase homogenization just at a time when the diversity of student needs and backgrounds is increasing. This would be unfortunate. It is likely to take thoughtful and lengthy efforts by faculty members and administrators to preserve a diversity of assessment procedures in the years ahead as pressures to standardize evaluation increase. Therefore, it would seem important for faculty members to consider the five variables related to global assessment suggested here and to be conscious of and explicit about the purposes and appropriateness of the assessment procedures they use.

Concluding Comments: Assessment, Grading, and Standards. We have remained purposely vague about the function to be served by assessment procedures in an undergraduate course or program. Although it is usually assumed that an assessment enables a faculty member to assign a grade, it need not. Students can benefit greatly from feedback on their performance even if a grade is never assigned.

One might go so far as to say that any educational institution provides two kinds of instructionally related services to students: teaching and assessment. Students will learn about the external world through the teaching process and about themselves through assessment of skills, knowledge, and attitudes. Unfortunately, assessment is usually tied to grades, thereby gaining a punitive and evaluative reputation. Any of the assessment tools described above can be used independent of grades to give students information about current levels of performance. This information can, in turn, be used by students and their advisers to make choices among future course offerings, major areas of study, careers, avocations, and so forth. These assessment tools need not be used for grading purposes.

A second important issue concerns the source of criteria by which a student is to be assessed. This is particularly problematic when the assessment is tied to grades. In American higher education, we are constantly confronted with the paradox of asking faculty members simultaneously to set standards for their students and to help the students achieve these standards. Because standards are not set by some external agency, instructors are caught in the paradoxical position of having to be "good teachers" (effective in helping students work toward a set of standards) while also being guardians of high standards (ensuring that not too many students achieve the standards and receive high grades). If all the students in a course receive As, this can be interpreted as an indication of either the instructor's excellent work as a teacher or the lowering of standards by the instructor. As long as the instructor works alone in setting standards, high grades for all students may not be justifiable.

As noted in our discussion of the personalized system of instruction, faculty members can often involve colleagues in setting standards or can rely on standards (criteria, tests, norms) that have been established by external agencies (testing services, disciplinary associations, external review panels, or graduate schools). To the extent that standards established by a faculty member have been verified by others, then the assessment of student performance is also, in part, an assessment of the faculty member's own performance. The better a student performs in a course (especially compared with the entering level of performance), the more effectively the faculty member is working. A large proportion of high grades thus reflects positively on the faculty member rather than being evidence of lowered standards.

Unfortunately, externally based standards are rarely formulated, partly because academic leaders cannot readily agree on the desired outcomes for most educational programs. This conflict can be avoided or covered over when one faculty member (the instructor) sets the standards. As the number of people involved in setting standards increases, the debate and potential conflict concerning outcomes will become more vociferous and complex. Attention shifts at this point from instructional assessment procedures to educational outcomes, the sixth curricular dimension, to which we turn in the next chapter.

— VI —

OUTCOMES

*Defining Intended Course
and Program Results*

One of the essential characteristics of any coherent system or organization is its goal-directedness. What differentiates a group of people or elements from a random assembly is the common direction in which each person or element is moving or at least wishes to move. An academic institution, like all other systems and organizations, finds its identity and continued existence in the purposes to which it assigns priority and in the goals toward which it strives. The role of purposes and goals in any organization is so central to its existence that a statement about the importance of educational outcomes to any academic institution—and, in particular, to the curriculum of the institution—borders on tautology.

There are two ways to describe the educational outcomes of a collegiate institution. One can examine the explicit statements that have been made in the catalogue, in the mission

250

statement of the institution, in the college's listing of required competencies, and so forth. Our discussion concerning the definition of outcomes will describe alternative approaches that can be taken in formulating and organizing these explicit statements.

Educational outcomes can also be approached from another perspective, which, because of its pervasive and often unrecognized character, may be particularly influential in defining the desired outcomes for a collegiate undergraduate education and, in turn, in determining critical characteristics of the curriculum that have been designed to provide this education. We refer to basic assumptions that are made about the nature of the "educated person" and the role to be played by education in the life of the individual and society. These assumptions can be thought of as the "paradigm" of collegiate curriculums (to borrow from and modify the concepts of Kuhn, 1970) or as the "tacit" knowledge that one holds about collegiate curriculums (to borrow from the philosophy of Polanyi, 1967). Given the central role these assumptions play in determining one's definition and assessment of educational outcomes, we will first consider their nature, origins, and implications for the college and university curriculum.

Assumptions About Education

One of the most penetrating and provocative discussions of alternative assumptions about education has been provided by William J. Bouwsma, a distinguished professor of history at the University of California. In an *American Scholar* article titled "Models of the Educated Man," Bouwsma (1975) identifies seven educational "ideals" that have been embraced by various people and institutions in the Western world: (1) aristocratic, (2) scribe, (3) civic, (4) personal self-cultivation, (5) Christian-secular, (6) romantic-naturalistic, and (7) research. He believes that these seven categories describe not only dominant working models of education in the past but also underlying, often implicit assumptions that we continue to make in our design of the modern collegiate curriculum: "All [these models] linger on in some part of our minds, obscurely clashing with one another and variously challenging, accusing, and confusing us" (1975, p. 209).

Bouwsma describes the role that societal needs play in the definition and ascendancy of each ideal and points out that these ideals are even more profoundly influenced by the under- lying "anthropological" presuppositions of a culture about (1) the degree to which human nature is malleable and the dimen- sions in which this malleability is evident, (2) the nature and character of the human organism and the value to be assigned to its various potentialities, and (3) the extent to which a human being is viewed as autonomous, unique, and free to determine his or her own ends as opposed to being "part of a larger system of reality—metaphysical, cosmological, or biological—that deter- mines objectively the proper shape and direction of human de- velopment" (p. 209).

Bouwsma (pp. 210-211) states that "the educational pro- posals in the past which have proved most influential have chief- ly put into words the values and convictions already implicit, if not in educational practice, at least in the more vigorous cul- tural movements of their times." Thus, the primary role of the faculty member or administrator who is designing a new curric- ulum is to make that which is tacit and implicit in our culture explicit in the college's curriculum. An academic leader must "not so much . . . create a new ideal for education as . . . sense what is already present in a latent form" (p. 212).

Following is a brief description of each of the seven ideals that Bouwsma has identified.

Aristocratic Ideal. This model of the educated person springs from the evolution of the ancient warrior from predator to hero, courtier, and gentleman. This ideal emphasizes con- spicuous achievement, prestige, leadership, and personal honor. It is a highly elitist ideal, which promotes the exceptional per- son above the average one. All dimensions of the human being are emphasized. Physical, moral, and social development are all appropriate aspects of education. Only intellectual development seems to be neglected, with an emphasis being placed on becom- ing something rather than learning about something.

Though dominant in educational institutions before the Enlightenment, the aristocratic ideal is not advocated explicitly by many contemporary colleges or universities, except as it is revealed in a recurrent collegiate interest in intercollegiate athletics and in the extolling of virtues and wisdom gained on the playing field. To the extent that a collegiate institution affirms the importance of pride in one's work, risk taking, and worldly accomplishment, it may be said to reflect this ideal implicitly. Bouwsma believes that this ideal emerged in response to the need for a more polished and flexible upper class. If real power still resides in corporate boardrooms and local country clubs, then this ideal may still be relevant in the preparation of leaders for our society.

Scribe Ideal. The second ancient ideal highlighted by Bouwsma arises from the need for a class of literate persons. Emphasis in this model is placed on acquisition of reading and writing skills. Education is equated with acquisition of knowledge from the Great Books; hence, schools and universities are required to hold these books, and faculty members are required to assist students in reading and interpreting them. Whereas the aristocratic ideal emphasis action and tangible achievements, the scribe ideal emphasizes prudence, calculation, foresight, and other virtues related to reflection and restraint.

The scribe ideal emphasizes the one dimension that is neglected by the aristocratic—intellectual development. During and after the Enlightenment, colleges and universities flourished under the dominance of this educational model. The scribe ideal continues to be salient today among those colleges and universities, such as St. John's, that espouse a classical liberal education and those that emphasize interdisciplinary scholarship rather than disciplinary research.

The Platonic ideal of the philosopher-king seems to be a hybrid of the aristocratic and scribe ideals, as is the "collegiate way" that prevailed in American colleges and universities before the Civil War (Rudolph, 1962). Although the colleges and universities of colonial and pre-Civil War America emphasized the scribe ideal in their formal curriculums, the decision to make these institutions residential and to provide students with many extracurricular diversions revealed the implicit acceptance of the aristocratic ideal as well.

Civic Ideal. This ideal "appeared first in the Greek polis, reappeared in Rome, and again during the Renaissance" (Bouwsma, 1975, p. 200). It is central to the continuing emphasis at all levels of American education on preparing students for responsible citizenship. The civic ideal borrows from the aristocratic in its emphasis on the physical, emotional, and moral aspects of education. From the scribe ideal it borrows an emphasis on literacy. A major point of tension in the civic ideal concerns a desire, on the one hand, to prepare citizens for the social order as it now exists and, on the other hand, to prepare citizens for the task of transforming and improving this social order (by encouraging the autonomous "rational man" of the Enlightenment to emerge).

In contemporary colleges and universities, one can see the civic ideal being expressed in several ways. Some institutions prepare students for a world of action by providing them with specific tools to solve social problems (a blend of the civic and aristocratic ideals), whereas many others advocate the role of the collegiate institution as a place for reflection and analysis rather than action (a blend of the civic and scribe ideals). At the latter type of institution, an assumption is often made (implicitly or explicitly) that we need to know much more about social problems before we try to solve them. An eminent professor of technology recently proposed, "Don't just do something, stand there!" and learn more about what is being confronted so that subsequent interventions are not ineffective or counterproductive.

Personal Self-Cultivation Ideal. This ideal, which first appeared in Hellenistic Greece, finds its modern-day equivalent in the emphasis on esthetics and culture to be found in many liberal arts colleges and in the inner-directed emphasis on sensation and personal growth that was prevalent in the late 1960s and early 1970s. Bouwsma points to Seneca and the Stoics of every age as advocates of this ideal: education is meant to free us from the concerns of this world. This sense of transcendence can easily become elitist, though the elitism comes not from position and power, as in the aristocratic ideal, but from intellect, as in the scribe ideal.

Christian-Secular Ideal. Bouwsma proposes that the Christian ideal for the educated person is inherently secular, for education, from the Christian perspective, cannot lead to spiritual advancement—which is a matter of grace or virtue—and hence can be devoted exclusively to the daily living of the student. Bouwsma describes Christian education as an educational ideal of limited scope that, unlike the aristocratic, scribe, civic, and personal self-cultivation ideals, is not proposing to address all facets of a person's life. By tracing the rise of secular education to the Christian perspective, Bouwsma calls into question the frequent labeling of Christian education as being impractical and "otherworldly."

Romantic-Naturalistic Ideal. According to Bouwsma, this ideal defines the task of education as protecting and aiding human nature as it unfolds according to its own innate principles of development. Whereas the five ideals already described are based on ends that lie outside ourselves, the romantic-naturalistic ideal places the human being at the heart of the educational process and relies heavily on biology, developmental psychology, and learning theory rather than theology, philosophy, or politics for inspiration. This ideal is more holistic than the others. All aspects of the person are considered equally important, because all are equally natural and inherent in the human condition. Yet, as in the aristocratic ideal, there is something of an anti-intellectual, antirational bias in this model, for intellectual development is often considered an advanced stage that can be deferred and replaced by concerns for emotional, social, creative, physical, and sensory development.

Research Ideal. The final ideal identified by Bouwsma is a product of the "knowledge revolution" and a growing image of the educated person as a specialist who knows more and more about less and less. Bouwsma points out that this image has led to a loss of consensus about an ideal, for the research ideal will differ in character and function from one area of specialization to another.

The research ideal is clearly prominent in many major

universities today and in liberal arts colleges that seek to emulate these universities. Although the research ideal is often said to be value-free, it is in fact imbued with many statements about worth and meaning. The educated person, according to the research ideal, is critical, industrious, imaginative, independent, active, innovative, and bold. Research and scientific knowledge are assumed to be essential to the effective solution of many kinds of problems, some of which are value-laden and perhaps more effectively addressed by one or more of the other educational ideals.

According to Bouwsma, no dominant ideal presently pervades the American higher education community or even a particular sector of this community. Not only does the research ideal take a different form in each academic discipline, it is also clearly not acceptable to colleges and universities that view their primary task to be education rather than research. There seem to be fragments and remnants of each of the seven ideals in most colleges. Furthermore, in many ways the ideals themselves have given way to pragmatic goals of the college or university that relate to survival. Many colleges and universities have ceased to pursue a distinctive and transcendent mission that speaks to the needs of society, the individual student, or a divine purpose. These institutions have become, instead, responsive to the immediate and transient needs of the marketplace. Rightly or wrongly, many students are currently being prepared for careers rather than life.

Certainly there are exceptions to this rather bleak portrait of contemporary colleges and universities, and there is a sense in which, if Bouwsma is correct in his analysis of history, a new ideal might emerge that reflects and integrates the more theoretical with practical concerns. The new ideal will build on the old, implicit ideals and undoubtedly will reflect the pluralism and complexity of contemporary education and culture.

Definition of Outcomes

Some ingredients in the creation of a new educational ideal can be found in the explicit statements of desired educational outcomes formulated by a variety of colleges, universities, commissions, testing agencies, and educational theorists. These statements tend to reveal the remnants of old ideals as well as hint at new ones.

Statements of educational outcomes vary along several dimensions. They differ not only in content but also in perspective and structure. Some outcome statements are defined mainly from an institutional or societal perspective, others from a student-learning perspective. The former perspective helps potential students identify the type of resources and priorities that they can expect to encounter on entering the institution. It also helps potential sponsors gain a clear idea about the probable use that will be made of their support and helps the institution's faculty members and administrators determine the direction toward which they should be working and the criteria by which to judge the worth of their own and their colleagues' work. In contrast, the student perspective indicates the institution's expectations about the desired characteristics or competencies of its graduates. This perspective is of benefit to both students and faculty in the formulation of clear and equitable assessment procedures. Whereas outcomes that are prepared from an institutional/societal perspective are meant for an external as well as an internal audience, student outcomes are often prepared exclusively for internal use.

With reference to the structure of outcome statements, some statements are formulated along a single dimension. Outcomes of comparable generality and importance are identified and listed. In other instances, outcome statements are listed hierarchally, different levels of generality and/or importance being identified through placement of some outcome statements in a subordinate relation to others.

The following discussion of outcome measures has been organized around perspective and structure: (1) institutional perspective/unilateral structure, (2) student perspective/unilateral structure, (3) institutional perspective/hierarchical structure, and (4) student perspective/hierarchical structure.

Institutional Perspective/Unilateral Structure. Some colleges and universities approach the process of identifying educational outcomes by asking what purposes they should serve in relation to their students, their supporting community (secular or religious), and/or society in general. Davis and Elkins College (W. Va.) has undertaken this task, identifying twelve goals for a liberal arts education. As stated in a recent college bulletin, engagement in liberal learning means—

* to undertake the practice of those human and humane competencies that free men and women to live life rather than to be lived by it;
* to grow that integrity that draws varied competencies and makes a life both single and singular;
* to grapple with ideas at increasing levels of complexity and with increasing degrees of integration, independence, and creativity;
* to experience the satisfaction and self-confidence that come from the reasonable mastery of some field of study or style of inquiry;
* to experience learning both as the art of detachment and the art of involvement, both as idea and as act;
* to enlarge the personal repertoire of styles, mental and moral, emotional and volitional, sensual and imaginative, for appropriate response to the varied demands life makes;
* to learn the kind of discrimination which complicates life by refusing to be content with simplicism or mere prejudice;
  * to strive for reason and order without giving up a tolerance for ambiguity;
  * to cultivate discipline without loss of spontaneity, and seriousness without losing a talent for play;
  * to value science without demeaning mystery;
  * to distinguish the truth of an idea from its popularity, and the worth of a man from the number of his detractors;
  * to hold one's absolutes provisionally;
* to improve decision-making skills in an environment which offers a real range of personal and academic alternatives, limits liability for any single decision or performance, minimizes irreversibility, and makes guidance readily accessible;
* to experience the tension between tenacity and compromise which all living together requires;
* to discover how to cope with unfamiliar surroundings, both intellectual and cultural;
* to achieve increasing clarity of moral and religious convictions; and
* to arrive at increasing clarity of vocation in order to help determine what the world will make of itself [Davis and Elkins College, 1977, p. 9].

A somewhat broader definition of educational goals is offered by St. Thomas Aquinas College (N.Y.) in its statement of goals and objectives:

To develop liberally educated persons through transmitting a knowledge of the arts and sciences and of their interrelatedness, developing reasoning and communication skills essential to lead a full and productive life; developing understanding of human relations: respect for an ability to relate to others, including those of different origins, cultures, and aspirations; developing competence in the processes of cultivating values, particularly the formation of spiritual, ethical, religious, and moral values that are essential to individual dignity and a humane civilization; providing opportunities for students to pursue learning in off-campus settings and in interinstitutional programs.

To develop students who possess advanced knowledge in specialized areas and are prepared to pursue further study through stimulating and encouraging academic achievement; fostering creative approaches to learning; facilitating the development of research skills; encouraging in-depth and broad reading in specialized areas; and providing opportunities for independent study.

To prepare men and women within the liberal arts tradition to pursue personally fulfilling careers through assisting students in exploring career options in the arts, sciences, and professions in relation to their own self-fulfillment and the needs of society; assisting students in integrating career planning with their personal and academic development; providing undergraduate programs for students preparing for medical, legal, and other professions; developing specific career competencies through programs in business administration and teacher education and reviewing, evaluating, designing, and redesigning programs in response to emerging needs.

To develop a college community conducive to mental, emotional, and physical well-being through the offering of lectures, formal course work, and field experience in the areas of mental, emotional, and physical health; providing appropriate counseling and referral services concerning mental, emotional, and physical well-being; facilitating communication between faculty and students both in formal advisement and in informal interaction; affording opportunities for religious, cultural, social, and recreational activities both on and off campus and requiring on admission and on other occasions a record of a recent medical examination.

To develop a college community responsive to the wider civic community through providing programs and events to meet the needs of diverse age and interest groups; encouraging the individual student to consider seriously and to commit himself willingly to his responsibilities as a participating member in a free society; helping the student to perceive the relevance of his educational experiences in improving the potential for contributing to the common good; inspiring the student with an essential hope in the capability of society to be improved through concerted effort; and providing and encouraging appropriate opportunities for students to participate in action directed to improving the quality of life [St. Thomas Aquinas College, 1976, pp. 6-7].

The Davis and Elkins statement of goals seems to reveal most clearly the personal self-cultivation ideal that Bouwsma has identified, secondary emphasis being given to the civic, Christian-secular, and romantic-naturalistic ideals. The Aquinas goal statement tends to emphasize both the personal self-cultivation and the civic ideals. Whereas Davis and Elkins tends to focus its attention on providing the best possible education for traditional college-age students, Aquinas has committed itself explicitly to serving a broad-based student population. In part, this difference in institutional goals can be attributed to differences in the geographic location of the two institutions. Whereas Davis and Elkins is located in a rural region of West Virginia, St. Thomas Aquinas College is located in the suburbs of New York City. Differences also might be attributable to the definitions and traditions of service in the two churches (Presbyterian and Catholic) that founded these colleges. As Bouwsma has noted, the educational ideal of a college or university is defined by the implicit needs and cultural characteristics of the community being served by, and providing support to, the institution.

Student Perspective/Unilateral Structure. Rather than addressing the issue of outcomes from the perspective of institutional goals and responsibilities, many colleges and universities as well as higher education commissions have addressed the issue from the perspective of the anticipated or desired characteristics or competencies of students who have successfully completed study at the institution. In 1947, the President's Commission on Higher Education identified eleven "objectives of general education." The commission (as reported by Gaff, 1980, p. 38) indicated that graduating students should be expected to—

1. Develop for the regulation of one's personal and civic life a code of behavior on ethical principles consistent with democratic ideals.
2. Participate actively as an informed and responsible citizen in solving the social, economic, and political problems of one's community, state, and nation.
3. Recognize the interdependence of the different peoples of the world and one's personal responsibility for fostering international understanding and peace.

4. Understand the common phenomena in one's physical environment, to apply habits of scientific thought to both personal and civic problems, and to appreciate the implications of scientific discoveries for human welfare.
5. Understand the ideas of others and to express one's own effectively.
6. Attain a satisfactory emotional and social adjustment.
7. Maintain and improve [one's] own health and to cooperate actively and intelligently in solving community health problems.
8. Understand and enjoy literature, art, music, and other cultural activities as expressions of personal and social experience, and to participate to some extent in some form of creative activity.
9. Acquire the knowledge and attitudes basic to a satisfying family life.
10. Choose a socially useful and personally satisfying vocation that will permit one to use to the fullest [one's] particular interests and abilities.
11. Acquire and use the skills and habits involved in critical and constructive thinking.

Similarly, in a 1977 report, the Carnegie Foundation for the Advancement of Teaching identified five purposes for general education that reflect directly on anticipated characteristics of graduates from liberal arts colleges and universities:

1. For its political well-being, society needs wise and effective leadership and an informed citizenry.
2. For its economic well-being, society needs able and imaginative men and women for the direction and operation of its institutions (broadly defined), for the production of goods and services, and for the management of its fiscal affairs. It also needs alert and informed consumers.
3. For its cultural advancement, society needs creative talent and appreciative and discriminating readers, viewers, and listeners. It also needs people who understand the common culture and its antecedents in other parts of the world.
4. For its survival, society needs members who understand the dependence of human beings on the resources provided in their natural environment and on one another.
5. For its moral and ethical integrity, society needs tone-setting models and persons who, as parents and teachers and [in] other capacities, are able to pass the nation's ideals and heritage along to future generations [Gaff, 1980, p. 56].

As one would expect, these two national commissions tend to emphasize the civic ideal (preparation for national and world citizenry) as well as the personal self-cultivation and

Christian-secular ideals. Both lists of outcomes also hint at more ancient ideals: leadership and cultivation (the aristocratic ideal) and acquisition of practical skills for the formulation and maintenance of public policy (the scribe ideal). These two ideals from antiquity also are revealed, as is the research ideal, in the recent goal statements of Harvard University (Mass.) in its reformulation of the core curriculum. Henry Rosovsky, the dean of the Faculty of Arts and Sciences, sets forth six criteria for determining the success of an educational program as reflected in the characteristics of its graduates:

1. An educated person must be able to think and write clearly and effectively. . . . Our students, when they receive their bachelor's degrees, must be able to communicate with precision, cogency, and force.
2. An educated person should have a critical appreciation of the ways in which we gain knowledge and understanding of the universe, of society, and of ourselves. . . . He or she should have an informed acquaintance with the mathematical and experimental methods of the physical and biological sciences; with the main forms of analysis and the historical and quantitative techniques needed for investigating the workings and development of modern society; with some of the important scholarly, literary, and artistic achievements of the past; and with the major religious and philosophical conceptions of man.
3. An educated American, in the last third of this century, cannot be provincial in the sense of being ignorant of other cultures and other times. It is no longer possible to conduct our lives without reference to the wider world or to the historical forces that have shaped the present and will shape the future. Perhaps few educated people will ever possess a sufficiently broad perspective. But it seems clear to me that a crucial difference between the educated and the uneducated is the extent to which one's life experience is viewed in wider contexts.
4. An educated person is expected to have some understanding of, and experience in, thinking about moral and ethical problems. While these issues change very little over the centuries, they acquire a new urgency for each generation when it is personally confronted with the dilemmas of choice. It may well be that the most significant quality in educated persons is the informed judgment that enables them to make discriminating moral choices.
5. We should expect an educated individual to have good manners and high esthetic and moral standards. By this, I mean the capacity to reject shoddiness in all its many forms and to explain and defend one's views effectively and rationally.

6. Finally, an educated individual should have achieved depth in some field of knowledge. Here I have in mind something that lies between the levels of professional competence and superficial acquaintance. In Harvard terminology, it is called a "concentration." The theory is straightforward: Cumulative learning is an effective way to develop a student's powers of reasoning and analysis. It is expected that in every concentration students will gain sufficient control of the data, theory, and methods to define the issues in a given problem, develop the evidence and arguments that may reasonably be advanced on the various sides of each issue, and reach conclusions based on a convincing evaluation of the evidence [Carnegie Foundation for the Advancement of Teaching, 1977, pp. 156-158].

Other colleges and universities have tended to focus more precisely on the scribe ideal, identifying educational outcomes that relate specifically to the intellectual faculties of graduating seniors. Mount Holyoke College (Mass.), for instance, emphasizes the problem-solving capacities of its students:

* the ability to recognize and to define a problem;
* the understanding to place it in its appropriate intellectual and temporal context;
* the competence to recognize and weigh evidence;
* the capacity to assess and to articulate with precision a proposition's implications for personal and social values; and
* the ability to act with compassion and an awareness of one's own fallibility [Greenberg, 1979, p. 20].

Focusing also on the intellectual faculties of students, Mars Hill College (N.C.) makes extensive use of Phenix's (1964) categorization of six realms of meaning: symbolic communication, empirics, esthetics, personal knowledge, ethics, and synoptic knowledge. Extrapolating from these six categories, Mars Hill indicates that its graduates should exhibit the following competencies:

1. A graduate of Mars Hill College is competent in communication skills (Communication).
2. A graduate of Mars Hill College can use knowledge gained in self-assessment to further his own personal development (Personal Knowledge).

3. A graduate of Mars Hill College comprehends the major values of his own and one foreign culture, can analyze relationships of values between the cultures, and can appraise the influence of those values on contemporary societal developments in the cultures (Cultural Values).
4. A graduate of Mars Hill College understands the nature of esthetic perception and is aware of the significance of creative and esthetic dimensions of his own experience, which he can compare to other cultures (Esthetics).
5. A graduate of Mars Hill College understands the basic elements of the scientific method of inquiry, applies this understanding by acquiring and analyzing information that leads to scientific conclusions, and appraises those conclusions (Sciences).
6. A graduate of Mars Hill College has examined several attempts to achieve a unified world view and knows how such attempts are made. The graduate is aware of the broad questions that have been posed in the history, philosophy, and religion of Western civilization and can assess the validity of answers given to these broad questions in terms of internal consistency, comparative analyses, and his own position (Humanities) [Grant and others, 1979, pp. 170-171].

The competencies identified for use in assessing general education outcomes by the Educational Testing Service (ETS) and the American College Testing (ACT) Program also tend to emphasize the scribe ideal. The ETS study focuses on four intellectual competencies: communication skills, analytic thinking, synthesizing ability, and awareness. ACT similarly attends to communication skills, problem solving, critical thinking, and values analysis (Wood and Davis, 1978).

One list of outcomes is offered that seemingly encompasses virtually all of Bouwsma's ideals. Formulated by Samuel Magill, past president of Simon's Rock College (Mass.), this list is deceptively simple:

> *Communication skills:* the capacity to write, speak, and listen effectively and to use symbolic language like mathematics and computer language;
> *Analytic skills:* the capacity to reason, to problem set, and to problem solve;
> *Interpersonal skills:* the capacity to emphasize, to develop and nurture intimate relationships, and to live and work effectively within group situations;
> *Re-creational skills:* the capacity to engage zestfully in activities that are personally self-renewing such as play and lifelong learning;

Citizenship skills: the capacity to live effectively and responsibly in the polis, one's society or state, and, in our time, in world society [Magill, 1977, p. 440].

Magill's list might prove to be a useful overall categorization scheme for a college's statement of outcomes. Several of the other lists (especially Mars Hill's extrapolation of Phenix's work) could be used to flesh out Magill's scheme, though several of his categories (interpersonal, re-creational, and citizenship) are underrepresented among the detailed outcome statements on the lists we have identified. Although the statements drawn up by Rosovsky and his Harvard colleagues do not provide sufficient detail about the desired characteristics or competencies of graduates, these statements can be of considerable value in deducing the rationale for including particular outcomes. Rosovsky's statements make explicit many of the implicit assumptions and educational ideals that undergird his list as well as the others.

We turn now to hierarchical lists of outcomes that in many instances provide not only the range of outcomes found in Magill's list and the level of detail and precision found in the Mars Hill list but also the depth of rationale and analysis found in Rosovsky's.

Institutional Perspective/Hierarchical Structure. In 1954 the College of Letters and Science at the University of California formulated a statement of objectives that identified not only the educational outcomes for this institution but also several levels at which these outcomes must be defined:

1. The fundamental aim of the College of Letters and Science is to increase man's understanding of nature and of himself. But this is a high-level abstraction and has little *direct* connection with immediate realities. What do we want our students to be like, when we have finished with them, so that they may possess understanding?

2. In order that our students may have the understanding referred to above, we believe that they should have (a) a comprehension of abstract thought, (b) an appreciation of the structure of ideas, (c) a feeling for style, and (d) a basis for forming value judgments. But these are also high-level abstractions, and they are the result of certain abilities which the student must develop. Hence we must go to a still less abstract level.

3. On the third level, upon which the qualities listed above are built, we may put those abilities that we believe can be developed by the educational process: (a) the development of intellectual curiosity and the awakening of new intellectual interests; (b) the development of the ability to recognize facts and their relationships, with consequent liberation from uncritical loyalties evidenced by prejudice and provincialism; (c) the development of mature habits of reading and observation; (d) the development of esthetic appreciation; and (e) the development of appreciation for the responsibilities and satisfactions arising from the exercise of free choice.

4. Underlying the abilities just specified and forming the foundation upon which they must be built is the considerable stock of knowledge that the student must have if he is to be, in any meaningful sense of the term, *an educated person.* The committee does not believe that education can be divorced from knowledge even though we meet now and then with unusual people who have the qualities of the educated person without the formal training.

5. At the fifth level, we come to a general statement of the program by which the student gains the knowledge specified in (4) above. It is the belief of the special committee that the present program of the college, *in its general characteristics,* can be the instrument by which the higher objectives can be reached. These general characteristics are (a) the experience of various different types of intellectual experience represented by the *breadth requirement* and (b) the advance in depth in a particular subject or field represented by the *major requirement.*

6. Finally, at the level of the completely specific, we have the particular programs that our students like [Carnegie Foundation for the Advancement of Teaching, 1977, pp. 153-154].

By identifying these six levels of abstraction, the University of California committee has added greater precision to the formulation of educational outcomes. A single-level list of educational outcomes often includes statements of varying levels of abstraction; hence, it is often difficult to determine where these outcomes should operate in the collegiate institution that formulated them. Do particular outcomes relate to an overarching institutional mission (curricular and extracurricular), to the overall curriculum of the institution, to the general education component of the curriculum, or to individual departments or program units?

Even the University of California's hierarchal list does not represent the full range of educational objectives, for this list stopped at the program level in terms of specificity, when one could penetrate to subunits of the program, even to particular instructional units. Whereas one often hears of the distinction among mission, goals, and objectives, the University of California analysis identifies at least five levels. Following is our suggested listing of eight outcome levels as derived from the university's list:

1. Fundamental aim of the institution—the reasons for the college's or university's existence (mission level one).
2. Attributes (knowledge, skills, attitudes) or competencies that students are expected to exhibit upon graduation from the institution (mission level two).
3. Attributes or competencies of the student that the institution expects to help students acquire or improve during their tenure at the institution (goal level one).
4. Resources that a student needs in order to acquire or improve the desired attributes or competencies (goal level two).
5. General characteristics of a program that will provide these resources to students (goal level three).
6. Characteristics and competencies that a student will be specifically expected to acquire as a function of participation in this program (objectives level one).
7. Description of activities that shall be initiated in order to facilitate the acquisition of these characteristics or competencies (objectives level two).
8. Description of specific behaviors that shall be exhibited or are expected to be exhibited by both staff and participants during successful performance of each program activity (objectives level three).

The second of these levels (overall characteristics or competencies of students) has attracted most of the attention regarding educational outcomes at American colleges and universities, though several of the taxonomies and student-based outcome statements to which we now turn penetrate to rather high levels of specificity.

Student Perspective/Hierarchical Structure. One of the most widely cited and discussed hierarchies of educational outcomes is contained in the three-volume *Taxonomy of Educational Objectives,* prepared by Benjamin Bloom and his colleagues over a twenty-five-year period (late 1940s to early 1970s). Bloom divided the overall set of objectives into three domains: cognitive, affective, and psychomotor (roughly corresponding to the ancient categories of cognition, affect, and conation). In each of these three domains, a taxonomy has been prepared that provides up to three levels of analysis. The most detailed analysis is provided in the cognitive domain. Krathwohl and others (1964) differentiate the affective domain less finely than the cognitive domain. A third taxonomy has been prepared more recently (1972) concerning the psychomotor domain, but it is generally not considered applicable to higher education and is rarely used by colleges or universities in formulating overall educational-outcome statements. The cognitive and affective taxonomies, by contrast, have received a great deal of attention in American higher education, some of this attention being highly critical.

Several of these criticisms have been identified by Wood and Davis (1978) in their monograph on curricular evaluation and development. First, they note that Paul Dressel "has criticized the separation of the cognitive from the affective domain, arguing that values underlie the selection of knowledge both by the learner (what the student selects to remember) and by the teacher (what he or she chooses to present and to emphasize)" (p. 35). In this criticism, Dressel joins many other contemporary educators and philosophers in cautioning us about the arbitrary and often destructive distinction that is made between thinking and feeling, objectivity and subjectivity, science and humanities. To the extent that Bloom contributes to the reification of this distinction, he may be reinforcing the overemphasis in higher education on one of these domains (usually the cognitive, though not always) at the expense of the other.

Wood and Davis also support Heywood's criticism of Bloom's taxonomies as being insensitive to the unique languages and activities of particular disciplines and fields. The learning objectives of medical education, for instance, would necessarily include a category involving diagnosis, while English literature needs categories regarding creativity, fluency, and organization. At the University of California, Los Angeles, the engineering faculty has identified ten categories in which to sort subject matter and outcomes: principle, law, precept, concept, definition, analysis or synthesis, skills, tools, factual data, and application. Several of these categories are not reflected in Bloom's taxonomies.

Many educators have also expressed concern about their inability to differentiate among Bloom's objectives when composing test items. Although the distinctions often seem clear on paper, they become elusive when the objectives are being assessed.

In the formulation of educational outcomes, Bloom's taxonomies must be used conservatively and with sensitivity. The taxonomic categories should be considered only tentative approximations to reality, should be only the starting points for formulating outcomes in individual disciplines, and should be only suggestive for test-item construction. It should be noted, however, that any list of outcomes suffers from these problems and must be used cautiously and with sensitivity in various educational settings.

Three more recent hierarchical lists produced at Bowling Green State University (Ohio), the College of Human Services (N.Y.), and Alverno College (Wisc.) represent distinctly different ways of organizing and establishing priorities for the educational outcomes of a college or university. In its general education program, Bowling Green has identified eleven objectives, of which five are "essential skills," five are "functional understandings," and one is a "capstone experience" (Travis, Facione, and Litwin, 1978). The essential skills are (1) problem solving and critical thinking, (2) reading and writing, (3) computation and mathematics, (4) listening and speaking, and (5) decision making and values-conflict resolution. Each of these skills-oriented objectives is defined, in turn, by several more specific skills. The first objective (problem solving and critical thinking) illustrates the subdivision of each objective into subareas, or skills.

Objective 1: Develop Essential Skills in Problem Solving
and Critical Thinking

Skill 1: Gathering information:

Design a method or procedure for using bibliographic resources to efficiently and thoroughly find information, data, or points of view concerning issues or problems from various areas of study.

Skill 2: Identifying issues:

Identify the central issues or questions being discussed in a speech, essay, report, or other body of material . . . designed essentially for persuasive as well as informative purposes.

Skill 3: Selecting arguments:

Identify the major answers or conclusions being presented, and identify the reasons presented in support of each conclusion or answer.

Skill 4: Determining hypotheses:

Design several initially plausible hypotheses relative to a set of data, identify competing hypotheses, and outline research strategies to confirm or reject competing hypotheses.

Skill 5: Evaluating positions:

Evaluate the overall acceptability of a variety of arguments which cover several different issues, in terms of errors of reasoning, the impact of unstated assumptions, the presence of vague or ambiguous language, the use of data and evidence, the absence of relevant information, the presence of fallacious elements in content or logical structure, and the reliance on logical and rational strategies of proof.

Skill 6: Formulating positions:

Formulate and present your own reasoned conclusion concerning each of several specific issues or controversies, making explicit the definitions of crucial terms, value priorities, and the reasons operative in your formulation.

Skill 7: Expressing alternatives:

Identify alternative positions to your own view that might be taken on each of several controversies given the same definitions, values, and reasons you hold and given reasonable variations in those definitions, values, or reasons for other groups [Travis, Facione, and Litwin, 1978, pp. 440-441].

The five functional understandings at Bowling Green are (1) literature, the fine arts, and the humanities, (2) the natural sciences and technology, (3) the social and behavioral sciences, (4) cultures other than our own, and (5) personal development (including physical fitness). Like the essential skills, each of these understandings is subdivided into several "outcomes." The second category, for instance, is defined by four outcomes:

Objective 7: Achieve a Functional Understanding of the
Natural Sciences and Technology

Outcome 1: Basics:

Demonstrate a working knowledge of the basic scientific vocabulary, principles, values, attitudes, and methodology employed in the natural sciences.

Outcome 2: Applications:

Apply this working knowledge to the completion of at least one scientific research project or study.

Outcome 3: Impact of science:

Demonstrate a functional understanding of the impact of the natural sciences on society by:

A.   Accurately reading and interpreting a series of articles and reports concerning scientific activities and/or research applications that are drawn from sources such as intellectually respected periodicals.

B.   Making reasonably accurate predictions concerning the effects of current and future societal and individual decisions on one's self, one's culture, and one's environment.

C.   Describing several major scientific advances and/or research issues that impact on individual or social concerns, articulating their significance for contemporary and future living.

Outcome 4: Impact of technology:

Demonstrate a working knowledge of the impact of technology in at least one aspect of our society and culture by:

A.   Describing the appropriate use, accurate application, and limitations of the use of technology from the scientific dimension.

B.   Assessing the impact of the application of technology in terms of its cultural, ethical, social, and political ramifications [Travis, Facione, and Litwin, 1978, p. 443].

The eleventh ("capstone") objective requires integration of the essential skills with the functional understandings of the curriculum. Students demonstrate their "ability to effect a functional synthesis of their general education through an analytical study of a given problem, issue, or question that has ramifications in several areas of the liberal arts" (as reported in Grant and others, 1979, p. 310).

At the College of Human Services (N.Y.), a "performance grid" has been created that identifies, classifies, and interrelates two kinds of competencies. Some of the competencies with which the college is concerned involve specific actions or functions that students are to initiate or serve (for example, "design and implement a learning-helping environment"). Other competencies concern an increased consciousness of one's own values associated with particular actions and increased understanding of the larger system within which the action is embedded. The interaction between these two types of competencies ("the combination of the accomplishment with an awareness of its value") constitutes a "professional performance" (as reported in Grant and others, 1979, pp. 312-313).

The performance grid in Figure 5 contains descriptions of the eight action-oriented competencies (vertical column) and five value/dimension-oriented competencies (horizontal row) identified by the college. Several professional performances (labeled "facets"), representing an interaction between one action-oriented and one dimension-oriented competency, have been placed in appropriate cells of the performance grid to illustrate how the college has used this grid to generate its list of educational outcomes.

The Bloom, Bowling Green, and College of Human Services lists differ significantly in the particular competencies or objectives they contain. Each has a dualistic concept of competencies or objectives, but Bloom differentiates between cognition and affect, whereas Bowling Green differentiates between skills (essential skills) and knowledge (functional understanding), and the College of Human Services seems to differentiate between skills/knowledge (action) and affect/knowledge (values/dimensions).

The most comprehensive of such hierarchical lists has been developed by the Alverno College (Wisc.) faculty and administration. This list not only touches on all or most of the dimensions considered by Bloom, Bowling Green, and the College of Human Services (as well as those represented in the unilateral student outcome lists presented above), it also provides an analysis of six levels of achievement for each of eight competencies that have been identified. The Alverno list is wide ranging, like the Magill list, though it does not define the dynamic interaction between various competencies or types of competencies, as does the College of Human Services list. (See Grant and others,

1979, pp. 273-275, for a listing of the Alverno competencies and levels.)

Each of the hierarchical lists we have presented serves a particularly useful function in addressing certain curricular issues. The Alverno list can be helpful to a college addressing the issue of assessment, for outcomes can be measured at several levels using the Alverno model. By contrast, the College of Human Services provides an organizational scheme that would be useful for colleges wishing to create or evaluate outcomes from a career-oriented or experientially oriented curriculum. As mentioned above, several of the unilateral lists (for example, Rosovsky's and Mars Hill's) are particularly applicable to one or more of the educational ideals, the College of Human Services list being directly applicable to the civic ideal. None of the lists is appropriate for all collegiate institutions or for all curricular purposes. The complexity of an educational-outcomes list should also be kept in mind, especially if one wishes to conceive of the student outcome list as only one in a series of lists that need to be generated to cover all levels of the college curriculum.

Multiple Perspective/Hierarchical Structure. The lists that have been offered are meant primarily to be suggestive of the diversity, breadth, and depth one can build into a statement of outcomes. To expand more fully on this diversity, depth, and breadth, we shall offer one more list of goals, which was completed by Howard Bowen (1977) for his book *Investment in Learning.* Bowen surveyed over 1,000 goal statements before preparing a catalogue of goals that incorporates both the student ("goals for individual students") and institutional/societal perspectives ("goals for society"), as well as offering a hierarchy in the tradition of Bloom and Bowling Green (Bowen, 1977, pp. 55-59):

I.   Goals for Individual Students
    A.   Cognitive Learning
        1.   *Verbal skills.* Ability to comprehend through reading and listening. Ability to speak and write clearly, correctly, and gracefully. Effectiveness in the organization and presentation of ideas in writing and in discussion. Possibly some acquaintance with a second language.

Figure 5. The Performance Grid with Sample Facets in One Competency.

Dimensions

Competencies	A. Purpose	B. Values	C. Self and Others	D. Systems	E. Skills
	Describe appropriate and realistic purposes and demonstrate reasonable success in achieving them	Demonstrate a clear understanding of your values and persistence in working for them.	Demonstrate an understanding of yourself and others in relation to your purposes.	Demonstrate an understanding of systems in relationship to your purposes.	Demonstrate an ability to make good use of necessary and appropriate skills in the achievement of your purposes.
I. Become an effective learner and potential professional, accepting the responsibility for identifying your learning goals and finding appropriate resources for achieving them.					
II. Establish professional relationships at the work site with coworkers and citizens.					
III. Work with others in groups, helping to establish clear goals and achieve optimum results.	Facet 3: Demonstrate reasonable success in helping a group to achieve its common purpose while working toward your individual purpose.	Facet 3: Describe your views on the issue of decision making in groups and explain how your views affect your performance (Locke, Mill, Dahl, Lindblom, Galbraith, Ibsen).	Facet 3: Demonstrate an understanding of alternative approaches to working in groups and their applicability to specific situations (Maslow, Lewin, Schwartz, Bion, Thelen).	Facet 4: Demonstrate an understanding of groups as cultural units (Kluckhohn, Barnouw, Greenwood, Goode, C. P. Snow).	Facet 3: Demonstrate in appropriate circumstances the ability to test and learn new interpersonal techniques (Miles).

IV. Function as a teacher, helping people to define and achieve appropriate learning goals.				
V. Function as a counselor, helping people to resolve problems in a manner that promotes their growth and independence.				
VI. Function as community liaison, working with the people and resources of the community to meet community needs.				
VII. Function as a supervisor, taking the responsibility for teaching, encouraging, and enabling other workers to make the best use of their abilities on behalf of citizens.				
VIII. Act as a change agent, planning, researching, and promoting programs to improve human service delivery.				

Source: Grant and others, 1979, pp. 312–313.

2. *Quantitative skills.* Ability to understand elementary concepts of mathematics and to handle simple statistical data and statistical reasoning. Possibly some understanding of the rudiments of accounting and the uses of computers.
3. *Substantive knowledge.* Acquaintance with the cultural heritage of the West and some knowledge of other traditions. Awareness of the contemporary world of philosophy, natural science, art, literature, social change, and social issues. Command of vocabulary, facts, and principles in one or more selected fields of knowledge.
4. *Rationality.* Ability and disposition to think logically on the basis of useful assumptions. Capacity to see facts and events objectively—distinguishing the normative, ideological, and emotive from the positive and factual. Disposition to weigh evidence, evaluate facts and ideas critically, and to think independently. Ability to analyze and synthesize.
5. *Intellectual tolerance.* Freedom of the mind. Openness to new ideas. Willingness to question orthodoxy. Intellectual curiosity. Ability to deal with complexity and ambiguity. Appreciation of intellectual and cultural diversity. Historical perspective and cosmopolitan outlook. (Appreciation of the local, provincial, and parochial is commendable. Values such as cosmopolitanism are not undesirable but perhaps they are most valuable when they occur in tension with their opposites, when the person achieves an appreciation of both the cosmopolitan and the provincial and a critical capacity to stress the merits and deficiencies of both.) Understanding of the limitations of knowledge and thought.
6. *Esthetic sensibility.* (Esthetic sensibility is often classified under affective development rather than cognitive learning. It contains elements of both.) Knowledge of, interest in, and responsiveness to literature, the fine arts, and natural beauty.
7. *Creativeness.* Imagination and originality in formulating new hypotheses and ideas and in producing new works of art.
8. *Intellectual integrity.* Understanding of the idea of "truth" and of its contingent nature. Disposition to seek and speak the truth. Conscientiousness of inquiry and accuracy in reporting results.
9. *Wisdom.* Balanced perspective, judgment, and prudence.
10. *Lifelong learning.* Love of learning. Sustained intellectual interests. Learning how to learn.

B. Emotional and Moral Development

1. *Personal self-discovery.* Knowledge of one's own talents, interests, values, aspirations, and weaknesses. Discovery of unique personal identity.

2. *Psychological well-being.* Progress toward the ability to "understand and confront with integrity the nature of the human condition" (Perry, 1968, p. 201). Sensitivity to deeper feelings and emotions combined with emotional stability. Ability to express emotions constructively. Appropriate self-assertiveness, sense of security, self-confidence, self-reliance, decisiveness, spontaneity. Acceptance of self and others.

3. *Human understanding.* Humane outlook. Capacity for empathy, thoughtfulness, compassion, respect, tolerance, and cooperation toward others, including persons of different backgrounds. Democratic and nonauthoritarian disposition. Skill in communication with others.

4. *Values and morals.* A valid and internalized but not dogmatic set of values and moral principles. Moral sensitivity and courage. Sense of social consciousness and social responsibility.

5. *Religious interest.* Serious and thoughtful exploration of purpose, value, and meaning.

6. *Refinement of taste, conduct, and manner.*

C. Practical Competence

1. *Traits of value in practical affairs generally.* Virtually all of the goals included under cognitive learning and emotional and moral development apply to practical affairs. In addition, the following traits, which are more specifically related to achievement in practical affairs, may be mentioned:

   a. *Need for achievement.* Motivation toward accomplishment. Initiative, energy, drive, persistence, self-discipline.

   b. *Future orientation.* Ability to plan ahead and to be prudent in risk-taking. A realistic outlook toward the future.

   c. *Adaptability.* Tolerance of new ideas or practices. Willingness to accept change. Versatility and resourcefulness in coping with problems and crises. Capacity to learn from experience. Willingness to negotiate, compromise, and keep options open.

   d. *Leadership.* Capacity to win the confidence of others, willingness to assume responsibility, organizational ability, decisiveness, disposition to take counsel.

2. *Citizenship.* Understanding of and commitment to democ-

racy. Knowledge of governmental institutions and procedures. Awareness of major social issues. Ability to evaluate
propaganda and political argumentation. Disposition and
ability to participate actively in civic, political, economic,
professional, educational, and other voluntary organizations. Orientation toward international understanding and
world community. Ability to deal with bureaucracies. Disposition toward law observance.

3. *Economic productivity*. Knowledge and skills needed for
    first job and for growth in productivity through experience
    and on-the-job training. Adaptability and mobility. Sound
    career decisions. Capacity to bring humanistic values to the
    workplace and to derive meaning from work.

4. *Sound family life*. Personal qualities making for stable fam-
    ilies. Knowledge and skill relating to child development.

5. *Consumer efficiency*. Sound choice of values relating to
    style of life. Skill in stretching consumer dollars. Ability to
    cope with taxes, credit, insurance, investments, legal issues,
    and so on. Ability to recognize deceptive sales practices
    and to withstand high-pressure sales tactics.

6. *Fruitful leisure*. Wisdom in allocation of time among work,
    leisure, and other pursuits. Development of tastes and skills
    in literature, the arts, nature, sports, hobbies, and commu-
    nity participation. Lifelong education, formal and infor-
    mal, as a productive use of leisure. Resourcefulness in over-
    coming boredom, finding renewal, and discovering satisfying
    and rewarding uses of leisure time.

7. *Health*. Understanding of the basic principles for cultivat-
    ing physical and mental health. Knowledge of how and
    when to use the professional health care system.

D. Direct Satisfactions and Enjoyments from College Education.
    1. During the college years.
    2. In later life.

E. Avoidance of negative outcomes for individual students.

II. Goals for Society (Note: These goals may be achieved through educa-
    tion, through research and related activities, or through public serv-
    ices.)

    A. Advancement of Knowledge
        1. Preservation and dissemination of the cultural heritage.
        2. Discovery and dissemination of new knowledge and ad-
            vancement of philosophical and religious thought, litera-
            ture, and the fine arts—all regarded as valuable in their own
            right without reference to ulterior ends.
        3. Direct satisfactions and enjoyments received by the popu-

lation from living in a world of advancing knowledge, technology, ideas, and arts.

B. Discovery and Encouragement of Talent.
C. Advancement of Social Welfare.
   1. Economic efficiency and growth.
   2. Enhancement of national prestige and power.
   3. Progress toward the identification and solution of social problems.
   4. "Improvement" in the motives, values, aspirations, attitudes, and behavior of members of the general population.
   5. Over long periods of time, exerting a significant and favorable influence on the course of history as reflected in the evolution of the basic culture and of the fundamental social institutions. Progress in human equality, freedom, justice, security, order, religion, health, and so on.
D. Avoidance of Negative Outcomes for Society.

Whether or not one chooses to use Bowen's list as a model for identifying and categorizing educational outcomes, its scope is useful in encouraging a curriculum-planning group to be explicit in its acceptance or rejection of particular goals and modes of organizing these goals. Ultimately, each college or university must create its own list of outcomes that accurately and explicitly reflects its underlying assumptions and educational ideals as well as the realities of the institution. The outcome statements also must be organized in a manner that is specifically tailored to the function being served by this list. The task of creating one's own statements of educational outcomes is often tiresome and seemingly without immediate benefit. Yet, over the long term, it is important, for a statement of outcomes should provide guidance and direction for the curriculum as it is being designed and implemented with reference to each of the other five curricular dimensions: time, space, resources, organization, and procedures.

Assessment of Outcomes

Bowen (1977, p. 27) has suggested that studies on the outcomes of higher education usually employ one of six means: "(1) investigation of changes in the achievements, personalities, attitudes, and behavior of students during the college years; (2) surveys of the views of students and alumni about their college experiences; (3) censuses, public opinion polls, and other explorations of attitudes, economic status, and behavior of adult respondents; (4) multiple regression studies for particular populations incorporating many variables and designed to sort out the separate impact of education on income, career choice, health, voting behavior, religion, and so on; (5) case histories of individuals; and (6) critical and analytical studies without empirical data." Some of these means of assessing outcomes focus on the specific impact of the academic world on students who are now enrolled in the college. Some of Bowen's methods concern very specific outcomes; others refer to more global and societal outcomes. In this section of the book, we will describe a variety of methods that are relevant to general assessment of undergraduate student-learning outcomes. More specific course-related assessment methods were described in Chapter Five.

Assessment of general student-based outcomes began in the early part of the twentieth century with the study by Richard Crane of 1,593 members of the graduate class of 1894 at Harvard, Wisconsin, California, Chicago, and ten other large colleges and universities. This study of alumni and many others that followed made extensive use of questionnaires, interviews, and other self-report measures as well as demographics, such as salary, location, and family status (Witmer, n.d.). More sophisticated control-group studies have followed, using more complex methods (for example, personality inventories, achievement tests, direct observation) to assess the acquisition of values, verbal and quantitative skills, vocational competencies, and so forth. Many of the findings from these studies are summarized in vol. 1 of Feldman and Newcomb's *Impact of College on Students* (1969) and methods used listed in vol. 2 of Feldman and Newcomb's report. Though now dated, this report stands as an excellent example of outcomes-oriented research and as a source of ideas for colleges and universities that are designing their own programs for evaluating undergraduate curriculums.

A large variety of methods are available to assess overall student-learning outcomes. Warren (1973) identifies seven methods: questionnaires, interviews, group meetings with students, trial programs to test student responses (temporary educational simulations), faculty/student retreats, student-run surveys and evaluations, and direct observations of student behavior. Much more exhaustive lists of methods are provided by Knapp and Sharon (1975), Lenning (1977), and Lenning and others (1977). Table 1 summarizes these lists and suggests several additional methods as well as bibliographic references where available.

Table 1. Methods for Assessing Student-Learning Outcomes.

Method	Reference
Paper-and-pencil tests	Boyd and Shimberg (1971)
	Lake, Miles, and Earle (1973)
	Maloney and Ward (1976)
	Opennheim (1966)
	Robinson, Athanasiou, and Head (1969)
	Robinson, Rusk, and Head (1968)
	Robinson and Shaver (1969)
	Shaw and Wright (1967)
	Wylie (1961)
Anecdotal records	
Audiovisual media procedures	Edling (1968)
Behavioral-events analysis	Pottinger (1975)
	Pottinger and Klemp (1976)
Card sorts	
Case studies	Bergquist and Phillips (1981)
Checklists	
Computer analysis (for example, computer grading of essays)	Levy and Fritz (1972)
Computer-assisted instruction	Bergquist and Phillips (1981)
Concerns conference	Witkin (1975)
Confrontation meeting	Beckhard (1967)
Critical-incident technique	Flanagan (1954)
Diaries	
Fact-finding and decision-making exercises	
Formal demonstration of support for a program (banquets, parades, and so on)	

(continued on next page)

Table 1 (Continued)

Method	Reference
Games/simulations	Bergquist and Phillips (1981)
Group problem-solving exercises	Bergquist and Phillips (1977, chap. 6)
In-basket technique	Bergquist and Phillips (1981)
Institutional records (and other secondary data)	Boyd and Westphall (1972)
Interviews (structured, unstructured, stress, panel)	
Inventories	
Job-element analysis	Primoff (1973)
	Pottinger (1975)
	Pottinger and Klemp (1976)
Leaderless group discussions	
Logs	
On-the-job assessment by supervisors	
Opinion polls	Witkin (1975)
Oral exams	Levine and McGuire (1970)
Oral presentations	
Organizational-climate technique	Pottinger (1975)
	Pottinger and Klemp (1976)
Performance tests	
Product testing and assessment	Bergquist, Lounibos, and Langfitt (1980)
Programmed cases	Pottinger (1975)
	Pottinger and Klemp (1976)
Questionnaire/rating forms	Bower and Renkiewicz (1977)
	Oppenheim (1966)
	Tull and Albaum (1973)
Ratings by expert judges	
Recorded observed behavior	Boyd and DeVault (1966)
Reverse-flow conferences	Witkin (1975)
Role playing	
Self-monitoring/self-charts	Mount and Tirrell (1977)
	Swenson (1974)
Self-observation reports	American College Testing Program (1973, pp. 304-319)
	Baird (1976)
	Berdie (1971)
	McMorris and Ambrosino (1973)
	Palola and Lehemann (1976)
Speak-ups	Witkin (1975)

Table 1 (Continued)

Method	References
Staffing conferences	Kelly and Dowd (1975)
Student evaluation of instruction	Bergquist and Phillips (1975, chap. 3)
Unobtrusive measures	Webb and others (1966)
Work samples	
Written diagnostic and trouble-shooting exercises	
Life histories	
Supervisor, peer, and/or clinical ratings	

Most of these methods can be placed in one of six categories. Four categories refer to the assessment of impact while the student is enrolled in a program or at its conclusion: (1) self-appraisal, (2) appraisal by another person, (3) achievement tests, and (4) on-campus activities. The other two forms of assessment require postprogram appraisal: (5) retrospective self-appraisal and (6) postgraduate activities and accomplishments. Following are brief descriptions of each of these six kinds of assessment.

Self-Appraisal. Typically, a student is asked to appraise his or her own learning outcomes through the use of questionnaires and rating forms, unstructured and structured interviews, checklists, card sorts, opinion polls, self-monitoring and self-charts, self-observation reports, and related single-person-report methods (for references for these and all other methods cited in this section, see Table 1). Occasionally, one or more group-report methods are used: concerns conferences, confrontation meetings, group and panel interviews, leaderless group discussions, juries, reverse-flow conferences, and speak-ups.

Recently more precision has been brought to the single-person self-report appraisal through use of the critical-incident checklist, which asks students not only to assess the extent to which they have acquired certain knowledge, skills, or attitudes or achieved certain developmental states but also to identify "critical incidents" (people, events, procedures, policies, and so on) that have contributed to this success (or failure). A related method, behavioral-events analysis, has been developed by David McClelland and his colleagues (Pottinger and Klemp, 1976, pp. 46-48). A behavioral-event analysis begins with the student's identification of "behavioral episodes" (incidents or events) that exemplify successful or unsuccessful achievement of a particular outcome. The report contains a description of the episode, of the events, decisions, and so on that led up to the episode, when and where the episode is likely to occur, and the student's feelings before, during, and after the episode. Usually conducted through the use of interviews, this procedure allows program evaluators to identify in a tangible way the characteristics and causes of successful or unsuccessful outcome achievement. Typically, students who have been particularly successful or unsuccessful are chosen to be interviewed. Critical-incident checklists and behavioral-event analysis are valuable in helping a college construct case studies of students who have particularly benefited from a given academic program (success-oriented analysis) or have received little benefit from this program (failure-avoidance analysis).

Another valuable source of information from students about academic programs is the evaluation reports they complete for the courses they are taking in the academic area being evaluated. Evaluation instruments such as *IDEA* (Kansas State University) and CASC's *Instructional Assessment System* (Bergquist and Phillips, 1975) ask students not only to rate the effectiveness of particular components of a course but also to assess the extent to which certain kinds of learning have occurred for them in the course.

A final set of assessment methods that have received increased attention are unobtrusive—that is, they do not disrupt the ongoing instructional process, being part of the process. This set of methods includes diaries and logs. Two of the assessment procedures described in Chapter Five (portfolios and global assessment) are also appropriate for assessing overall program outcomes. Students can be asked to document or help assess their overall achievements in the program much as they do in documenting and assessing their achievements in individual components of the program.

With reference to the assessment of knowledge, skills, attitudes, or developmental stages, most precise self-appraisal assessment involves some paper-and-pencil psychometric device. In the many studies of student attitudes that are reviewed by Feldman and Newcomb (1969, vol. 2), self-appraisal inventories or rating scales are by far the most common means of assessment. Rarely in the studies surveyed by Feldman and Newcomb were students asked to appraise their own levels of knowledge or skills. Rather, the students were given some performance test (see discussion below). The most commonly used attitude scales have been the Allport-Vernon Study of Values, Thurstone-Chave's Religious Attitudes Scales (Attitude Toward the Church Scale and Attitude Toward the Reality of God Scale), the California F (Fascism) and E (Ethnocentrism) Scales, Rokeach's Dogmatism Scale, and the Strong-Campbell Vocational Interest Blank. General personality and developmental assessment tools that Feldman and Newcomb (1969, vol. 2) frequently reported being used include the Omnibus Personality Inventory, the Sixteen Personality Factor Test, the California Personality Inventory, the Bernreuter Personality Inventory, Edwards Personal Preference Schedule, the Guilford-Zimmerman Temperament Survey, the Myers-Briggs Type Indicator, and the Minnesota Multiphasic Personality Inventory (MMPI). These scales and others are fully described in the *Mental Measurements Yearbook* (Buros, 1972). Other excellent sources of information about attitudes and personality scales are Robinson and Shaver's (1969) *Measures of Social Psychological Attitudes,* Robinson, Rusk, and Head's (1968) *Measures of Political Attitudes,* and Lake, Miles, and Earle's (1973) *Measuring Human Behavior.* Several of these scales are particularly noteworthy with regard to the sophistication and sensitivity of the instrument, richness of theoretical constructs underlying the scale, and/or appropriateness of the instrument for a collegiate population. These scales are the Allport-Vernon Study of Values (though somewhat dated), Rokeach's Dogmatism Scale, the Strong-Campbell Vocational Interest Blank, the Omnibus Personality Inventory, Edwards Personal Preference Schedule, and the Myers-Briggs Type Indicator. One of the most frequently used personality inventories, the MMPI, should be avoided unless carefully used by someone with rather extensive training and experience in its use and interpretation.

In recent years, with an increased interest in the developmental stages of students, researchers and assessors of student-learning outcomes have often been dissatisfied with the general information about developmental stages and concerns that is obtained from multipurpose personality inventories. On occasion, questionnaires and inventories have been designed to assess students' developmental stages. Douglas Heath (1968), for instance, has developed the Self-Image Questionnaire and Perceived Self-Questionnaire (as well as using the MMPI, Allport-Vernon Study of Values, and Strong-Campbell Vocational Interest Blank) to study maturation among college students. Roy Heath (1976) has similarly developed a Modes of Existence Test and Jane Loevinger (Loevinger and Wessler, 1970) a Sentence Completion Test to aid in assessing the developmental stages of students. Many other developmental theorists (for example, Piaget, Kohlberg, and Perry) begin with the assumption that development is closely linked with, and dependent on the acquisition of, certain cognitive skills (see Kneflecamp, Widick, and Parker, 1978). Accordingly, these theorists usually use performance tests (see discussion below), rather than self-appraisals, to assess developmental stages. Most of the developmental theorists have also been inclined to make use of in-depth interviews and observations rather than psychometric devices when assessing developmental stages.

Appraisal by Another Person. Like self-appraisal, the appraisal of student-learning outcomes by another person can be done through questionnaires and rating scales, structured and unstructured interviews, checklists, card sorts, and opinion polls. Various group assessment methods can also be used, including concerns conferences, confrontation meetings, group and panel interviews, leaderless group discussions, juries, reverse-flow conferences, and speak-ups.

In the assessment of another person's behavior, several of the other methods discussed above with reference to self-appraisal are appropriate. The critical-incident checklist encourages an assessor to focus on specific behavior or outcomes or on the causes or consequences of specific behavior or outcomes. Raters can make use of behavioral episodes identified by successful and unsuccessful student interviewees to determine categories for assessing the outcomes of other students.

One method is uniquely suited to the appraisal by another person of a student's learning: recorded observation of student behavior. A trained observer can determine the frequency and success with which certain skills are being used or the frequency with which certain behavior occurs that reveals acquisition of particular knowledge or attitudes or achievement of particular developmental stages.

Achievement Tests. The most commonly used measures of achievement are general intelligence tests and various scholastic aptitude tests that students take when seeking to enter particular levels of higher education. Feldman and Newcomb (1969, vol. 2) frequently mention the Otis IQ Test as well as the College Entrance Examination Board tests, the Scholastic Aptitude Test, and the American College Testing Battery. One might also make use of Graduate Record Examinations to test for higher-level achievement in verbal and quantitative skills or acquisition of knowledge in a particular discipline.

A variety of other performance tests are available to measure the acquisition of knowledge and skills. The Educational Testing Service has recently developed a series of general education tests that assess four academic competencies: communication skills, analytic thinking, synthesizing ability, and awareness. These tests are specifically designed for pre- and postmeasurement to determine the success of a general education program. Similar tests have been developed by the American College Testing Program (the College Outcome Measures Project), focusing on communication skills, problem solving, critical thinking, and values analysis. Both sets of tests make use of a variety of assessment procedures (for example, multiple choice, short answer, essay, oral response) and are acceptable to many faculty members, who are particularly skeptical of paper-and-pencil assessment of complex, subtle conceptual skills. Pace (1979) has provided an excellent review of the use of achievement tests to measure college outcomes.

The work of Diederich (1974) and Cooper and Odell (1977) on the assessment of writing skills is also noteworthy. They have surveyed a variety of methods for measuring student growth in written communication and have provided writing samples to be used in assessing on several dimensions the current level of student writing. A similar procedure might be used in preparing samples of effective oral communication, problem solving, or analytic thinking.

Several methods have been used to assess critical thinking. The Watson-Glaser Test, probably the most widely used test of critical thinking, asks the student to recognize the critical element in an argument, whereas the Thematic Analysis Test, developed by Winter (Pottinger and Klemp, 1976), requires that the test taker actively produce a critical argument. The Sentence Completion Test of Critical Thinking, developed by Schroder in conjunction with the cognitive-development model of Harvey, Hunt, and Schroder (1961), also asks a student to construct a statement that reflects critical thinking. Klemp's General Integrative Model of Assessment expands on the critical thinking work by requiring a student to demonstrate "his/her ability to integrate the following abilities: (a) to observe, (b) to extract relevant information; (c) to analyze and integrate this information; (d) to ask appropriate questions; (e) to process new information in response to such questions; (f) to utilize this information and one's knowledge in making sound and logical recommendations; (g) to develop main and contingency plans; (h) to set meaningful goals; and (i) to feed back this new information into the process for better problem analysis and solutions" (Pottinger, 1975, p. 21). Further and more extensive discussions on the nature, promotion, and assessment of critical thinking are to be found in Young's (1980) small volume, *Fostering Critical Thinking.*

Interpersonal sensitivity and judgment are elusive generic skills that have recently been assessed in a variety of ways. Pottinger and Klemp (1976) have developed a series of "programmed cases" that require students to choose among several responses to an interpersonal incident. Certain responses have been identified by expert judges as more appropriate than others. Similar use is made of the case-study method for assessment purposes by many corporate groups. Pottinger, Klemp, and their colleagues have made use of content-filtered speech to assess levels of student sensitivity ("empathy") to other people's nonverbal messages (Pottinger and Klemp, 1976, p. 16). In the near future, we are likely to find case studies, simulations, role playing, and related activities being much more extensively used for the assessment of student competencies. Alverno College (Wisc.) is already making extensive use of these methods in assessing the basic competencies of Alverno students.

On-Campus Activities. Although performance tests can be effectively used to measure a student's capacity to perform certain functions, they usually do not measure a student's interest in or willingness to perform these functions. By observing what a student actually does while attending the college, one can obtain an immediate sense of how a particular academic program has affected a student's attitudes. These direct observations or recordings of actual behavior often yield more tangible and convincing information than attitude scales do. These latter scales are as likely to indicate what students believe their public attitudes should be as to indicate what students really believe.

On-campus activities can be assessed in a variety of ways: unstructured and structured interviews, questionnaires, anecdotal records, recorded observed behavior, unobtrusive measures, card sorts, checklists, critical-incident technique, logs, diaries, group interviews, institutional records, leaderless group discussion, self-monitoring/self-charting, and life histories. The major distinction between the use of these methods for recording on-campus behavior and the self-appraisals noted above is that students are not being asked to indicate the extent to which they think they have attained certain outcomes or manifest certain attitudes, knowledge, skills, or developmental stages. Rather, they are asked to indicate what they do daily at the college (or at home, at work, in the community, and so on). The assessors (not the students) need to take the next step in determining whether these activities indicate that a particular set of outcomes has been attained.

One of the most useful questionnaires for assessing cam-

pus activities is George Stern's Activities Index, which was frequently cited in Feldman and Newcomb's (1969, vol. 2) student outcome studies. In assessing the outcomes of an academic
program, one might wish to review the list of outcome criteria
generated by the Project on Outcomes in Postsecondary Education and compiled by the National Center for Higher Education
Management Systems (NCHEMS; Lenning and others, 1977,
Appendix B; Micek and Wallhaus, 1973).

The critical-incident technique and behavioral-events
analysis materials described can also be useful in examining on-
campus activities if the critical incidents or behavioral episodes
are determined by the assessors rather than the students. Students are given a checklist of critical incidents or episodes and
asked how often these incidents or episodes have occurred in
their own lives during a particular period of time on campus.

Because the assessment of on-campus activities seems obvious and minimally obtrusive (compared with self-appraisal and
performance tests, which are very obtrusive), it is surprising
how rarely this mode of assessment is used. More colleges and
universities should consider ways in which valued knowledge,
skills, attitudes, and developmental stages are immediately evident in their students' on-campus behavior. This mode of assessment is inappropriate only if these outcomes are not expected
to be evident until after the students graduate—in which case
the fifth and sixth modes of assessment, to which we now turn,
are appropriate.

Retrospective Self-Appraisal. Like assessment while a student is in college, assessment of outcomes for students after
graduation takes several forms: a "soft" self-appraisal and a
"hard" documentation of activities and achievements after graduation. Self-appraisal usually involves a questionnaire sent to
alumni. Alumni are asked the extent to which the college
helped them progress toward certain objectives, such as writing
clearly and effectively or developing social competence. In his
excellent review of alumni surveys, Pace (1979) notes that this
mode of self-appraisal has been used in major studies conducted
at Syracuse University (1948) and UCLA (1969) and by the National Opinion Research Council (1968), the Higher Education

Research Institute (1974-75), and the Associated Colleges of the Midwest (1976).

In many of these studies, alumni were also asked to generally rate the effectiveness of their college in preparing them for their first job, current job, and/or current life situation. These questions were also asked of alumni in the NCHEMS student-outcomes questionnaire (Gray and others, 1979).

Postgraduate Activities and Achievements. Much more common than the alumni's self-appraisal of outcomes is the description by alumni of their current activities and/or activities engaged in immediately after graduation and their current status and achievements in such areas as vocation, culture, family, and community service. Many of the alumni surveys reviewed by Pace (1979), beginning with the 1937 University of Minnesota survey and culminating in the 1978 NCHEMS alumni surveys, ask questions about current income, current occupational level, job satisfaction, relation of job to major field of study in college, and current political, community, and/or cultural activities. As Pace notes, there is need for much more work in this area and more sophisticated instruments. The NCHEMS project has been valuable in developing comparable instruments for assessing graduating students, "program completes," former students, entering students, nonreturning students, and recent alumni. However, the NCHEMS questionnaires may be inadequate for many colleges and universities. The original list of outcomes and outcome taxonomies developed by NCHEMS provides direction for more complex instruments (Lenning and others, 1977; Micek and Wallhaus, 1973). Clearly, much more needs to be done in developing tools and procedures for the effective assessment of student-learning outcomes while students are enrolled as well as after they graduate.

CONCLUSION

Using Curriculum Option Analysis for Program Design

In generating new ideas for an academic program, it is often valuable for a planning team to examine systematically all the various options available concerning the six basic dimensions of the college curriculum: time, space, resources, organization, procedures, and outcomes. Each of these dimensions has been extensively reviewed in this book. One or more members of an academic planning team might be encouraged to read these descriptive materials before beginning the design of a new academic program that will effectively serve undergraduate students.

In addition, this planning team might wish to explore these six dimensions and the descriptive materials associated with each dimension in a more engaging and creative manner through the use of a tool called "curriculum option analysis" (COA). Derived from a technique called "morphological analysis" (Ignatovich, 1974), COA has been used recently in collegiate course and curriculum design. An exercise called "Dial-a-

Course," for instance, makes use of COA-type analysis to facilitate nonconventional thinking about course design among faculty members, administrators, and students (Bergquist and Phillips, 1977, pp. 150-154).

When used to promote creativity in the design of a new academic program, curriculum option analysis is a four-step operation. First, each of the six dimensions of the undergraduate curriculum is reviewed. One or more members of a planning team might be assigned to each dimension and asked to read the appropriate chapters in this book as well as other relevant sources referenced in these chapters or known to members of the team. One member, for instance, might read extensively about various uses of time in the college curriculum, while another might specialize in curricular procedures.

Second, for each of the six curricular dimensions, or for each of the subcategories (such as "calendar" and "clock" under the dimension of time), a range of possible options is identified. As a rule, this range should consist of five or six options and should incorporate the most traditional approaches as well as some of the more experimental, more innovative, or less frequently used options. With regard to the dimension of time, for instance, the following five options might be selected for the subcategory of clock: (1) weekday/daytime, (2) weekday/evening, (3) weekday/marginal time, (4) weekend, and (5) extended time. Similarly, for the subcategory of calendar, five options might be identified: (1) semester/early semester/trimester, (2) quarter, (3) 4-1-4/4-4-1, (4) block/module scheduling, and (5) unspecified/unlimited duration.

Table 2 is a list of five suggested options that are appropriate for each subcategory of the six curricular dimensions identified and discussed in this book. This list can readily be modified by differentiating more finely between some options, adding a sixth option, collapsing several options together, or separating others. New subcategories can be added, and some subcategories or even entire dimensions can be ignored. Many planning teams, for instance, may have no control over the calendar or modes of crediting and hence will want to eliminate these subcategories from further consideration.

The third step in COA requires that the planning team

Table 2. Options for Each Curricular Dimension.

I.　*Time Dimension*
    A.　*Calendar*
        Option 1:　Semester/early semester/trimester
        Option 2:　Quarter
        Option 3:　4-1-4/4-4-1
        Option 4:　Block/module scheduling
        Option 5:　Unspecified/unlimited duration
    B.　*Clock*
        Option 1:　Weekday/daytime
        Option 2:　Weekday/evening
        Option 3:　Weekday/marginal time
        Option 4:　Weekend
        Option 5:　Extended time

II.　*Space Dimension*
    A.　*On Campus*
        Option 1:　Instructional (classroom/laboratory/studio)
        Option 2:　Quasi-instructional (library/auditorium/chapel)
        Option 3:　Noninstructional (dormitory/service center/outdoors)
        Option 4:　Media-based (closed-circuit television/electronic blackboard)
        Option 5:　Personally defined (study area)
    B.　*Off Campus*
        Option 1:　Instructional (conference center, retreat, church camp)
        Option 2:　Noninstructional (store, government building, internship site)
        Option 3:　Mobile classroom/laboratory
        Option 4:　Media-based (television, radio, newspaper)
        Option 5:　Wilderness

III.　*Resource Dimension*
    A.　*People*
        Option 1:　Faculty member(s) (instructor, teaching assistants, visiting faculty)
        Option 2:　Instructional support staff (counselors, librarians, secretarial staff)
        Option 3:　Noninstructional/off campus
        Option 4:　Peers/family/neighbors
        Option 5:　Student
    B.　*Materials and Equipment*
        Option 1:　Print (books, journals, magazines)

Table 2 (Continued)

Option 2:	Audiovisual (blackboard, overhead projector, videotape, slides, holography)	
Option 3:	Laboratory/studio equipment	
Option 4:	Packaged instructional materials (programmed texts, simulations, games)	
Option 5:	Computer	

IV. *Organization Dimension*
    A. *Organization of Program*
        Option 1:   Single unified program
        Option 2:   Concentration with general education and electives
        Option 3:   Multiple concentration (dual major/interdisciplinary major)
        Option 4:   Multiple track (honors track, remedial track, alternative instructional modalities/alternative percentage of required courses)
        Option 5:   Contracted program
    B. *Arrangement of Academic Administrative Units*
        Option 1:   Disciplinary units
        Option 2:   Multidisciplinary units
        Option 3:   Interdisciplinary units
        Option 4:   Matrix units
        Option 5:   Temporary units (institute, center)

V. *Procedures Dimension*
    A. *Program Planning*
        Option 1:   Faculty/institution-prescribed
        Option 2:   Prescribed curriculum with some student options
        Option 3:   Student/faculty-negotiated
        Option 4:   Student-defined goals/faculty-based instruction
        Option 5:   Student-defined goals/student-based instruction
    B. *Crediting*
        Option 1:   Successful completion of instructional unit
        Option 2:   Transfer of college credits
        Option 3:   Assessment of competence
        Option 4:   Assessment of prior experience
        Option 5:   No credits given
    C. *Teaching*
        Option 1:   Content-based/auditory (lecture, question and answer, recitation)

(continued on next page)

Table 2 (Continued)

| | Option 2: | Content-based/multimedia (reading, audiotutorial, programmed instruction, suggestopedia) |

Option 2: Content-based/multimedia (reading, audiotutorial, programmed instruction, suggestopedia)

Option 3: Interaction-based/auditory (seminars, symposia, debates, Socratic dialogue, peer learning)

Option 4: Interaction-based/multimedia (case studies, simulations, role playing)

Option 5: Student-based (independent study, tutorial, learning contract)

D. *Assessing*

Option 1: Written tests (multiple choice, true/false, essay)

Option 2: Documentation (academic products, portfolio)

Option 3: Behavioral performance tests

Option 4: Observation of performance in field setting

Option 5: Global assessment (self/instructor/panel)

VI. *Outcomes Dimension*

A. *Mode of Definition*

Option 1: Institutional perspective/unilateral structure

Option 2: Student perspective/unilateral structure

Option 3: Institutional perspective/hierarchal structure

Option 4: Student perspective/hierarchal structure

Option 5: Multiple perspective/hierarchal structure

B. *Emphasis*

Option 1: Cultural/intellectual

Option 2: Skills/vocational

Option 3: Citizenship/problem-oriented

Option 4: Personal/developmental

Option 5: Research/disciplinary

C. *Assessment*

Option 1: Self-appraisal

Option 2: Appraisal by another person

Option 3: Achievement tests

Option 4: On-campus activities

Option 5: Retrospective appraisal and activities

---

choose one of two tracks. It can focus on each individual dimension (or subcategory) of the curriculum and discuss the positive and negative aspects of each option as it relates to the academic program in question. When looking at the clock subcategory of the time dimension, for instance, a team working on a new general education requirement may want to determine what a general education course or program might look like if offered at other than daytime hours—for example, at night, during marginal hours of the day, during weekends, or over a condensed period of time.

Although the separate examination of each dimension or subcategory is a valuable exercise, the COA technique acquires its full power only when a second track is chosen: the six dimensions (or fifteen subcategories) are considered simultaneously. The planning team examines each possible (or many possible) combination(s) of the various options contained in the six dimensions or fifteen subcategories. To perform this analysis, the group first must construct a matrix such as is found in Figure 6, which lists the dimensions and subcategories vertically and the options associated with each dimension or subcategory horizontally.

The team then randomly selects one option from each of the dimensions/subcategories. This can be done by picking numbers (1, 2, 3, 4, 5) out of a hat or rolling a die (ignoring the number 6 when it is rolled) for each dimension/subcategory and then identifying the option associated with the corresponding number. A team that is working on a general education program, for instance, might randomly generate the following numbers: 4, 4, 1, 3, 1, 2, 5, 1, 3, 2, 5, 2, 1, 3, and 1. Using the options listed in Table 2 and Figure 6, the group would have selected the following options for further discussion: block scheduling (calendar option 4), weekend scheduling (clock option 4), instructional space (on-campus option 1), mobile space (off-campus option 3), faculty resource (people option 1), audiovisual resources (equipment option 2), contracted program (program-organization option 5), disciplinary units (academic-arrangement option 1), student/faculty-negotiated program (program-planning option 3), transfer of college credits (crediting option 2), student-based teaching (teaching option 5), documentation (assessing option 2), institutional perspective/unilateral structure (mode-of-defining-outcomes option 1), citizenship/problem orientation (outcomes-emphasis option 3), and self-appraisal (outcomes-assessment option 1).

The team is then given the challenge of designing an aca-

Figure 6. Matrix for Curriculum Option Analysis.

Dimension	Subcategory	Option Number				
		1	2	3	4	5
I. Time	A. Calendar	Semester Early semester Trimester	Quarter	4-1-4 4-4-1	Block Module scheduling	Unspecified Unlimited duration
	B. Clock	Weekday Daytime	Weekday Evening	Weekday Marginal time	Weekend	Extended time
II. Space	A. On campus	Instructional	Quasi-instructional	Noninstructional	Media-based	Personally defined
	B. Off campus	Instructional	Noninstructional	Mobile classroom Laboratory	Media-based	Wilderness
III. Resources	A. People	Faculty	Instructional support staff	Noninstructional	Peers Family Neighbors	Student
	B. Materials and equipment	Print	Audiovisual	Laboratory Studio equipment	Packaged instructional materials	Computer
IV. Organization	A. Organization of program	Single unified program	Concentration with gen. ed. and electives	Multiple concentration	Multiple track	Contracted program
	B. Arrangement of academic administrative units	Disciplinary units	Multidisciplinary units	Interdisciplinary units	Matrix units	Temporary units

		Faculty/institution-prescribed	Prescribed curriculum with some student options	Student/faculty-negotiated	Student-defined goals Faculty-based instruction	Student-defined goals Student-based instruction
V. Procedures	A. Program planning	Faculty/institution-prescribed	Prescribed curriculum with some student options	Student/faculty-negotiated	Student-defined goals Faculty-based instruction	Student-defined goals Student-based instruction
	B. Crediting	Successful completion of instructional unit	Transfer of college credits	Assessment of competence	Assessment of prior experience	No credits given
	C. Teaching	Content-based Auditory	Content-based Mutimedia	Interaction-based Auditory	Interaction-based Multimedia	Student-based
	D. Assessing	Written tests	Documentation	Behavioral performance tests	Field observation	Global assessment
VI. Outcomes	A. Mode of definition	Institutional perspective Unilateral structure	Student perspective Unilateral structure	Institutional perspective Hierarchal structure	Student perspective Hierarchal structure	Multiple perspective Hierarchal structure
	B. Emphasis	Cultural Intellectual	Skills Vocational	Citizenship Problem-oriented	Personal Developmental	Research Disciplinary
	C. Assessment	Self-appraisal	Appraisal by others	Achievement tests	On-campus activities	Retrospective appraisal and activities

demic program that incorporates or is responsive to each of
these randomly selected options. This is the third step. In our
hypothetical example, the planning group would be asked to design a general education program that is scheduled in large
blocks, is held on weekends, emphasizes both traditional classroom space and mobile space (bus, boat, and so on). It will also
be a program that makes extensive use of faculty members and
audiovisual resources, involves student learning contracts, and is
run by an academic department. The program will be planned
jointly by students and faculty members and will emphasize
transfer of college credit from other colleges and student-based
teaching methods. Student performance will be assessed primarily on the basis of documentation. Outcomes will be structured on a unilateral basis, mainly from a student perspective,
with a citizenship/problem-oriented emphasis—the student
being asked to appraise his own achievement of stated outcomes.

A planning group would be facing a major task if it were
to explore fully the implications of each of these options, let
alone the combination of all of them. The primary function to
be served by the curriculum option analysis, however, is not to
generate serious discussion about a particular combination of
options, but rather to stir up new curricular images and expand
the vision of group members about viable options. Hence, a
planning team should play for one or two hours at most with
the combination of options that is randomly generated—tossing
out ideas, freely exploring various alternatives (some of which
may be humorous or bizarre).

After briefly exploring one set of options, the team should
freely explore a second set by once again randomly generating
a set of numbers and selecting the corresponding options. At
least two or three other sets of options should be similarly explored. Ideally, six to eight concentrated hours should be set
aside for this exercise.

The fourth and final step involves reflections on the curriculum option analyses just performed. If a first, shorter track
were followed during step three, this reflection should take
place after the consideration of each curricular dimension. If a

second, longer track were followed, the reflection should occur after all the various sets of options have been generated and discussed. The following questions should be addressed, regardless of the track taken: (1) Which of the options are truly viable for this academic program? For this institution? Why? (2) Which options need to be eliminated from further consideration? Why? (3) What new ideas have been generated from this exercise that we want to keep in mind when designing our academic program? (4) Are there any ways in which we want to modify the basic structure or nature of this academic program (for example, scheduling of program, type of student, sequencing or level of courses) to accommodate one or more particularly interesting options?

After the planning team has addressed these four questions, it will have extracted much of the insight to be gained from a curriculum option analysis and can proceed with new vision to the task of preparing the design for a new or revised academic program.

REFERENCES

Abt, C. C. *Serious Games.* New York: Viking Press, 1970.

American College Testing Program. *Assessing Students on the Way to College: Technical Report for the ACT Assessment Program.* Iowa City: American College Testing, 1973.

American Council on Education (ACE). "Institutional Survey." Memo prepared by ACE Office on Educational Credit and Credentials, September 9, 1980.

Andrews, R. S. "Customizing Geology in the Self-Instruction Mode." *Journal of Geological Education,* 1977, *25,* 108-111.

Antioch College. *Antioch College Bulletin.* Yellow Springs, Ohio: Antioch College, 1977.

Association for Experiential Education. "Directory of Higher Education Programs in Experiential Education." *Journal of Experiential Education,* 1979, *2* (1), 17-27.

Austin College. *The Austin College Bulletin 1980-81.* Sherman, Texas: Austin College, 1980.

Baird, L. L. *Using Self-Reports to Predict Student Performance.* New York: College Entrance Examination Board, 1976.

Barnes McConnell, P. "Leading Discussion." In O. Milton and Associates, *On College Teaching: A Guide to Contemporary Practices.* San Francisco: Jossey-Bass, 1978.

Bateson, G. *Mind and Nature.* New York: Dutton, 1979.

Beckhard, R. "The Confrontation Meeting." *Harvard Business Review,* 1967, *45,* 149-155.

Berdie, R. F. "Self-Claimed and Tested Knowledge." *Educational and Psychological Measurement,* 1971, *31,* 629-636.

Bergquist, W. H. "Eight Curricular Models." In A. W. Chickering and others (Eds.), *Developing the College Curriculum: A Handbook for Faculty and Administrators.* Washington, D.C.: Council for the Advancement of Small Colleges, 1977.

Bergquist, W. H. "Given Everything . . . Success?" Evaluation report on the Institutional Development Program presented to the University of Bridgeport, Bridgeport, Conn., May 1979.

Bergquist, W. H., Lounibos, J., and Langfitt, J. *The College 1 Experience: Integrating Work, Leisure, and Service.* Washington, D.C.: Council for the Advancement of Small Colleges, 1980.

Bergquist, W. H., and Phillips, S. R. *A Handbook for Faculty Development.* Vol. 1. Washington, D.C.: Council for the Advancement of Small Colleges, 1975.

Bergquist, W. H., and Phillips, S. R. *A Handbook for Faculty Development.* Vol. 2. Washington, D.C.: Council for the Advancement of Small Colleges, 1977.

Bergquist, W. H., and Phillips, S. R. *A Handbook for Faculty Development.* Vol. 3. Washington, D.C.: Council for the Advancement of Small Colleges, 1981.

Berk, R. A. "Teaching Statistics in an Intensive Semester Program." *Improving College and University Teaching,* 1979, *27* (2), 87-88.

Bloom, B. S., and others. *Taxonomy of Educational Objectives.* Vol. 1. New York: McKay, 1956.

Boettcher, K. D. *An Experimental Program Offering Junior College Remedial English Instruction Simultaneously to High*

School Seniors and Junior College Freshmen via Open Circuit Television. U.S. Educational Resources Information Center, ERIC Document ED 021 559, 1968.

Bouwsma, W. J. "Models of the Educated Man." *American Scholar,* 1975, *44,* 195-212.

Bowen, H. R. *Investment in Learning: The Individual and Social Value of American Higher Education.* San Francisco: Jossey-Bass, 1977.

Bower, C. P., and Renkiewicz, N. K. *A Handbook for Using the Student Outcomes Questionnaires.* Boulder, Colo.: National Center for Higher Education Management Systems, 1977.

Boyd, H. W., and Westphall, R. *Marketing Research.* (3rd ed.) Homewood, Ill.: Irwin, 1972.

Boyd, J. L., and Shimberg, R. *Directory of Achievement Tests for Occupational Education.* Princeton, N.J.: Educational Testing Service, 1971.

Boyd, R. D., and DeVault, V. "The Observation and Recording of Behavior." *Review of Educational Research,* 1966, *36,* 529-551.

Boyer, E. L. "Changing Time Requirements." In D. W. Vermilye (Ed.), *Learner-Centered Reform: Current Issues in Higher Education 1975.* San Francisco: Jossey-Bass, 1975.

Boyer, E. L., and Kaplan, M. "Educating for Survival." *Change,* 1977, *9,* 22-23.

Brown, J. W., and Thornton, J. W., Jr. *College Teaching: A Systematic Approach.* (2nd ed.) New York: McGraw-Hill, 1971.

Bruffee, K. A. "The Brooklyn Plan: Attaining Intellectual Growth Through Peer Group Tutoring." *Liberal Education,* 1978, *64,* 449.

Buros, O. K. *The Seventh Mental Measurements Yearbook.* Highland Park, N.J.: Gryphon Press, 1972.

Campbell, D. T., and Fiske, D. W. "Convergent and Discriminant Validation by the Multitrait-Multimethod Matrix." *Psychological Bulletin,* 1959, *56,* 81-105.

Carnegie Foundation for the Advancement of Teaching. *Missions of the College Curriculum: A Contemporary Review with Suggestions.* San Francisco: Jossey-Bass, 1977.

Charland, W. A., Jr. *A New Look at Lifelong Learning.* Monograph 3. Yellow Springs, Ohio: Union Press, Union for Experimental Colleges and Universities, 1976.

Chickering, A. W., and others. *Developing the College Curriculum.* Washington, D.C.: Council for the Advancement of Small Colleges, 1977.

Chickering, A. W., and Associates. *The Modern American College: Responding to the New Realities of Diverse Students and a Changing Society.* San Francisco: Jossey-Bass, 1981.

Churchill, R. J., Lord, W., and Maxwell, L. M. "University and College Cooperation in Engineering: Project CO-TIE." *Journal of Engineering Education,* 1971, *61* (8), 898-901.

Clark, C. *Brainstorming.* Garden City, N.Y.: Doubleday, 1958.

Clark, T. "Creating Contract Learning." In O. Milton and Associates, *On College Teaching: A Guide to Contemporary Practices.* San Francisco: Jossey-Bass, 1978a.

Clark, T. "The Nontraditional Setting." In J. Lindquist (Ed.), *Designing Teaching Improvement Programs.* Washington, D.C.: Council for the Advancement of Small Colleges, 1978b.

College of the Atlantic. *College of the Atlantic Catalogue for 1978-79.* Bar Harbor, Maine: College of the Atlantic, 1978.

Collins, A., and others. "Effectiveness of an Interactive Map Display in Tutoring Geography." *Journal of Educational Psychology,* 1980, *70,* 1-7.

Cooper, C. R., and Odell, I. *Evaluating Writing: Describing, Measuring, Judging.* Urbana, Ill.: National Council of Teachers of English, 1977.

Council for the Advancement of Experiential Learning. *Directory of Members.* Columbia, Md.: Council for the Advancement of Experiential Learning, 1979-80.

Cox, C. R. *Flexible Scheduling To Fit the Firefighters.* U.S. Educational Resources Information Center, ERIC Document ED 037 191, 1969.

Cross, K. P. "Learner-Centered Curricula." In D. W. Vermilye (Ed.), *Learner-Centered Reform: Current Issues in Higher Education 1975.* San Francisco: Jossey-Bass, 1975.

Cross, K. P. "Adult Learners: Characteristics, Needs, and Interests." In R. Peterson and Associates, *Lifelong Learning in America: An Overview of Current Practices, Available Re-*

sources, and Future Prospects. San Francisco: Jossey-Bass, 1979.

Dambrot, F. "General Psychology over Closed-Circuit Television." *AV Communication Review,* 1972, *20* (2), 181-193.

"Data Processing on the Move." *Nation's Schools and Colleges,* 1975, *2,* 49-50.

Davis and Elkins College. *Davis and Elkins College Bulletin: 1977-78.* Elkins, W. Va.: Davis and Elkins College, 1977.

Davis, S. M., and Lawrence, P. R. "Data Processing on the Move." *Nation's Schools and Colleges,* 1975, *2,* 49-50.

Davis, S. M., and Lawrence, P. R. *Matrix.* Reading, Mass.: Addison-Wesley, 1977.

Dennis, L. E. *The Other End of Sesame Street.* U.S. Educational Resources Information Center, ERIC Document ED 050 672, 1971.

Diederich, P. *Measuring Growth in English.* Urbana, Ill.: National Council of Teachers of English, 1974.

Dowd, R. "Core Program in the Humanities: School of New Resources of New Rochelle." *Liberal Education,* 1979, *65,* 14.

Dressel, P. *College and University Curriculum.* Berkeley, Calif.: McCutchan, 1971.

Duley, J. "Editor's Notes." In J. Duley (Ed.), *New Directions for Higher Education: Implementing Field Experience Education,* no. 6. San Francisco: Jossey-Bass, 1974.

Dye, G. R., and Stephenson, J. B. "Learning Ethics Through Public Service Internships: Evaluation of an Experimental Program." *Liberal Education,* 1978, *64,* 343.

Eddy, M. S. "Recycling Academic Calendars." *American Association of Higher Education Bulletin: Research Currents,* October 1979, pp. 7-10.

Edling, J. V. "Educational Objectives and Educational Media." *Review of Educational Research,* 1968, *38,* 177-194.

Eldred, M. D., and Marienau, C. "Adult Baccalaureate Programs." *American Association of Higher Education: Higher Education Research Report,* 1979, *9,* 43-55.

Emory & Henry College. *To Be: The Emory and Henry Bulletin.* Emory, Va.: Emory & Henry College, 1978.

Evergreen State College. *The Evergreen State College Bulletin: 1977-79.* Olympia, Wash.: Evergreen State College, 1977.

Farley, J. *Chenango Development Project: Peoplemobile Project Evaluation.* U.S. Educational Resources Information Center, ERIC Document ED 096 093, 1971.

Feldman, K. A., and Newcomb, T. M. *The Impact of College on Students.* (2 vols.) San Francisco: Jossey-Bass, 1969.

Fey, P. A. "Family College: A Future Form of Lifelong Learning." *Community and Junior College Journal,* 1977, *48* (2), 18-20.

Fisher, C. "Being There Vicariously by Case Studies." In O. Milton and Associates, *On College Teaching: A Guide to Contemporary Practices.* San Francisco: Jossey-Bass, 1978.

Flanagan, J. C. "The Critical Incident Technique." *Psychological Bulletin,* 1954, *51,* 327-358.

Freidman, W. *Class Scheduling Preferences: Full-Time Students and Faculty.* U.S. Educational Resources Information Center, ERIC Document ED 176 669, 1979.

Fromm, E. *The Art of Loving.* New York: Harper & Row, 1956.

Fund for the Improvement of Postsecondary Education. *Special Focus Program—Adapting Improvements: Better Strategies for Educating Adults.* Washington, D.C.: U.S. Government Printing Office, 1978.

Fund for the Improvement of Postsecondary Education. *Designing for Development: Four Programs for Adult Undergraduates.* Washington, D.C.: U.S. Government Printing Office, 1979a.

Fund for the Improvement of Postsecondary Education. *Resources for Change: A Guide to Projects 1978-79.* Washington, D.C.: U.S. Government Printing Office, 1979b.

Gaff, J. G. "Objectives for Students." In J. Gaff and others (Eds.), *General Education: Issues and Resources.* Washington, D.C.: Association of American Colleges, 1980.

Gaff, J. G., and Associates. *The Cluster College.* San Francisco: Jossey-Bass, 1970.

Gagnon, G. O. "Prison Education Network Impacts Total Program." *Community and Junior College Journal,* 1977, *48* (2), 26-28.

Giese, M., and Lawler, M. "Development and Implementation of a PSI Course in Human Physiology." *Journal of Allied Health,* 1978, 7, 268-273.

Goddard College. *The Goddard College Catalogue: 1978-80.* Plainfield, Vt.: Goddard College, 1978.

"Going to School at Sea." *Time,* January 28, 1980, pp. 54-55.

Goldberger, N. "Simon's Rock: Meeting the Developmental Needs of the Early College Student." In E. M. Greenberg, K. O'Donnell, and W. Bergquist (Eds.), *New Directions for Higher Education: Educating Learners of All Ages,* no. 29. San Francisco: Jossey-Bass, 1980.

Gordon, W. *Synectics.* New York: Collier, 1961.

Governors State University. *1978 Catalogue.* Park Forest South, Ill.: Governors State University, 1978. (Modified by personal correspondence with C. L. McCray, Provost, July 7, 1980.)

Grand Valley State Colleges. *Undergraduate Catalogue: 1977-79.* Allendale, Mich.: Grand Valley State Colleges, 1977.

Grant, G., and others. *On Competence: A Critical Analysis of Competence-Based Reforms in Higher Education.* San Francisco: Jossey-Bass, 1979.

Gray, R. G., and others. *Student-Outcomes Questionnaires: An Implementation Handbook.* Boulder, Colo.: National Center for Higher Education Management Systems, 1979.

Greenberg, E. M. "The University Without Walls Program at Loretto Heights College: Individualization for Adults." Unpublished paper, 1972.

Greenberg, E. M. "The Community as a Learning Resource." *Journal of Experiential Education,* 1978, 1 (2), 22-25.

Greenberg, E. M. "Toward an Hypothesis for Advancing Quality Undergraduate Education in the Small Independent College." Unpublished paper prepared for the Council for the Advancement of Small Colleges, Washington, D.C., 1979.

Greenberg, E. M. "The University Without Walls (UWW) Program at Loretto Heights College: Individualization for Adults." In E. M. Greenberg, K. M. O'Donnell, and W. H. Bergquist (Eds.), *New Directions for Higher Education: Educating Learners of All Ages,* no. 29. San Francisco: Jossey-Bass, 1980.

Greenberg, E. M., and Charland, W. A., Jr. "Project Transition at Loretto Heights College: Designing for Transition." In E. M. Greenberg, K. M. O'Donnell, and W. H. Bergquist (Eds.), *New Directions for Higher Education: Educating Learners of All Ages,* no. 29. San Francisco: Jossey-Bass, 1980.

Greenberg, E. M., O'Donnell, K. M., and Bergquist, W. H. (Eds.), *New Directions for Higher Education: Educating Learners of All Ages,* no. 29. San Francisco: Jossey-Bass, 1980.

Hall, E. T. *The Hidden Dimension.* Garden City, N.Y.: Doubleday, 1966.

Hall, K. A. "The Development and Utilization of Mobile CAI for the Education of Nurses in Remote Areas." ERIC Document No. ED-121-261. Unpublished manuscript, 1976.

Halliburton, D. "Curricular Design." In A. W. Chickering and others (Eds.), *Developing the College Curriculum.* Washington, D.C.: Council for the Advancement of Small Colleges, 1977.

Harvey, O. J., Hunt, D. E., and Schroder, H. M. *Conceptual Systems and Personality Organization.* New York: Wiley, 1961.

Hassett, M. J., and Thompson, R. B. "PSI in College Mathematics." *American Mathematical Monthly,* 1978, *85,* 760-763.

Havighurst, R. *Developmental Tasks in Education.* New York: Longmans Green, 1948.

Heath, D. *Growing Up in College.* San Francisco: Jossey-Bass, 1968.

Heath, R. "The Modes of Existence Test." Unpublished manuscript, 1976, cited by L. Knefelcamp, C. A. Parker, and C. Widick, "Roy Heath's Model of Personality Typologies." In L. Kneflecamp, C. Widick, and C. A. Parker (Eds.), *New Directions for Student Services: Applying New Developmental Findings,* no. 4. San Francisco: Jossey-Bass, 1978.

Hefferlin, J. L. *Dynamics of Academic Reform.* San Francisco: Jossey-Bass, 1969.

Heiss, A. *An Inventory of Academic Innovation and Reform.* Berkeley, Calif.: Carnegie Commission on Higher Education, 1973.

Henry, M., and Ramsett, D. "The Effects of Computer-Aided Instruction on Learning and Attitudes in Economic Principles

Courses." *Journal of Economic Education*, 1978, *10*, 26-34.

Hill, J. E., and Nunnery, D. N. *The Educational Sciences.* Bloomfield, Mich.: Oakland Community College Press, 1973.

Hofstetter, F. T. "Instructional Design and Curricular Impact of Computer-Based Music Education." *Educational Technology*, 1978, *18*, 50-53.

Hofstra University. *Hofstra University Bulletin: 1978-79.* Hempstead, N.Y.: Hofstra University, 1978.

Horn, R. E. "How Students Can Make Their Own Simulations." In D. W. Zuckerman and R. E. Horn (Eds.), *The Guide to Simulations: Games for Education and Training.* (2nd ed.) Lexington, Mass.: Information Resources, 1973.

Horn, R. E. *The Guide to Simulations: Games for Education and Training.* (3rd ed.) Cranford, N.J.: Didactic Systems, 1977.

Hughes, L. J., and others. "Origins of Life: An Interdisciplinary Course in Chemical Evolution for Undergraduates." *Journal of Chemical Education*, 1978, *55*, 521-524.

Huizinga, J. *Homo Ludens.* Boston: Beacon Press, 1955.

Hurt, R. D. "The University of Mid-America: An Open University Approach to Higher Education." *Peabody Journal of Education*, 1977, *54* (2), 120-122.

Ignatovich, F. "Morphological Analysis." In S. Hencley and J. Yates (Eds.), *Futurism in Education.* Berkeley, Calif.: McCutchan, 1974.

Jenkins, O. L. H. *Weekend College: A Cooperative Approach to Teaching Children with Handicaps.* U.S. Educational Resources Information Center, ERIC Document ED 157 338, 1978.

Kalmbach, J. A. "Success Characteristics of Students in an Audio-Tutorial College Course: A Descriptive Study." *NSPI Journal*, 1980, *19*, 43-46.

Keating, L. A., Cervi, M., and Cypert, S. "Integrating Natural and Human Environments." *Journal of Physical Education and Recreation*, 1978, *49* (1), 33-34.

Keller, F. "Goodbye Teacher . . . ." *Journal of Applied Behavior Analysis*, 1968, *1*, 83.

Kelly, F. D., and Dowd, E. T. "The Staffing Conference: An Approach to Student Evaluation." *Counselor Education and Supervision,* 1975, *15,* 135-139.

Keogh, R. N. *Instructional Television Programming in the Biological Sciences: A Restructured Format.* U.S. Educational Resources Information Center, ERIC Document ED 062 834, 1970.

Knapp, J., and Sharon, A. *A Compendium of Assessment Techniques.* Princeton, N.J.: Educational Testing Service, 1975.

Kneflecamp, L., Widick, C., and Parker, C. A. (Eds.). *New Directions for Student Services: Applying New Developmental Findings,* no. 4. San Francisco: Jossey-Bass, 1978.

Knowles, M. S. *Self-Directed Learning: A Guide for Learners and Teachers.* New York: Association Press, 1975.

Krathwohl, D. R., and others. *Taxonomy of Educational Objectives.* Vol. 2: *Affective Domain.* New York: McKay, 1964.

Kuhn, T. *The Structure of Scientific Revolutions.* (2nd ed.) Chicago: Rand McNally, 1970.

Lake, D. G., Miles, M. B., and Earle, R. B., Jr. *Measuring Human Behavior.* New York: Teachers College Press, Columbia University, 1973.

Laramee, W. A., and Spears, P. U. "Linking Work and Academic Learning." *Liberal Education,* 1978, *53,* 321.

Larson, I., and others. "Performance Modules of Undergraduate Students in Computer-Assisted Information in Elementary Logic." *Instructional Sciences,* 1978, *7,* 15-35.

Lavin, B. F. "Can Computer-Assisted Instruction Make a Difference?" *Teaching Sociology,* 1980, *7,* 163-179.

Lenning, O. T. "Assessing Student Progress in Academic Achievement." In L. Baird (Ed.), *New Directions for Community Colleges: Assessing Student Academic and Social Progress,* no. 18. San Francisco: Jossey-Bass, 1977.

Lenning, O. T., and others. *A Structure for the Outcomes of Postsecondary Education.* Boulder, Colo.: National Center for Higher Education Management Systems, 1977.

Levine, A. *Handbook on Undergraduate Curriculum.* San Francisco: Jossey-Bass, 1978.

Levine, A., and Weingart, J. *Reform of Undergraduate Education.* San Francisco: Jossey-Bass, 1973.

Levine, H. G., and McGuire, C. H. "The Validity and Reliability of Oral Examinations in Assessing Cognitive Skills in Medicine." *Journal of Educational Measurement,* 1970, *7,* 63-74.

Levinson, D. *The Seasons of a Man's Life.* New York: Knopf, 1978.

Levy, L. B., and Fritz, K. V. *Status Report on the Computer Grading of Essays.* Madison: Counseling Center, University of Wisconsin, 1972.

Lichtman, J. *Bring Your Own Bag: A Report on Free Universities.* Washington, D.C.: American Association for Higher Education, 1973.

The Lindenwood Colleges. *The Lindenwood Colleges Bulletin: 1976-1977.* St. Charles, Mo.: Lindenwood Colleges, 1976.

Loevinger, J. *Ego Development: Conceptions and Theories.* San Francisco: Jossey-Bass, 1976.

Loevinger, J., and Wessler, R. *Measuring Ego Development I: Construction and Use of a Sentence Completion Test.* San Francisco: Jossey-Bass, 1970.

Loretto Heights College. *University Without Walls: Loretto Heights College.* Denver, Colo.: Loretto Heights College, 1971.

Luskin, B., and Zigerell, J. "Community Colleges in Forefront of Telecourse Development." *Community and Junior College Journal,* 1978, *48* (8), 8-9; 44-45.

Lyon, D. N. "Embryo: A Radical Experiment in Learning." *Journal of Higher Education,* 1979, *50* (1), 33.

McAnliffe, D. G. "How a College System Joined TV Network." *Community and Junior College Journal,* 1978, *48* (8), 40-41.

McCart, B. R. "The Career Awareness Micro-Internship Program." *Liberal Education,* 1978, *64* (3), 331-332.

McMorris, R. F., and Ambrosino, R. J. "Self-Report Predictors: A Reminder." *Journal of Educational Measurement,* 1973, *10,* 13-17.

MacMurray College. *MacMurray College: 1975-1977.* Jacksonville, Ill.: MacMurray College, 1977.

Magada, V., and Moore, M. "The Humanities Cluster College at Bowling Green State University: Its Middle Years." *Liberal Education,* 1976, *62* (1), 100-113.

Magill, S. H. "The Aims of Liberal Education in the Post-Modern World." *Liberal Education,* 1977, *63,* 440.

Maloncy, M. P., and Ward, M. P. *Psychological Assessment: A Conceptual Approach.* New York: Oxford University Press, 1976.

Mars Hill College. *Emphasis: 1979-80.* Mars Hill, N.C.: Mars Hill College, 1979.

Martin, W. B. "The Limits to Diversity." *Change,* 1978, *10,* 41-45.

Maslow, A. *Motivation and Personality: Toward a Psychology of Being.* New York: Harper & Row, 1970.

Mathews, D. Speech given at the banquet of the National Center for Independent Colleges and Universities, National Conference of the Association of American Colleges, Philadelphia, February 9, 1976.

Mayhew, L. B., and Ford, P. J. *Changing the Curriculum.* San Francisco: Jossey-Bass, 1971.

Mayville, W. V. *Interdisciplinarity: The Mutable Paradigm.* Washington, D.C.: ERIC Clearinghouse, 1978.

Meyer, P. *Awarding College Credit for Non-College Learning: A Guide to Current Practices.* San Francisco: Jossey-Bass, 1975.

Micek, S. S., and Wallhaus, R. A. *An Introduction to the Identification and Uses of Higher Education Outcome Information.* Technical Report No. 40. Boulder, Colo.: National Center for Higher Education Management Systems, 1973.

Michael, D. N. *On Learning To Plan—and Planning To Learn: The Social Psychology of Changing Toward Future-Responsive Societal Learning.* San Francisco: Jossey-Bass, 1973.

Mignault, L. B. "Suggestopedia: Is There a Better Way to Learn?" *Canadian Modern Language Review,* 1978, *34,* 695-701.

Miles, J. S. *Report on a Survey of CATV-MATV-TV Distribution Systems at Colleges and Universities.* U.S. Educational Resources Information Center, 1972. ED 066 864.

Milivojevic, D. "New Directions in Foreign Language Teaching." *Journal of Thought,* 1979, *14,* 273-279.

Mittelstet, S. K. "Telecourses Recruit in Dallas." *Community and Junior College Journal,* 1978, *48* (8), 20-22.

Moss, L. "Evaluation of a Television Course." *Educational Forum,* 1970, *34* (3), 401-406.

Mount, M. K., and Tirrell, F. J. "Improving Educational Scores through Self-Monitoring." *Journal of Educational Research,* 1977, *71,* 70-73.

Nash, P. C., and Voth, G. L. "GENTRAIN: An Instructional Delivery System at Monterey Peninsula College." *Liberal Education,* 1979, *65* (1), 45.

New College at the University of Alabama. *Bulletin of the New College: 1975.* Tuscaloosa: University of Alabama, 1975.

Newby, M. R., and Harker, B. "In-Service Education Hits the Road." *Adult Leadership,* 1976, *24,* 209-214.

Newman, F., and others. *Report on Higher Education.* Washington, D.C.: U.S. Department of Health, Education and Welfare, 1971.

Oppenheim, A. N. *Questionnaire Design and Attitude Measurement.* New York: Basic Books, 1966.

Ottawa University. *Ottawa University Bulletin.* Ottawa, Kans.: Ottawa University, 1976.

Pace, C. R. *Measuring Outcomes of College.* San Francisco: Jossey-Bass, 1979.

Padgett, J. "Making Learning Relevant to Living." *Liberal Education,* 1969, *55* (2), 296.

Palola, E. G., and Lehemann, T. "Student Outcomes and Institutional Decision-Making with PERC." In O. T. Lenning (Ed.), *New Directions for Higher Education: Improving Educational Outcomes,* no. 16. San Francisco: Jossey-Bass, 1976.

Payne, D. *The Specification and Measurement of Learning Outcomes.* Waltham, Mass.: Blaisdell, 1968.

Perry, W. G., Jr. *Forms of Intellectual and Ethical Development in the College Years: A Scheme.* New York: Holt, Rinehart and Winston, 1968.

Phenix, P. *The Realms of Meaning.* New York: McGraw-Hill, 1964.

Philp, M. J. "Learning on the Big Bay." *Community and Junior College Journal,* 1978, *48* (8), 30-33.

Polanyi, M. *The Tacit Dimension.* Garden City, N.Y.: Doubleday, 1967.

Polanyi, M. "Sense-Giving and Sense-Reading." In M. Polanyi, *Knowing and Being.* Chicago: University of Chicago Press, 1969.

Pottinger, P. S. *Comments and Guidelines for Research in Competency Identification: Definition and Measurement.* Syracuse, N.Y.: Educational Policy Research Center, Syracuse University Research Corporation, 1975.

Pottinger, P. S., and Klemp, G. *Concepts and Issues Related to the Identification, Measurement, and Validation of Competence.* Boston: McBer, 1976.

Primoff, E. *How to Prepare and Conduct Job Element Examinations.* Washington, D.C.: Bureau of Policies and Standards, U.S. Civil Service Commission, 1973.

Prince, G. *The Practice of Creativity.* New York: Harper & Row, 1970.

Racle, G. L. "Can Suggestopedia Revolutionize Language Teaching?" *Foreign Language Annuals,* 1979, *12,* 39-49.

Raser, J. R. *Simulation and Society.* Boston: Allyn & Bacon, 1969.

Resnick, S., and Kaplan, B. "College Programs for Black Adults." *Journal of Higher Education,* 1971, *42* (3), 202-218.

Richmond, M. J., Jr. "A Flexible All-Year Curriculum for Post-secondary Education." *College Student Journal,* 1977, *11* (1), 135-138.

Robinson, J. P., Athanasiou, R., and Head, K. B. *Measures of Occupational Attitudes and Occupational Characteristics.* Ann Arbor: Institute for Social Research, University of Michigan, 1969.

Robinson, J. P., Rusk, J. G., and Head, K. B. *Measures of Political Attitudes.* Ann Arbor: Institute for Social Research, University of Michigan, 1968.

Robinson, J. P., and Shaver, P. R. *Measures of Social Psychological Attitudes.* Ann Arbor: Institute for Social Research, University of Michigan, 1969.

Rockler, M. J. "Applying Simulation/Gaming." In O. Milton and Associates, *On College Teaching: A Guide to Contemporary Practices.* San Francisco: Jossey-Bass, 1978.

Rogers, C. R., and Stevens, B. *Person to Person.* New York: Pocket Books, 1971.

Rubin, E., and Howe, F. "Women's Studies Programs, 1980." *The Women's Studies Newsletter,* Winter 1980, *8* (1).

Rudolph, F. *The American College and University.* New York: Knopf, 1962.

St. Andrews Presbyterian College. *St. Andrews Presbyterian College Bulletin: 1979-1980.* Laurinburg, N.C.: St. Andrews Presbyterian College, 1977.

St. Thomas Aquinas College. *St. Thomas Aquinas College: 1976-1977.* Sparkill, N.Y.: St. Thomas Aquinas College, 1976.

Schiller, W., and Markle, S. "Using the Personalized System of Instruction." In O. Milton and Associates, *On College Teaching: A Guide to Contemporary Practices.* San Francisco: Jossey-Bass, 1978.

Schmidtlein, E. Personal correspondence. Columbia, Mo., July 16, 1980.

Schultz, J. "The Story Workshop Method: Writing from Start to Finish." *College English,* 1977, *39,* 411-436.

Sexton, R. F., and Stephenson, J. B. "Institutionalizing Experiential Learning in a State University." In J. Duley (Ed.), *New Directions for Higher Education: Implementing Field Experience Education,* no. 6. San Francisco: Jossey-Bass, 1974.

Shaw, M. E., and Wright, J. W. *Scales for the Measurement of Attitudes.* New York: McGraw-Hill, 1967.

Shirts, R. G. "Notes on Defining 'Simulation.'" *Occasional Newsletter About Simulations and Games,* 1972, no. 15, pp. 14-23.

Shumway, K. Personal correspondence. Ottawa, Kans., July 25, 1980.

Sommer, R. *Personal Space.* Englewood Cliffs, N.J.: Prentice-Hall, 1969.

Stadsklev, R. (Ed.). *Handbook of Simulation and Gaming in Social Education.* Tuscaloosa: Institute of Higher Education Research and Services, University of Alabama, 1975.

Stephens College. *1979 Catalogue.* Columbia, Mo.: Stephens College, 1979. (Modified by personal correspondence with E. Schmidtlein, Dean of Faculty, July 16, 1980.)

Stewart, A. W. "The 4-4-1 Plan." *Improving College and University Teaching,* 1976, *24* (3), 188.

Stitt, D. "Stop Shop, and Learn." *Nation's Schools and Colleges,* 1975, *2,* 43-46.

Stitt, D. "An Inner City Mobile Counseling Unit." *Vocational Guidance Quarterly,* 1976, *4,* 368-371.

"Stop, Shop, and Learn." *Nation's Schools and Colleges,* 1975, *2,* 43-46.

Swenson, L. C. "The Effects of Reinforcing Self-Charting of Course Progress on Course Work Productivity in College Courses." Paper presented at the annual convention of the Western Psychological Association, San Francisco, April 1974.

Tough, A. *Adults' Learning Projects.* (2nd ed.) Austin, Texas: Learning Concepts, 1979.

"Tracking Civilization on GENTRAIN: Snapshots of Global History." *Change,* 1978, *10* (7), 38.

"Transitions: A Four-Program Television Series for Adult Experiential Learners." Athens: WOUB-TV, Adult Learning Services, Ohio University, 1981.

Travis, R. G., Facione, P. A., and Litwin, J. L. "Beyond the Core Curriculum: An Outcome Approach to General Education." *Liberal Education,* 1978, *64,* 435-446.

Tull, D. S., and Albaum, G. S. *Survey Research: A Decisional Approach.* New York: Intext Educational Publishers, 1973.

Tussman, J. *Experiment at Berkeley.* New York: Oxford University Press, 1969.

Twelker, P. A. (Ed.). *Instructional Simulation Systems: An Annotated Bibliography.* Corvallis: Oregon State University Press, 1969.

Union for Experimenting Colleges and Universities. *University Without Walls: A First Report.* Yellow Springs, Ohio: Union for Experimenting Colleges and Universities, 1972.

Vaughn, G. B. "Learning in Transit at Mountain Empire." *Community and Junior College Journal,* 1974a, *44,* 54-55.

Vaughn, G. B. "Busing—Community College Style." *College Management,* 1974b, *9,* 20-21.

Votaw, R. G., and Farquhar, B. B. "Current Trends in Computer-Based Education in Medicine." *Educational Technology,* 1978, *18,* 54-56.

Walton, W. W. *Productive Delivery Systems for Nontraditional*

Learning. U.S. Educational Resources Information Center, ERIC Document ED 115 281, 1975.

Warner, G. E. "Two ITV Consortia in California." *Audiovisual Instruction,* 1976, *21,* 20-21; 68.

Warren, J. R. "Who Wants To Learn What? Evaluation with a Changing Clientele." In C. R. Pace (Ed.), *Evaluating Learning and Teaching.* San Francisco: Jossey-Bass, 1973.

Washburn, J. E. *Jabberwockey.* Santa Rosa, Calif.: J. E. Washburn (P.O. Box 6855), 1971.

Watson, G., and Johnson, D. *Social Psychology.* (2nd ed.) Philadelphia: Lippincott, 1972.

Watson, N. E., and Luskin, B. J. "A Credit Telecourse." *Community and Junior College Journal,* 1975, *45* (8), 10-11.

Weathersby, R. "A Developmental Perspective on Adults' Use of Formal Education." Unpublished doctoral dissertation, School of Education, Harvard University, 1977.

Weathersby, R., and Tarule, J. H. "Adult Development: Implications for Higher Education." Research Report No. 4. Washington, D.C.: American Association of Higher Education/ERIC, 1980.

Webb, E. J., and others. *Unobtrusive Measures: Nonreactive Research in the Social Sciences.* Chicago: Rand McNally, 1966.

Western Washington State University. *Western Washington State University General Catalogue: 1977-79.* Bellingham: Western Washington State University, 1977.

William Jewell College. *William Jewell College Bulletin.* Liberty, Mo.: William Jewell College, 1978.

Willingham, W. *Principles of Good Practice in Assessing Experiential Learning.* Columbia, Md.: Council for the Advancement of Experiential Learning, 1977.

Witkin, B. R. *An Analysis of Needs Assessment Techniques for Educational Planning at State, Intermediate, and District Levels.* Hayward, Calif.: Office of Alameda County Superintendent of Schools, 1975.

Witmer, D. R. *The Outcomes of Higher Education.* La Crosse: University of Wisconsin, n.d.

Wood, L., and Davis, B. G. *Designing and Evaluating Higher Education Curricula.* Washington, D.C.: American Association for Higher Education, 1978.

Wylie, R. C. *The Self-Concept: A Critical Survey of Pertinent Research Literature.* Lincoln: University of Nebraska Press, 1961.

Youmans, H. L. "Students Are Differing Folk: An Operational System of Placing Students in Chemistry." *Journal of College Science Teaching,* 1976, *6,* 92-93.

Young, R. (Ed.). *New Directions for Teaching and Learning: Fostering Critical Thinking,* no. 3. San Francisco: Jossey-Bass, 1980.

Zajano, N. C., and Arnoff, S. M. *Mobile Career-Education Resource Unit.* U.S. Educational Resources Information Center, ERIC Document ED 146-466, 1976-1977.

Zand, D. E. "Collateral Organization: A New Change Strategy." *Journal of Applied Behavioral Science,* 1974, *10* (1), 63-89.

Zigerell, J., and Luskin, B. "Community Colleges in Forefront of Telecourse Development." *Community and Junior College Journal,* 1978, *48* (8), 8-9; 44-45.

Zuckerman, D. W., and Horn, R. E. *The Guide to Simulations: Games for Education and Training.* (2nd ed.) Lexington, Mass.: Information Resources, 1973.

INDEX